Frommer's®

W9-ATW-378

PORTABLE

Banff & Jasper National Parks

4th Edition

by Christie Pashby

Here's what the critics say about Frommer's:

"Amazingly easy to use. Very portable, very complete."

—*Booklist*

"Detailed, accurate, and easy-to-read information for all price ranges."

—*Glamour Magazine*

"Hotel information is close to encyclopedic."

—*Des Moines Sunday Register*

"Frommer's Guides have a way of giving you a real feel for a place."

—*Knight Ridder Newspapers*

John Wiley & Sons Canada, Ltd.

JOHN WILEY & SONS CANADA, LTD

6045 Freemont Blvd.
Mississauga, ON L5R 4J3

Copyright © 2008 John Wiley & Sons Canada, Ltd. All rights reserved.
No part of this work covered by the copyright, herein may be reproduced
or used in any form or by any means—graphic, electronic or mechanical—
without prior written permission of the publisher. Any request for photo-
copying, or other reprographic copying of any part of this book shall be
directed in writing to The Canadian Copyright Licensing Agency (Access
Copyright). For an Access Copyright license, visit www.accesscopyright.ca
or call toll free, 1-800-893-5777.

FROMMER'S is a registered trademark of Arthur Frommer. Used under
license.

Library and Archives Canada Cataloguing in Publication Data
Pashby, Christie
  Frommer's Banff & Jasper National Parks/by Christie Pashby. — 4th ed.

Includes index.
ISBN 978-0-470-15346-8

  1. Banff National Park (Alta.) —Guidebooks. 2. Jasper National Park
(Alta.) —Guidebooks. I. Title. II. Title: Frommer's Banff and Jasper
National Parks. III. Title: Banff & Jasper National Parks. IV. Title: Banff
and Jasper National Parks.

FC3663.P38 2007   917.123'32   C2007-905867-1

Editor: Robert Hickey
Project Manager: Elizabeth McCurdy
Project Coordinator: Pamela Vokey
Cartographer: Mapping Specialists
Publishing Services Director: Karen Bryan
Publishing Services Manager: Ian Koo
Production by Wiley Indianapolis Composition Services

Front cover photo: Canoe on Moraine Lake in Banff National Park:
Dallas & John Heaton/Stock Connection/Alamy

SPECIAL SALES

For reseller information, including discounts and premium sales, please call
our sales department: Tel. 416-646-7992. For press review copies, author
interviews, or other publicity information, please contact our marketing
department: Tel. 416-646-4584; Fax: 416-236-4448.
Manufactured in Canada

1   2   3   4   5   TRI   11   10   09   08   07

Contents

List of Maps

ABOUT THE AUTHOR

Christie Pashby is the co-author of *Frommer's Argentina* and has authored *Frommer's Banff* for each of its four editions. She is the former editor of the *Canmore Leader* newspaper and *Wildlife*, a Bow Valley arts and entertainment newsmagazine. Her travel stories have also been published in major Canadian dailies and wide-ranging magazines. She was a staff reporter at the *Tico Times* in San Jose, Costa Rica. An avid traveler, Christie makes her home in Canmore, Alberta, and Patagonia, Argentina. Her website is www.patagonia living.com.

ACKNOWLEDGMENTS

I'd like to thank Gloria Keyes-Brady in Jasper and the staff at Parks Canada in Banff. Also, I'm grateful to my friends in Canmore who keep me current on life in the Rockies while I'm on the other side of the equator.

—Christie Pashby

AN INVITATION TO THE READER

In researching this book, we discovered many wonderful places—hotels, restaurants, shops, and more. We're sure you'll find others. Please tell us about them, so we can share the information with your fellow travelers in upcoming editions. If you were disappointed with a recommendation, we'd love to know that, too. Please write to:

Frommer's Banff & Jasper National Parks, 4th Edition
John Wiley & Sons Canada, Ltd. • 6045 Freemont Blvd.
Mississuaga, ON L5R 4J3

AN ADDITIONAL NOTE

Please be advised that travel information is subject to change at any time—and this is especially true of prices. We therefore suggest that you write or call ahead for confirmation when making your travel plans. The authors, editors, and publisher cannot be held responsible for the experiences of readers while traveling. Your safety is important to us, however, so we encourage you to stay alert and be aware of your surroundings. Keep a close eye on cameras, purses, and wallets, all favorite targets of thieves and pickpockets.

FROMMER'S STAR RATINGS, ICONS & ABBREVIATIONS

Every hotel, restaurant, and attraction listing in this guide has been ranked for quality, value, service, amenities, and special features using a **star-rating system.** In country, state, and regional guides, we also rate towns and regions to help you narrow down your choices and budget your time accordingly. Hotels and restaurants are rated on a scale of zero (recommended) to three stars (exceptional). Attractions, shopping, nightlife, towns, and regions are rated according to the following scale: zero stars (recommended), one star (highly recommended), two stars (very highly recommended), and three stars (must-see).

In addition to the star-rating system, we also use seven feature icons that point you to the great deals, in-the-know advice, and unique experiences that separate travelers from tourists. Throughout the book, look for:

Finds	Special finds—those places only insiders know about
Fun Fact	Fun facts—details that make travelers more informed and their trips more fun
Kids	Best bets for kids and advice for the whole family
Moments	Special moments—those experiences that memories are made of
Overrated	Places or experiences not worth your time or money
Tips	Insider tips—great ways to save time and money
Value	Great values—where to get the best deals

The following **abbreviations** are used for credit cards:

AE	American Express	DISC	Discover	V	Visa
DC	Diners Club	MC	MasterCard		

FROMMERS.COM

Now that you have this guidebook to help you plan a great trip, visit our website at **www.frommers.com** for additional travel information on more than 3,600 destinations. We update features regularly to give you instant access to the most current trip-planning information available. At Frommers. com, you'll find scoops on the best airfares, lodging rates, and car rental bargains. You can even book your travel online through our reliable travel booking partners. Other popular features include:

- Online updates of our most popular guidebooks
- Vacation sweepstakes and contest giveaways
- Newsletters highlighting the hottest travel trends
- Online travel message boards with featured travel discussions

Welcome to Banff & Jasper National Parks

In the distance, an avalanche rumbles down a slope. You can hear songbirds chirping, marmots whistling, and the clearness of your own deep breath. You've earned this perfect picnic by hiking 4 hours along a mountain creek to this glorious alpine lake nestled beneath towering peaks. Watching the sun shine on a distant glacier, you feel miles away from normal. Welcome to the Canadian Rockies.

Banff and Jasper national parks are both located in the province of Alberta. They have more than this geographical location in common, but they are also quite different. Banff, with a total area of 6,641 sq. km (2,564 sq. miles) is by far the most popular of Canada's national parks, with more than four million visitors per year. It's a destination that draws travelers year-round for its endless photo opportunities, pristine wilderness, and first-class alpine skiing, not to mention a good selection of restaurants, shopping, and nightlife—amenities not usually found in a national park. An unfortunate side effect of Banff's popularity is the crowds. In the heart of downtown Banff, particularly in summer, you may feel less like you're visiting a protected wilderness area than a shopping mall. North of Banff, Jasper National Park has excellent lodging, including small cabins and rustic bungalows for rent, nestled in a large, unspoiled wilderness. Although larger than Banff, with a total area of 10,878 sq. km (4,199 sq. miles), Jasper nevertheless receives fewer visitors (closer to two million per year). Its remote location compared to Banff and its less developed nature allow Jasper to offer a more quiet charm than does its neighbor to the south.

The Fairmont hotel chain has a big presence in both parks, capitalizing on the truth that some visitors to the parks, though they want to enjoy the nature around them, also want an excellent meal and a soft bed to retire to. Luxury hotels like the Fairmont Chateau Lake Louise and Fairmont Banff Springs, in Banff, and the slightly more rustic Fairmont Jasper Park Lodge, in Jasper, cater to this. But

---

(*Tips* **If It's Solitude You Seek**

While it would be ideal to have the time and money to visit Banff *and* Jasper, it may not be possible for everyone. Banff National Park is almost always the top draw, and most people will head straight there. If you have already seen Banff, have a few extra days to spend, or are looking for quieter streets and backcountry trails, head to Jasper or Yoho national parks. Note, however, that if you visit in July or August things still will be quite busy. Though less crowded than Banff, these joints will still be jumping. If you want a meaningful encounter between you and Mother Nature with few distractions, plan to visit in spring or fall. A day trip to nearby Kootenay National Park is another option in the hunt for crowd-free wilderness.

---

for another group of visitors, a trip to one of these parks is all about the landscape. When you've got this kind of wilderness all around you, having a nice glass of wine to go with it is simply a bonus. So for the most part, hotels and restaurants in the parks try to be subtle and not outshine nature.

History buffs will find much in the parks to delight. The first area in Canada to be declared a national park, and the third-oldest national park in the world, Banff has dozens of heritage homes and historic sites that bring to life the early days of wilderness tourism. Jasper is rich in fur trade, railroad, and exploration history.

The highways that crisscross the parks are logical starting points for planning your trip. They include the Trans-Canada Highway (Hwy. 1), the Yellowhead Highway (Hwy. 16), and the Icefields Parkway (Hwy. 93). Although they're often quite busy, they're also extremely scenic and pleasant to drive. You won't take your vehicle far from these main roads during your trip, but try to do so when you can.

To better experience Banff and Jasper national parks, you'll want to get out of your car. Local outfitters offer rafting, canoeing, and float trips on mountain rivers. Horseback, hiking, and climbing trips are available, either alone or in groups. Winter activities include skiing, snowboarding, skating, and snowshoeing.

Banff and Jasper national parks, along with Yoho and Kootenay national parks and three provincial parks in the neighboring province of British Columbia, have been declared World Heritage Sites by UNESCO (United Nations Educational, Scientific and Cultural Organization), and represent one of the largest tracts of protected mountain wilderness in the world. See the sections in chapter 9, "Radium Hot Springs, British Columbia & Kootenay National Park" and "Golden, British Columbia & Yoho National Park" for details on making a side trip to Kootenay or Yoho, both gateways to Banff National Park.

National parks are a country-wide system of protected natural areas deemed significant by the government of Canada. By law, they are protected for public understanding, appreciation, and enjoyment, while being maintained in an unimpaired state for future generations. Protection of this natural and cultural legacy is a responsibility all visitors share.

1 Banff National Park Today

Banff is Canada's oldest national park—in fact, it's the third-oldest national park in the world. It is Canada's crown jewel, famous for dramatic mountain scenery and first-rate hotels, restaurants, and nightlife. Some come to Banff to explore the backcountry. Many more come to browse the shops of Banff Avenue, soak in the Upper Hot Springs, and have their picture taken in front of Lake Louise.

There are two towns in the national park: Banff and Lake Louise. They complement the wilderness, adding a note of culture and comfort, although Banff sometimes borders on tacky and overflows with tourists. Still, it's this pairing of nature (in the form of the surrounding wilderness) and nurture (in the form of the hotels, restaurants, and shopping) that makes Banff National Park a unique destination. There are two mountain ranges in the park (the Front and Eastern Main Ranges), and nearly 277 species of birds, 69 species of mammals, 15 species of reptiles and amphibians, and 41 species of fish.

In winter, Banff becomes a wonderland of snowy activities and has some of the best alpine skiing and snowboarding in North America at Mount Norquay, Sunshine Village, and the Ski Lake Louise area.

However, be forewarned that you're not the only one planning a trip to Banff National Park. Even with close to 7,000 sq. km (2,600 sq. miles) of protected wilderness, it can get downright crowded here. It's not uncommon to have difficulty finding hotel vacancies in the heart of summer, or to be turned away from a very large, but very full, campground. Scoring a parking spot in Lake Louise's busy Samson Mall or on bustling Banff Avenue is a World Cup sport here.

Partly in response to human traffic accidents and partly as an effort to protect wildlife that have been killed trying to cross a busy transcontinental highway, the government of Canada has doubled the width of the Trans-Canada Highway all the way through Banff. It's now easier for wildlife to avoid the highway. (A reduced speed limit—70kmph versus 90kmph—on the Trans-Canada Highway at Lake Louise has been put in place to help protect bears.) This particular project notwithstanding, construction and expansion of any kind is heavily restricted throughout the park. Development within the town of Banff is also under very strict regulations—another tight balancing act between economics and environment.

On the ecological front, in 2003 Banff National Park completed a massive prescribed fire in the Carrot Creek area (on the north side of the Trans-Canada Hwy., between Canmore and Banff) in an effort to bring forests back to their natural cycles of fire. It's hard to miss the burned mountain slopes. "Ecological integrity"—a Parks Canada buzzword—means that all park policy must put healthy ecosystems at the top of priority lists. In that vein, Banff National Park's website (www.pc.gc.ca/banff) now has fun new features like avalanche maps and wildflower notes.

Changes have also been approved at the area's major alpine ski centers—Sunshine Village, Lake Louise, and Banff Mount Norquay—to keep up with the ever-evolving ski industry. Newer, bigger, and faster chairlifts are the draws.

A note on the town of Banff: You will hear people refer to it as both the "Town of Banff" and the "Banff Townsite." The names are used interchangeably here, and the practice is carried on throughout this guide.

2 The Best of Banff National Park

This section is designed to take you to all points of Banff National Park and show you the best of what's out there. Never fear, every attraction in these lists is covered in full detail later on in the book.

THE BEST INTERPRETIVE TRAILS

The trails listed below, and others, are detailed under "Day Hikes" in chapter 4, except for the Fenland Trail, which is located right in downtown Banff. For more details about it, see "What to See & Do in Banff Townsite" in chapter 3.

- **Johnston Canyon** (Bow Valley Pkwy., Hwy. 1A): This trail follows a narrow river as it roars through what is probably the most popular canyon in the Canadian Rockies. The 2.2km (1.4-mile) trail includes a suspended walkway and narrow tunnel-like sections. You can extend it into a half-day hike and head for the Upper Falls.

- **Peyto Lake/Bow Summit** (Icefields Pkwy., Hwy. 93): A short, 20-minute stroll heading out from the Icefields Parkway, Highway 93, this trail takes you to a jaw-dropping viewpoint of lovely Peyto Lake and Peyto Glacier, and the Mistaya Valley. Interpretive displays along the 1.2km (.7-mile) loop explain the basics of the subalpine and alpine landscape.

- **Sulphur Mountain Boardwalk** (Banff Townsite): There are 367 steps (1km/.6 mile) along an elevated boardwalk from the top of the Sulphur Mountain Gondola to the summit of Sanson Peak and the historic Sanson Peak Meteorological Station. En route, informative placards describe the truly stunning views that stretch below you. Geology, weather, and history all come alive here in one of the world's most stunning and accessible ridgewalks. A Rocky Mountain high!

THE BEST SHORT DAY HIKES

Hiking is Banff's premier outdoor activity. And getting beyond the parking lot into the mountains doesn't necessarily require an entire day. These short hikes take only a few hours to complete. Combine them with other outdoor or sightseeing activities. See "Day Hikes" in chapter 4 for more information on these and other hikes in Banff.

- **Bourgeau Lake** (Bow Valley Pkwy./Castle Junction area): Though the climb is gradually long and steep, the reward is a beautiful lake tucked away in an alpine meadow below the rugged rock wall of Mount Bourgeau. Snowy into late June, this 15km (9.3-mile) trail passes through prime wildlife habitat. This hike takes around 5 hours to complete, round-trip.

- **Parker Ridge** (Icefields Pkwy., Hwy. 93): A mere 2-hour round-trip, this 5km (3-mile) trail will take you up to a ridge

---

Fun Fact **What Is an Interpretive Trail?**

Unlike a hiking trail, which isn't regularly maintained, an interpretive trail is well groomed and includes informative displays, placards, signs, and mounted photographs that relate the significance of the area. Most walks are less than 3km (1.9 miles) in length and many are wheelchair-accessible. These are great places to get out of the car for a stretch and learn about where you are.

top with expansive views of the Columbia Icefield and Saskatchewan Glacier, one of the largest alpine valley glaciers in the Rockies. Keep an eye on the lower slopes for grizzly bears and mountain goats. Be prepared for cold and windy weather up here!

- **Plain of the Six Glaciers** (Lake Louise): This 5-hour, 11km (6.8-mile) round-trip hike is an ideal way to appreciate the wonders of the Lake Louise area. Leave early in the morning to avoid crowds. Head up the narrow path at the back of the lake to an exposed moraine below Victoria Glacier for a fantastic view of six other glaciers. Stop at the Plain of the Six Glaciers Teahouse for lunch or a cup of tea and a warm biscuit. If you've still got some stamina left, continue another half-hour to the Victoria Glacier Viewpoint.

THE BEST LONGER DAY HIKES

If you can devote 6 or 8 hours to hiking, you'll be able to access areas of the mountains that are much more moving and dramatic than what you can see from the road. "Day Hikes" in chapter 4 describes these longer hikes in more detail.

- **Nigel Pass** (Icefields Pkwy., Hwy. 93): Often used as a jumping-off point for a backpacking trip into Jasper National Park, the 15km (9.3-mile) round-trip trek is the best day hike in the part of the Icefield area that falls within the Banff boundary. Look behind you to see the looming forms of Parker Ridge, Mount Saskatchewan, and the Hilda Glacier. Ranked moderate. Give yourself at least 5 hours to complete.

- **Paradise Valley/Larch Valley:** (Lake Louise) This 17km (10.5-mile) hike takes you through an alpine meadow, below high peaks, beside thundering falls, and over a majestic pass before ending at spectacular Moraine Lake. This hike is ranked difficult; expect it to take you 7 or 8 hours to complete. It also doesn't hurt to be in shape.

THE BEST OVERNIGHT BACKPACKING TRIPS

While overnight trips do require a fair bit of organizing, the reward of sleeping out in the open under the Rocky Mountain stars and waking to the peace and solitude of the mountains is unbeatable. See chapter 4 for more on these and other suggested trails, and chapter 5 for campsites.

- **Egypt Lakes** (2–6 days): Surrounded by beautiful larch trees, Egypt and its neighboring lakes are stunning and easy to get to.

Don't miss the side trips to Whistling Pass and Haiduk Creek, and be sure to spend a night at the Shadow Lake campground.

- **Skoki Valley** (Lake Louise; 3–5 days): At the convergence of a series of valleys in the Slate Range, the Skoki Valley area is the place to go if you want to see a new lake every day, take in plenty of wildlife, and experience a rich human history.
- **Sunshine Meadows/Mount Assiniboine** (3 days): Access Mount Assiniboine, known as the "Matterhorn of the Rockies," via Sunshine Village ski area. Virtually the entire route consists of stunning alpine valleys. It ends at the Mount Shark trail head in nearby Kananaskis Country.

THE BEST PLACES TO SEE WILDLIFE

Beyond squirrels and chipmunks, your chances of seeing bighorn sheep and elk are quite good in Banff. Early morning and dusk are the best times of day. Refer to chapter 10 for a park nature guide.

- **Minnewanka Loop:** This stretch of road just outside the Town of Banff is a prime place to spot bighorn sheep.
- **Trans-Canada Highway Overpasses between Banff and Castle Junction:** Look up when you pass underneath the two wildlife bridges that cross the Trans-Canada Highway (Hwy. 1)—they allow deer, bear, coyotes, and elk access to the Bow River.
- **Waterfowl Lake** (Icefields Pkwy., Hwy. 93): You won't be surprised to see mallard ducks and loons on this lake. What may well surprise you, however, is spotting a moose. Summer evenings are the best time.

THE BEST HISTORICAL SITES

Banff's history comes alive at a number of well-presented historical sites and museums. Learning about those who were here before you will give you insight into the issues facing the park today. These and other historical sites worth visiting are detailed under "What to See & Do in Banff Townsite" in chapter 3. You can visit the Lake Agnes Teahouse as part of the Lake Agnes/Beehives hike, which is reviewed under "Day Hikes" in chapter 4.

- **Cave and Basin National Historic Site** (Banff Townsite; © **403/762-1566**): In an easy 20 minutes, hike the Discovery Trail to the source of the hot springs, discovered in 1883, which led to the creation of Banff National Park.
- **Lake Agnes Teahouse** (Lake Louise): Built in 1901 by the Canadian Pacific Railway to draw tourists to the mountains, the teahouse was named for the wife of Sir John A. Macdonald,

Canada's first prime minister. Home-baked treats and warm teas are served daily from June to early October. It's a 2-hour hike from the Fairmont Chateau Lake Louise.

• **Spiral Tunnels** (in Yoho National Park): Relive the challenges and wonder of the Canadian Pacific Railway as it makes its way down the steep west side of mighty Kicking Horse Pass, known as "The Big Hill." If your timing's right, you can actually see a train loop through Mt. Stephen. There are great placards explaining the engineering feat that dates to 1909.

THE BEST CULTURAL ACTIVITIES

When you're ready to take a break from mountain mania, check out these first-rate cultural attractions, all in Banff Townsite. Dance, opera, film, and drama lovers, refer to "What to See & Do in Banff Townsite," in chapter 3 for more.

• **Banff Summer Arts Festival** (© **403/762-6301**): Drama, opera, ballet, plus classical, jazz, and pop music are on offer at this summer-long festival that runs from mid-July to the end of August. Many events are free, others are "pay as you wish."

• **Canada House Gallery** (© **403/762-3757**): For more than 30 years, this has been the premier commercial art gallery in the Canadian Rockies. Showcasing Canadian artists, there are regular artist receptions on Saturdays during the summer at 201 Bear St. It's a vibrant and inspiring place, much like Banff itself.

• **Whyte Museum of the Canadian Rockies** (© **403/762-2291**): It's rare to find such an interesting and unique museum in a small town. The Whyte is the only museum in North America that specializes in the history and culture of the Canadian Rockies.

THE BEST PLACES TO SWIM

These swimming spots are all located within a 10-minute drive from the Town of Banff. See "Other Activities" in chapter 4 for more outdoor activities in Banff.

• **Johnson Lake:** This is one of the few lakes around the Town of Banff that actually reaches a temperature that's warm enough to swim in. There's a picnic area and a sandy beach to toss a Frisbee back and forth. This is where the locals escape to on a hot summer day.

• **Upper Hot Springs** (© **403/762-1515**): Making time for a soak in these warm mineral waters is a must for all visitors to

Banff. The pools are rich in heritage, have lovely views, and are open into the evenings throughout the year—for romantic, starry nights.

- **Willow Stream Spa** (© 403/762-1772): A soak in the Hungarian mineral pools at this exclusive spa inside the Fairmont Banff Springs hotel is the ultimate getaway and a luxurious treat for hiking-tired muscles. But it's pricey, and you must have a reservation. Sign up for the least expensive treatment—say, a manicure for C$55/US$51—and enjoy the services for an entire day.

THE BEST PLACES FOR WINTER SPORTS

Banff may be somewhat dormant in October and November, but the winter season, December to April, is an exciting time to visit. See "Winter Sports & Activities" in chapter 4.

- **Ice-Skating on Lake Louise:** On a crisp winter day, there's nothing more spectacular than tying on your blades and going for a skate on frozen Lake Louise. It's equally lovely in the evening, when hot chocolate is served and an open fire crackles. Rent skates at the Fairmont Chateau Lake Louise. November to April.
- **Ski Lake Louise** (© 877/253-6888): One of the best ski resorts in the world for both snow and scenery, Lake Louise is a great destination for skiers. Snowboarders will particularly enjoy the snowboard obstacle or "terrain" park, and steep terrain. There are beginner runs from every chair, so novices aren't limited to the bottom slopes.
- **Spray River Loop:** This 2.2km (1.4-mile) cross-country ski trail starts from the Town of Banff, crosses the Banff Springs golf course, and follows a fire road along the bottom slopes of the picturesque Mount Rundle. You can extend the trail to 10.8km (6.7 miles).
- **Sunshine Village** (© 877/542-2633): Situated high in the Rockies, this world-class ski resort has lots of powder snow and so much terrain you'll need a week to ski it all. There's a great ski school plus on-hill dining and lodging.

THE BEST ACTIVITIES FOR KIDS

It can be a real challenge to entertain little people for days on end. Let these kid-friendly attractions and their helpful staff take over for a while and give you a break!

- **Canada Place** (© 403/762-1338): Great interactive kid-friendly exhibits here tell the remarkable story of the "Great White North." Shoot the rapids with fur traders, check out Canada's role in space travel, and make a video about what Canada means to you.

- **Lake Louise Sightseeing Gondola** (② **403/522-3555**): The gondola is located at the Lake Louise ski area. Take the lift up Whitehorn Mountain for a spectacular view—particularly in the summertime. There's a great grizzly bear–themed interpretive tour—bring binoculars to look for bears! It's cool to see the ski hill looking like a vertical golf course! The focus is on fun and nature education.
- **Junior Naturalists** (② **403/762-8918**): Drop your kids by Banff's Tunnel Mountain campground afternoons at 4:15 Wednesday through Saturday. Park staff will entertain them with an "inside scoop" peek at wildlife and the complexities of the local ecosystems.

THE BEST RV PARKS AND CAMPGROUNDS

Banff's RV parks and campgrounds are maintained to very high standards by Parks Canada staff. "Frontcountry Camping in Banff National Park" in chapter 5 includes more detailed information about these and other Banff campgrounds.

- **Castle Mountain:** A good halfway point between Banff and Lake Louise, this campground hosts both tenters and RVers and has a wonderful view of the spectacular west ridge of Castle Mountain.
- **Tunnel Mountain Village:** Located just outside the Town of Banff, this campground is accessible and open year-round. With more than 1,000 well-spaced sites of every size and shape, it's big enough to have an entire section known as the "Trailer Court," with full RV hookups and nightly activities.
- **Waterfowl Lake** (Icefields Pkwy., Hwy. 93): This medium-size campground is near Saskatchewan Crossing, at the south end of beautiful Waterfowl Lake. The setting is intimate and just plain gorgeous.

THE BEST BACKCOUNTRY CAMPSITES

Here are my picks for the best places to pitch your tent if you're heading out to spend the night in the Banff backcountry. See "Exploring the Backcountry" in chapter 4 for more suggestions and information on reserving a backcountry campsite.

- **Egypt Lake:** On the crest of the Continental Divide you'll find both a park-operated shelter and a popular campground—a good base for day hiking in the area.

- **Merlin Meadows** (Lake Louise): Along the Skoki Loop, this site is just below Merlin Lake and past the historic Skoki Lodge. It's a great base for exploring the Skoki Valley.

THE BEST LODGING

There are dozens of hotels in Banff National Park, most in the Town of Banff. There are others in Lake Louise, and a few scattered in more remote parts of the park. This list is a sampling of the best in a variety of categories. Some of the finest lodging options in the Canadian Rockies are in Banff's neighbor, Yoho National Park. See chapter 9 for more information. See "Lodging in Banff National Park" in chapter 5 for full reviews and other lodging suggestions.

- **Fairmont Banff Springs** (Banff Townsite; ✆ **800/441-1414**): World-renowned and regularly considered one of the top hotels anywhere, the Banff Springs is in a category all its own. Incredible amenities—8 restaurants, a spa, bowling center, tennis courts, skating rink, golf course, just to mention a few— make up for the notoriously cramped rooms.
- **Num-Ti-Jah Lodge** (Icefields Pkwy., Hwy. 93; ✆ **403/522-2167**): On the shores of Bow Lake in Banff's northern reaches, this is one of the few hotels in the park that is secluded and surrounded completely by nature.
- **Post Hotel** (Lake Louise; ✆ **800/661-1586**): A Relais & Château luxury lodge with excellent service and a tranquil atmosphere, this inn combines the best of the old with the most modern amenities in a classic mountain style.
- **Ptarmigan Lodge** (Banff Townsite; ✆ **800/661-8310**): A great choice for families and those ready to jampack their time in Banff. The location, in the heart of downtown Banff, is great. The price point makes it a great value.

THE BEST RESTAURANTS

With numerous restaurants to choose from, eating in Banff can be as much of an adventure as exploring the wilderness. Generally, the food here is innovative, interesting, and fresh. Eating isn't a challenge, but getting a reservation often is. These restaurants offer both casual and classy dining at reasonable prices. More Banff restaurants are reviewed under "Where to Eat in Banff National Park" in chapter 5.

- **The Bison Mountain Bistro** (✆ **403/762-5550**): Serving Rocky Mountain "comfort food," the Bison is critically acclaimed and focuses on the seasonal and the regional. Think elegant rustic. It also has the best patio in town.

- **Coyotes Deli and Grill** (© **403/762-3963**): This is the best place for lunch in Banff. It's a casual bistro with a Southwestern-influenced menu that highlights freshness and creativity.
- **Melissa's Restaurant and Bar** (© **403/762-5511**): The best family dining in Banff is a classic, with local hospitality, a long and varied menu, and a chance to sample Alberta's famous AAA beef. Big servings, a kids' menu, and a heated patio are other perks.
- **The Station Restaurant at Lake Louise** (Lake Louise; © **403/ 522-2600**): If you're heading for a day-trip exploration of the stunning Lake Louise area, plan to make this your stop for lunch. The food is thoroughly modern and fresh. On a warm summer day, sit in the heritage building's courtyard.

3 Jasper National Park Today

Jasper is for those who love open spaces. It has an expansive feel to it. It's the largest of the Canadian Rocky Mountain National Parks, with an area of 10,878 sq. km (4,200 sq. miles)—in which there are more than 1,200km (700 miles) of hiking trails. You'll notice many more hikers in the Town of Jasper than in the Town of Banff. This doesn't mean that Jasper can't offer the varied lodging and dining options that Banff can (it can and does), just that the feel up here is a bit more adventurous and decidedly more rustic. It's a backcountry mecca.

Almost all of Jasper National Park is wilderness. You could hike up here for a month and not run into a single road or another soul. Even though most visitors choose to see the park from the road, since the highway system through the park is so well developed and scenic, I encourage you to take a few hikes, go rafting or canoeing, and get away from the highway. That's how you'll see the beauty of this park and come to appreciate the grandeur of the mountains.

Like Banff, Jasper National Park has a main population center—alternatively called "the Town of Jasper" or "Jasper Townsite." It's worth noting that Jasper and Banff are unique in that they have a substantial town inside the park boundaries (which happen to have the same names as the parks themselves). Many national parks in Canada, the United States, and other countries have strict limits on commercial development inside park boundaries. In a move to perhaps stem the development tide in parks like Banff and Jasper, the *National Parks Act* legislates fixed boundaries of communities in parks and restricts commercial development in those communities. Granted, with only 5,000 residents, Jasper's a small town, but it's one with a thriving permanent community and all the amenities a visitor could need. It's here that you'll find almost all of the hotels, lodges, restaurants, and outfitting companies.

4 The Best of Jasper National Park

This list will help give you a head start on your planning.

THE BEST INTERPRETIVE TRAILS

Take an hour or so to explore the park on these easy trails, where you'll stretch, learn, and let your imagination soar. For more interpretive trails, see "Day Hikes" in chapter 7.

- **Path of the Glacier** (Cavell Rd./Hwy. 93A): This 1.6km (1-mile) loop is tucked below the base of the imposing Mount Edith Cavell. Check out how far the Angel Glacier has receded in only 55 years.
- **Pocahontas Coal Mine Trail** (Jasper east): A short, wheelchair-accessible loop along the Athabasca River Valley tells the tale of the coal mine that thrived here in the early 1900s. The view of the Athabasca Valley and the Pocahontas Ponds is gorgeous. The trail is particularly lovely in the fall.

THE BEST SHORT DAY HIKES

Jasper specializes in the short or half-day hike. There are so many to choose from, you could spend weeks exploring one after the other. Here's a sampling from different areas of the park. For full descriptions of these and other hikes, see "Day Hikes" in chapter 7.

- **Bald Hills** (Maligne Lake): If you want to get up to a high point fast, head to this trail. The steep ascent of this 10.4km (6.4-mile) round-trip trail is worth it once you step on to the gentler ridge and take in the panoramic views and blooming flowers. It'll take you about 4 hours to complete the entire trip.
- **Cavell Meadows** (Hwy. 93A): For a chance to see mountain wildflowers at their most colorful, hike this 8km (5-mile) loop trail in July. This moderate-ranked 5-hour hike is popular, so go in the early morning to beat the crowds. You'll also have the best light at this time of day.
- **Wilcox Pass** (Icefields Pkwy.): This short but moderately challenging 8km (5-mile) half-day hike takes you above the Icefields Parkway (Hwy. 93) to a stunning view of the Athabasca

Glacier. A great supplement to a day exploring the Columbia Icefield area, accessible from either Jasper or Banff.

THE BEST LONGER DAY HIKES

Remember to bring along snack food and water on these longer hikes. Also be aware that, even if you leave in early or midmorning, you can expect to be on the trail well into the afternoon. See "Day Hikes" in chapter 7.

- **Geraldine Lakes** (Hwy. 93A): There are several hikes of varying distances and difficulty here. You can decide which one suits you best. It's only a 20-minute hike from the trail head to the first lake, and the other three lakes are pleasantly spread out on a progressively more difficult trail. It's 20km (12.4 miles) round-trip if you hike up the valley staircase to the highest lakes set below the walls of Mount Fryatt.

- **Saturday Night Lake** (Jasper Townsite): It won't require too much effort or time to get to the trail head for this 24.6km (15.3-mile) loop hike, since it's just outside the townsite. That leaves you the entire day to explore the series of lakes along the trail that culminates in Saturday Night Lake.

THE BEST OVERNIGHT BACKPACKING TRIPS

You could spend weeks exploring the corners of Jasper National Park. If you have a week to 10 days head to Athabasca Pass, or to the North or South Boundaries. If your time is more limited, choose one of these trails to see what glories lie in the backcountry. Check out "Exploring the Backcountry" in chapter 7 for more overnight trips.

- **Fryatt Valley** (3–4 days): This trip promises a wonderland of lakes, rivers, meadows, peaks, and glaciers. It'll take you 1 day of steep climbing from the trail head near Athabasca Falls on the Icefields Parkway (Hwy. 93), but once you've made it to Fryatt Valley you won't want to leave.

- **Skyline Trail** (2–4 days): This is by far the most popular trip in Jasper. The trail head is 45 minutes from the townsite. Most of the trail runs above the tree line along the top of a ridge with maximum exposure to unforgettable views. A true mountain experience.

- **Tonquin Valley** (3–5 days): A network of trails starting near Mount Edith Cavell winds its way through pristine mountain landscapes and culminates in the fortress-like wall of the Ramparts. Hike in, pick a site as a base camp, and spend a few days exploring this beautiful valley.

THE BEST PLACES TO SEE WILDLIFE

Whether it's bears, mountain goats, or majestic elk you're hoping to spot, your chances will be good at any one of these places—as long as you're quiet and patient. See chapter 10 for a guide to Jasper's flora and fauna.

- **Highway 16 East of Jasper Townsite:** Here, in an ideal elk-grazing habitat, you're likely to see some of these white-bottomed relatives of deer and moose roaming alongside the highway. Watch for signs lowering the speed limit.
- **Icefields Parkway:** Pull over at the Goats and Glaciers Viewpoint (which is well marked) and scan the hills for white mountain goats clinging to the slopes.
- **Maligne Lake Road:** Bighorn sheep and black bears both like to hang around here. Keep your eyes peeled on the roadside slopes for bears and on the shoulders for sheep.

THE BEST HISTORICAL SITES

There's plenty of history to soak up during your wilderness experience in Jasper National Park. These are my top picks; there are more in "What to See & Do in Jasper Townsite" in chapter 6.

- **Curly Phillips' Boathouse:** Visit this pioneer outpost on Maligne Lake and walk along the Mary Schaffer Trail to learn about the first non-Native woman to see this lake, as well as the early mountain settlers who once had this whole park to themselves.
- **Jasper: A Walk in the Past** (✆ 780/852-4767): A 2-hour early-evening stroll shows you the history of the town and its founders. The tour includes visits to some of the oldest buildings in town—and in the entire park, for that matter. An outstanding tour.

THE BEST CULTURAL ACTIVITIES

These and other cultural activities are reviewed in more detail in "What to See & Do in Jasper Townsite" in chapter 6.

- **Full Moon Hike** (✆ 780/852-4767): Join Jasper locals for a monthly evening hike under the moonlit sky. Organized by the prolific and friendly members of the Friends of Jasper, it's a great way to meet new friends, discover new trails, and soak up the magic of the mountains.
- **Jasper Heritage Folk Music Festival** (✆ 780/852-3615): Held every 2 years (the next one will be in 2009); join some

5,000 music lovers the first weekend in August in the field at Centennial Park to take in music from across Canada and around the world.

THE BEST PLACES TO SWIM

Jasper has hundreds of lakes, but only a few are actually warm enough to take a dip in.

- **Jasper Activity Centre** (© 780/852-3381): Great on a rainy day, there's a huge indoor pool, diving boards, waterslide, whirlpools, and a sauna at the town's public pool. Kids will enjoy themselves.
- **Lake Annette:** Just east of town, this is one of the only lakes in the Rocky Mountains where the water is warm enough to swim. There's a sandy beach and picnic tables. It's a local favorite.
- **Miette Hot Springs** (© 780/866-3939): An hour east of the Town of Jasper, these springs are kept at a temperature of 104°F (40°C), making for an ideal post-hike soak.

THE BEST PLACES FOR WINTER SPORTS

Although Jasper seems quite dormant in the fall and spring, it's a vital place in wintertime. From December to late March, the sun shines almost every day and the air is cool and crisp. If you're lucky, a goodly amount of snow will fall within 1 week, transforming the park into a true winter wonderland. These and other winter activities are described in more detail in "Winter Sports & Activities" in chapter 7.

- **Lac Beauvert** (© 780/852-3301): Go ice-skating on this frozen lake in front of the Jasper Park Lodge, and you'll feel like you're in a scene right out of a holiday greeting card. Music, a campfire, and plenty of hot chocolate keep the spell going.
- **Maligne Lake:** There's a variety of cross-country ski trails for all levels here, and the snow is in great condition well into spring.
- **Ski Marmot Basin** (© 780/852-3816): This ski and snowboard resort has the same great powder snow and wide-open terrain as other ski hills in the Rockies—without the crowds. It's rustic and expansive, much like Jasper itself.

THE BEST ACTIVITIES FOR KIDS

Here's what's on offer in the park for your little ones.

- **Jasper Tramway** (© 780/852-3093): This is the fastest and safest way to get your family above the tree line. Kids can roam the high alpine region and have fun figuring out where their hotel or campground is, way down below.

- **Junior Naturalist Program** (✆ **780/852-4767**): In just 1 hour, your kids will learn about the wonders of nature and have fun exploring the wilderness around Whistlers Campground.
- **Maligne Lake Cruise to Spirit Island** (Maligne Lake; ✆ **780/852-3370**): On a quest for mystery and adventure sure to excite your kids, the cruise ventures out to seemingly unvisited lakeside nooks and crannies. Kids love to take binoculars out to the back deck to watch the hills for eagles and mountain goats. The cruise docks at Spirit Island for a short tour before returning to the Maligne Lake boathouse.

THE BEST RV PARKS AND CAMPGROUNDS

After a long day of exploring in Jasper National Park, look no further than these campgrounds for a good night's sleep. See "Frontcountry Camping in Jasper National Park" in chapter 8 for more suggestions.

- **Snaring River Campground:** If you're pitching a tent and don't want to be dwarfed by RVs, head to this campground east of the Town of Jasper. (There are no RV hookups.) It's a little more rustic, the rates are cheaper, and it's just a better outdoor experience.
- **Wabasso Campground:** Even though it has a whopping 288 sites, this campground feels cozy and private since it's in a forested valley. It's best for RVers and trailers, although tents are welcome. Try to get a site next to the Athabasca River.
- **Wilcox Creek Campground:** This is the only spot where vans, trailers, and RVs can stay alongside tenters on the Icefields Parkway (Hwy. 93). You can wake up early and get a head start on exploring the fascinating Icefield area before the crowds come. The campground is located on a steep hill, so almost every site has a great view of the mountains. It's terraced, so there's plenty of privacy. But it can get chilly at night!

THE BEST BACKCOUNTRY CAMPSITES

These are the best of the designated campsites located strategically, and often scenically, along Jasper's backcountry hiking trails. See "Exploring the Backcountry" in chapter 7 for more backcountry campsites and instructions on how to reserve one.

- **Amethyst Lake:** Pitch a tent in the backcountry here and use it as your base camp for exploring the Tonquin Valley. The Ramparts, a 1,000m-high (3,280-ft.) quartzite wall, stands tall above you.
- **Four Point:** This campsite is located on the very popular Brazeau trail system. It's a great base for exploring the southern ranges of Jasper National Park.
- **Tekarra:** Camp here on your last night on the Skyline Trail— if the sky is clear, you'll remember the sunset forever. Great views of all the familiar peaks around Jasper Townsite.

THE BEST LODGING

Almost all the hotels are located within a 15-minute drive of the Town of Jasper. There is a wide selection of hotels, lodges, inns, bed-and-breakfasts, and bungalows. These are my top picks. "Lodging in Jasper National Park" in chapter 8 has complete reviews of these and other Jasper accommodations.

- **Alpine Village** (© 780/852-3285): Come here for understated luxury and solitude. Staying in one of these cabins will make you dream about the cottage you've always wanted. The style is pure Rocky Mountains and the staff are delightfully attentive and caring.
- **Fairmont Jasper Park Lodge** (© 800/441-1414): This hotel sets the standard for lodges across the country. The grounds are outstanding, the amenities first class, the peace and solitude remarkable for a lodge with 446 guest rooms. Even if you aren't staying here, stop by for a meal and a stroll—or a round of golf. It's centrally located in the middle of the park, just outside the Town of Jasper.
- **Pine Bungalows** (© 780/852-3491): Offering rustic privacy in cabins tucked along the Athabasca River, the very reasonably priced Pine Bungalows is Jasper as it used to be, before the motor inns moved in. I can't help but love the unpretentious enthusiasm and obvious nostalgia here. Reserve one of the recently renovated riverfront cabins.
- **Park Place Inn** (© 780/852-9770): City slickers will feel at home in this lovely inn, as downtown as it gets here. It's Jasper's answer to mountain chic. There are fabulous linens, huge bathtubs, and a trendy cowboy flair.

THE BEST RESTAURANTS

There's everything from fine cuisine to grab-it-and-go here. See "Where to Eat in Jasper National Park" in chapter 8 for full reviews on these, my top choices, and other restaurants in and around Jasper.

- **Andy's Bistro** (© **780/852-4559**): Fine dining with a friendly smile, Andy's has a fresh and inspired regional Canadian menu with European and Asian influences.
- **Bear's Paw Bakery** (© **780/852-2253**): With a new branch opening at 610 Connaught St.—known as "The Other Paw"—and the original at 4 Cedar Ave., these are Jasper's coziest, healthiest, and yummiest places to pick up a coffee and muffin in the morning, a loaded sandwich for the trail, or an afternoon tea and treat.
- **Tekarra Restaurant** (© **780/852-4624**): A place this out-of-the-way has got to be good. It's upscale yet casual, and the menu is crafted with a focus on the fresh. There's a fabulous breakfast buffet and a great lunch, too. It's definitely worth the search.

2

Planning Your Trip

Holiday planning includes plenty of patience, investigation, and decision making. But don't be intimidated by the work ahead! Once you've made a few key decisions, your vacation in the Canadian Rockies will be straightforward—and the payoff is unbeatable! Since you are competing against millions of other visitors who are probably heading to the same attractions you are, you need to strategize. Decide whether you want to do what most people do when they come to Banff or Jasper national parks—stay in hotels in the main townsites and see the parks primarily from your vehicle—or venture out of your car or RV and into the wilderness on foot, boat, bike, or ski. If you're interested in getting beyond the parking lots and highways, there's plenty of information out there to help you find the right adventure. This book is a good place to start.

1 Getting Started: Information & Reservations

It used to be very difficult to get information about a place you were planning to visit before you actually got there. Not anymore. Advances in technology have liberated the curious. There's now so much information out there, you need a special guidebook just to navigate your way through it all. Be careful about the reliability of your sources, however—particularly your online sources. Though many websites contain accurate, up-to-date information, many others are nothing more than marketing vehicles for a hotel or restaurant chain masquerading as information repositories. Be a savvy surfer.

For travel information on the entire province of Alberta, contact **Travel Alberta** (© **800/252-3782;** www.travelalberta.com). Travel Alberta runs a large information center just outside Banff's eastern entrance gate, right off Highway 1, the Trans-Canada Highway (2801 Bow Valley Trail, Canmore, AB T1W 3A2; © **800/661-8888** or 403/678-5277).

Banff and Jasper are both in the province of Alberta but border on the province of British Columbia to the west. You may be passing through BC on your trip. For information about visiting British

Tips   Online & On Your Way

There are dozens of websites that purport to tell you all about Banff and Jasper national parks with just a click of your mouse. But do they deliver the goods? Many are simply hidden sales tools. Here are eight that I find particularly useful for trip planning:

Canadian Rockies, General Information

- **www.canadianrockies.net**: A well-designed website with information on hiking, fishing, and skiing. Locals contribute their own insider tips to help you plan your trip.
- **www.mountainnature.com**: This site has great information about the natural history of the area.
- **www.peakfinder.com**: A wonderful resource with information on the geology and history of dozens of mountains in the Canadian Rockies.
- **www.icefieldsparkway.ca**: A new, interactive website that gives you a virtual tour of one of the world's most beautiful drives.

Banff

- **www.pc.gc.ca/banff**: The online home of **Banff National Park** has up-to-date information on trails, weather, events, and planning your trip to this mountain paradise.
- **www.banff.com**: A site with events listings, virtual tours, weather updates, and a listing for everything from restaurants to ski rental shops.

Jasper

- **www.explorejasper.com**: This locally run site has links to many businesses and hotels in the Town of Jasper, as well as a calendar of events.
- **www.jaspercanadianrockies.com**: The main portal for **Jasper Tourism and Commerce,** this site has links to services, hotels, restaurants, and activities in Jasper.

Columbia, get in touch with **Travel British Columbia** (✆ **800/435-5622;** www.hellobc.com).

GATEWAY TOWNS   The main gateways to Banff and Jasper national parks each have their own tourism centers all set to distribute

The Canadian Rockies

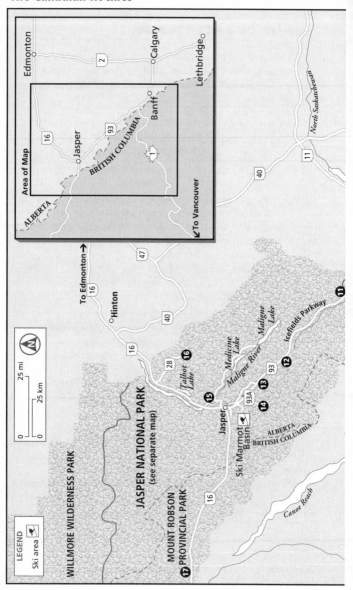

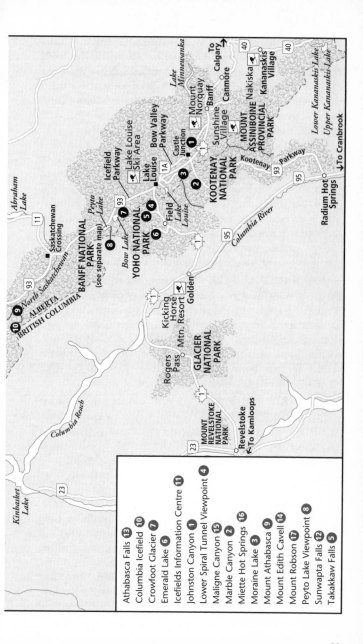

Athabasca Falls ⑬
Columbia Icefield ⑩
Crowfoot Glacier ⑦
Emerald Lake ⑥
Icefields Information Centre ⑪
Johnston Canyon ①
Lower Spiral Tunnel Viewpoint ④
Maligne Canyon ⑮
Marble Canyon ②
Miette Hot Springs ⑯
Moraine Lake ③
Mount Athabasca ⑨
Mount Edith Cavell ⑭
Mount Robson ⑰
Peyto Lake Viewpoint ⑧
Sunwapta Falls ⑫
Takakkaw Falls ⑤

useful information on weather, road conditions, lodging, and attractions. In Canmore, **Tourism Canmore** has a booth in the **Travel Alberta** center, mentioned just above. To the northwest of Banff, you may visit the town of Golden, in British Columbia's Columbia Valley, on the west side of Yoho National Park. Contact the **Golden Chamber of Commerce** (500 Tenth Ave. N, Golden, BC V0A 1H0; ⓒ **800/622-4653;** www.goldenchamber.bc.ca).

South of Golden and west of Banff and its neighbor Kootenay National Park is the small town of Radium Hot Springs, also in British Columbia. Contact the **Radium Chamber of Commerce** (7556 Main St. E, Radium Hot Springs, BC V0A 1M0; ⓒ **800/ 347-9704;** www.radiumhotsprings.com). See chapter 9 for information on accommodations, restaurants, and fun things to do in these gateway towns—enough that you may want to incorporate one of them into your trip as an excursion, or even base your trip at one of them. They can be more affordable than Banff!

BANFF NATIONAL PARK   The main contact number for the park is ⓒ **403/762-1550.** The website is www.parkscanada.gc.ca/ banff. For maps, books, and information on educational programs, a great source is the not-for-profit **Friends of Banff National Park** (P.O. Box 2590, Banff, AB T1L 1C3; ⓒ **403/762-8918;** www. friendsofbanff.com). You can also contact or visit the **Banff/Lake Louise Tourism Bureau** (P.O. Box 1298, Banff, AB T1L 1B3; ⓒ **403/762-8421;** www.banfflakelouise.com).

JASPER NATIONAL PARK   The main contact number for the park is ⓒ **780/852-6176,** and the website is at www.parkscanada. gc.ca/jasper. For maps and details on educational programs, the **Friends of Jasper National Park** (P.O. Box 992, 415 Connaught Dr., Jasper, AB T0E 1E0; ⓒ **780/852-4767;** www.friendsofjasper. com) is a good bet, as is the **Jasper Tourism and Commerce** office (P.O. Box 98, Jasper, AB T0E 1E0; ⓒ **780/852-3858;** www.jasper canadianrockies.com).

For information on backcountry huts, contact the **Alpine Club of Canada** (ⓒ **403/678-3200;** www.alpineclubofcanada.ca). If you're planning on going the hostelling route, contact **Hostelling International Canada** (ⓒ **866/762-4122;** www.hostellingintl.ca). **Rocky Mountain Reservations** (ⓒ **877/902-9455;** www.rocky mountainreservations.com), one of a number of private booking agencies in the area, will find you a hotel and book you a room for a nominal fee.

USEFUL PUBLICATIONS   The following books will enhance your visit to Banff and Jasper national parks. All are available at bookstores, gift shops, and information centers in the parks; many are available throughout North America. *Handbook of the Canadian Rockies,* by Ben Gadd (Jasper: Corax Press) is an excellent nature guide. See also *Canadian Rockies Access Guide,* by John Dood and Gail Helgason (Edmonton: Lone Pine Publishing). *Walks and Easy Hikes in the Canadian Rockies,* by Graeme Pole (Canmore, AB: Altitude Publishing), is a good resource for families looking for hikes to take. The most complete hiking guide to the area is *The Canadian Rockies Trail Guide,* by Brian Patton and Bart Robinson (Banff: Summerthought). See also *Backcountry Banff,* by Mike Potter (Banff: Luminous Compositions); *Backcountry Biking in the Canadian Rockies,* by Doug Eastcott (Calgary: Rocky Mountain Books); *Scrambles in the Canadian Rockies,* by Alan Kane (Calgary: Rocky Mountain Books); *Compact Guide to Birds of the Rockies,* by Geoffrey L. Holroyd and Howard Coneybeare (Edmonton: Lone Pine Publishing); *Birding in Jasper National Park,* by Kevin Van Tighem and Andrew LeMesurier (Jasper: Parks and People); *The Canadian Rockies Guide to Wildlife Watching,* by Michael Kerr (Calgary: Fifth House Publishers); *Compact Guide to Wildflowers of the Rockies,* by C. Dana Bush (Edmonton: Lone Pine); and *A Hunter of Peace,* Mary Schäffer (Banff: The Whyte Foundation).

The **Banff Book and Art Den** (94 Banff Ave.; ℂ **866/418-6613** or 403/762-3919; www.banffbooks.com) is a wonderful bookstore for local guides, maps, and great books in general. In Jasper, there's **Counterclockwise Books** (627 Patricia St.; ℂ **780/852-3152**). Most of these books are also available online at www.chapters.ca or www.amazon.com.

2 When to Go

Like most people, you're likely planning to visit Banff or Jasper in summertime. And that's a logical choice: The kids are out of school, the weather is warm and sunny, the hiking trails are open, and the days are long. This is the most enjoyable time of the year to be in the Canadian Rockies. However, it's far and away the most crowded and expensive time of the year, too. Most hotels double their prices during the high season, which as a rule stretches from June through September.

To avoid lineups, I suggest visiting in **June,** when the days are luxuriously long and you can catch the early wildflowers in bloom and perhaps even some migrating caribou, or in **September,** when the aspen and larch trees turn golden, but the midday temperature stays gloriously warm.

The Canadian Rockies are also a great destination in winter; by turns cozy, romantic, and peaceful, but also brimming with fun outdoor activities. Banff's star ski resorts—**Sunshine Village, Mount Norquay,** and **Lake Louise**—are among the best in North America, surely on the top of most skiers' wish lists. With hundreds of acres of skiable terrain and excellent powder snow, Jasper's **Marmot Basin** is also worth a visit. Both parks have ice-skating facilities, cross-country skiing, and backcountry ski touring to boot. Just outside the parks, there is dogsledding, helicopter skiing, and snowmobiling. And don't forget all those snowmen and women waiting to be built and evening strolls waiting to be taken under star-studded skies, often active with the stunning aurora borealis ("northern lights"). The main businesses in the Town of Banff stay open year-round, with many hotels dropping their prices substantially during the winter season, which runs from **December to late March.** In Jasper, by contrast, most of the lodges that are not located in the townsite close in winter. The Fairmont Jasper Park Lodge and Pyramid Lake Resort are the exceptions to this. Hotels, shops, and restaurants in town stay open year-round. There are often road closures throughout the Canadian Rockies, especially in the high mountain passes. See "Winter Sports & Activities" in chapters 4 and 7 for coverage of what's on offer when the snow flies in Banff and Jasper, respectively.

Average Daytime Temperatures & Precipitation in Banff & Jasper National Parks

	Jan	Feb	Mar	Apr	May	June	July	Aug	Sept	Oct	Nov	Dec
High Temp. (°C)	−4	0	4	9	14	19	22	22	16	10	1	−4
High Temp. (°F)	25	32	39	48	57	66	72	72	61	50	34	25
Low Temp. (°C)	−14	−10	−7	−2	2	5	7	7	3	0	−7	−13
Low Temp. (°F)	7	14	19	28	36	41	45	45	37	32	19	9
Days of Precipitation	12	10	11	11	13	14	13	13	12	9	10	12

THE CLIMATE   Despite the Canadian Rockies' northerly latitude, the climate actually resembles that of the Rocky Mountains south of the United States border. This is because the elevation in the Canadian Rockies isn't as high as it is in the US. Snow at lower elevations usually disappears by May, but sometimes hangs around the higher elevations well into the summer. The lower the elevation, the warmer the temperature. Although it usually rains for at least a week in June, and July is often assaulted by one cold rain/wet snowfall, the summer climate is very pleasant, with warm days and low humidity. Rain clouds do often gather along the Continental Divide, however, so don't be disappointed to come all the way here and not be able to see the high peaks right away. July temperatures typically hit 68° to 77°F (20°–25°C). Spring and fall days are usually fine and bright, though evenings can be cool. **Indian summers** in September and October can be lovely, as everyone enjoys the prolonged warmer temperatures. In January, though the lows can drop way down to –22°F (–30°C), the winter sunshine and blue skies are the stuff of legend.

AVOIDING THE CROWDS To beat the crowds, hit the most popular attractions in the early morning or late afternoon. The streets of Banff's main drag, **Banff Avenue,** get very busy during summertime. It isn't a place to be if you are in a hurry. Peak hours are usually between 10am and 3pm and the evening rush runs 5 to 8pm. (Locals use the back alleys.) In the summer the days are long, so make use of the later part of the day to get out and see the attractions. The parking lot at **Mount Edith Cavell,** in Jasper National Park, tends to start clearing out at around 3:30pm, but the sun doesn't set until 9pm in summertime. The **Jasper Tramway** and the **Sulphur Mountain Gondola** in Banff are other great late-day outings. You'll avoid the lineups and get to watch the sun set and the lights of the townsites sparkle.

As far as hiking goes, the season is quite short. Summer is, again, the period when the trails are busiest. But the traffic thins out as fall approaches, so I suggest going either late in the high season (late Aug) or early in fall (Sept). If you're considering a spring hike (anytime up until the end of June), be wary about heading out too early. You may find some passes still closed by snowpacks, and trails that aren't so much paths as puddles. For up-to-date trail reports in Banff National Park, call © **403/760-1305.**

If you're coming for a ski vacation, the busiest times are over the Christmas-to–New Year holiday, mid-March, and Easter. Avoiding these periods and skiing midweek are good ways to have more of the slopes to yourself.

3 Money

Although visitors from the United States will find that, with the stronger Canadian dollar, the exchange rate is not as agreeable as it has been in the past (at press time the Canadian dollar was worth US93¢; by the time you read this, the exchange rate will likely be one-to-one, or greater), enjoying your vacation in Banff or Jasper (which could mean anything from outfitting yourself for a back-country trip to renting a room at a scenic lodge or shelling out for kids' activities) is still generally less expensive than a similar vacation in the US. Banff, however, is quite expensive compared to other Canadian resorts. All hotels, restaurants, gift shops, and services charge the 6% **goods and services tax (GST)** on all purchases. (*Note:* A program that allowed foreigners to receive a rebate for the GST spent during their time in Canada was canceled in 2007.) There is no provincial sales tax in Alberta.

Most guides, drivers, restaurant servers, taxi drivers, hosts and hostesses, housecleaners, and concierges who have done a good job should be tipped. The standard rate is 15%.

Please note that rates in US dollars in this book are, in most cases, rounded to the nearest dollar.

4 Permits

Every visitor to a national park requires a permit (also known as a pass). You can pick one up at a **park gate** or **information center** inside the parks. Permits are valid in all Canadian Rocky Mountain National Parks (Banff, Jasper, Yoho, Kootenay, Waterton Lakes, and Glacier national parks). A day pass costs C$8.90 (US$8.30) for adults, C$7.65 (US$7.15) for seniors, and C$4.45 (US$4.15) for children. More economical is the Annual National Pass, which is a good idea if you're planning to stay for a few days and visit more than one park. It's valid for 1 year from the purchase date for unlimited entries to 27 National Parks and 78 National Historic Sites coast to coast. Individual rates are C$62 (US$58) for adults, C$54 (US$50) for seniors, and C$32 (US$30) for children ages 6 to 12. The pass is free for children under age 6. For groups of 2 to 7, this pass costs C$124 (US$116), making it the best deal for most visitors.

Although it's not necessary, you can order both a day pass and an Annual National Pass ahead of time by calling **Parks Canada** (© **800/ 748-7275**). They have no online payment system. There is no limit to the number of passes issued, and no chance they could ever be sold out. I suggest you pick up your permit when you get to the park gates.

(See the section "Getting There," below, for locations of the various gates into Banff and Jasper national parks.)

BACKCOUNTRY PERMITS   Unlike getting your permit to simply gain entry to the parks, if you are planning an overnight trip into the backcountry you *do* need to book your **backcountry campsite** well in advance, especially if you're planning to go between **late June and early September.** While you're booking your campsite, you'll also need to pick up a backcountry permit, which allows you to camp in the wilderness. You'll need this permit in addition to a park pass (see above). The permit you're looking for in this case is a **Wilderness Pass.** It's required for backcountry trips in both Banff and Jasper national parks and costs C$9.90 (US$9.25) per person per night. Or, you can buy an **annual backcountry pass**—a great idea if you plan to spend at least a week in the backcountry. The annual pass costs C$69 (US$65) per person. This gives you clearance to camp in the backcountry for a whole year from the purchase date. Get your permit and reserve your campsite by calling the respective park office (**Banff:** C 403/762-1550; banff.vrc@pc.gc.ca) (**Jasper:** C 780/852-6177; jnp_info@pc.gc.ca). The earlier you call, the better. Both offices accept reservations up to 3 months in advance. A C$12 (US$11) reservation fee is charged—well worth it, I think, to get the peace of mind that comes with knowing that, after a long day's hike, you're getting the campsite you want.

Value Parks Canada's Annual Pass

If you have been in the park for a few days, have been purchasing your permits day-to-day, and then decide you want to stay on, redeem the cost of your previous permits against the cost of an **Annual Pass**. The pass costs C$62 (US$58) each for adults, C$54 (US$50) each for seniors and students, and C$32 (US$30) each for children ages 6 to 12. It's free for children under age 6. Just be sure to show your receipts at the park center when you buy the pass.

Aside from the savings, perhaps the best thing about the Annual Pass is that it gives you entry to 27 National Parks and 78 National Historic Sites across Canada—including the four in the Rocky Mountains—for 1 whole year from the date of purchase. Now that's a deal!

FRONTCOUNTRY PERMITS Campsites in some of Banff National Park's 13 road-accessible campgrounds and most of Jasper National Park's major campgrounds can now be reserved online at Parks Canada's campground reservation system. To make your reservation, visit www.pccamping.ca or call ✆ **877/737-3783.** The cost is C$12 (US$11) per reservation. A number of good sites are set aside for drive-up first-come, first-served campers. (Frontcountry campgrounds are vehicle-accessible, suitable for RVs and car camping.)

OTHER PERMITS Fishing and boating permits are not available in advance, either. Pick them up once you get to the park at an information center or sporting goods store. They're C$9.90 (US$9.25) per day or C$35 (US$32) annually. In Banff, you can get both fishing and boating permits at **Standish Home Hardware** (223 Bear St.; ✆ **403/762-2080**). In Jasper, buy a fishing permit at **The Source for Sports** (406 Patricia St.; ✆ **780/852-3654**) or at **On-Line Sport & Tackle** (600 Patricia St.; ✆ **780/852-3630**).

5 Getting There

BY PLANE Both the **Calgary International Airport** (✆ **877/254-7427** or 403/735-1200; www.calgaryairport.com) and the **Edmonton International Airport** (✆ **800/268-7134;** www.edmontonairports.com) service the Canadian Rockies. If you are heading to **Banff National Park,** fly to Calgary and from there take either the **Banff Airporter** (✆ **888/449-2901** or 403/762-3330; www.banffairporter.com; C$50/US$47 one-way or C$93/US$87 return trip), or **Sundog Tours'** (✆ **888/786-3641** or 403/762-2711; www.sundogtours.com) airport shuttle, which is the only one that will take you to Lake Louise or Jasper from the Calgary Airport in both summer and winter. (Banff is 129km/80 miles west of Calgary. It's about 90 min. by car from the airport.) If you want to visit **Jasper National Park** first, fly to Edmonton (363km/225 miles east of Jasper; a 4-hr. trip by car). Many people visiting Jasper go first to Banff via Calgary and then drive north. Others do the trip in reverse. To inquire about flights into Calgary and Edmonton, contact **Air Canada** (✆ **888/247-2262;** www.aircanada.ca), **Continental Airlines** (✆ **800/231-0856;** www.flycontinental.com), **Delta** (✆ **800/221-1212;** www.delta.com), **Northwest** (✆ **800/225-2525;** www.nwa.com), or **WestJet** (✆ **888/937-8538;** www.westjet.com). Many airlines from Europe and the United Kingdom fly to Calgary and Edmonton as well.

It takes about 3½ hours to drive between Banff and Jasper with no stopping.

BY TRAIN   VIA Rail Canada (① 888/842-7245; www.viarail.ca) services **Jasper National Park** on its Edmonton–Vancouver run, which takes about 16 hours direct. Most trains from major Canadian and US centers connect to this route. Check with VIA Rail Canada or with Amtrak (① 800/872-7245; www.amtrak.com). There is no VIA Rail Canada service to Banff or Calgary; however, **Rocky Mountaineer Railtours** (① 877/460-3200; www.rockymountaineer. com) has a stunning overnight trip that departs from Vancouver and stops in either Banff or Jasper (you select your destination at the changeover in Kamloops, BC). **Royal Canadian Pacific Luxury Rail Tours** (① 877/665-3044; www.royalcanadianpacific.com) has a 6-day tour on a luxury heritage rail car that leaves Calgary, passes through the Canadian Rockies south of Banff, and loops back through Golden and Banff to Calgary.

BY BUS   Greyhound (① 800/661-8747; www.greyhound.ca) and **Brewster** (① 877/791-5500; www.brewster.ca) have daily trips from Vancouver to Edmonton and Jasper, including a 2-day drive that includes an overnight midway. Their routes from Vancouver to Calgary stop in Canmore, Banff, Field, and Golden.

BY CAR   Most visitors to Banff and Jasper national parks will fly to either Calgary or Edmonton and rent a car to get to the parks. Though shuttle service is available from the Calgary International Airport to several locations around Banff (see the section on getting there by plane, above), it's a good idea to rent your own car and enjoy its use for the duration of your trip. Car-rental agencies at the Calgary and Edmonton international airports include **Budget** (① 800/268-8900; www.budget.ca), **Hertz** (① 800/654-3131; www.hertz.ca), **National** (① 800/227-7368; www.nationalcar.ca), and **Thrifty** (① 800/847-4389; www.thrifty.com). They also have offices in the towns of Banff and Jasper.

If you're driving into Banff National Park from the east, take the **Trans-Canada Highway (Hwy. 1)** west from Calgary. The Park's eastern gate is 129km (80 miles) west of the **Calgary International Airport,** just west of the town of Canmore. If you are coming to Banff from the west, you have two options. From central British Columbia, you can take the Trans-Canada Highway east via the town of **Golden, BC,** and Yoho National Park, and enter Banff just west of the village of Lake Louise. The other option, from southeastern

Highway Access to Banff and Jasper National Parks

British Columbia, is to take Highway 93 north into Banff via the town of **Radium Hot Springs, BC,** and Kootenay National Park. See chapter 9 for more information on planning a side trip to Golden, BC, or Radium Hot Springs, BC, both gateways to Banff National Park.

If you're approaching the parks from the city of Edmonton, which is to the north, you'll get to Jasper National Park first. Take **Highway 16 (the Yellowhead Hwy.)** west to Jasper National Park's eastern gate (363km/225 miles west of **Edmonton International Airport**). From north-central British Columbia, you can take Highway 16 east to Jasper National Park via **Prince George, BC,** and Mount Robson Provincial Park.

Vancouver is 858km (532 miles) west of Banff and 863km (535 miles) west of Jasper.

6 Getting Around

There are a number of shuttle services to help ease your travel between Banff and Jasper national parks. **Sundog Tours** (© 888/786-3641 or 780/852-4056; www.sundogtours.com) runs between Banff, Lake Louise, and Jasper daily (except on poor winter-driving days and from Nov through late Dec). Some daily departures hit all the major attractions along the way; others go directly from Jasper to Lake Louise or Banff. The Jasper–Banff trip costs C$59 (US$55) per adult and C$35 (US$33) per child 12 and under; the Jasper–Lake Louise trip costs C$53 (US$50) per adult and C$29 (US$27) per child. **Brewster** (© 877/791-5500 or 403/762-6700; www.brewster.ca), the original tour company in Banff and Jasper, has a slew of shuttle services and day tours between Banff, Jasper, Calgary, and Edmonton, including a 9 1/2-hour day trip that starts in Banff and ends in the Town of Jasper. It costs C$134 (US$125) for adults and C$67 (US$63) for children ages 5 to 15. Children under age 5 ride free.

Taxis are another way to see Banff or Jasper and not be tied to your vehicle. Often, there are set rates for certain destinations. It never hurts to ask first. In Banff, try **Banff Taxi** (© 403/762-4444),

---

Tips The Rental Advantage

If you're staying in the Town of Banff and not really planning any trips outside of it, you can take a shuttle from the airport and then walk or take a short cab ride to most attractions in town. But if you take a cab it's still probably going to cost you more than renting a car! If you plan on seeing any of the rest of the park, including Lake Louise, as well as making a trip up to Jasper, then having your own vehicle is a major advantage. There is little to no public transport in the Canadian Rockies, and shuttle and taxi services are very expensive—not to mention restricting, since your movements are governed by their schedule. The roads are in good condition most of the year (you don't really need to rent an expensive four-wheel-drive sport utility vehicle, although they are very popular) and driving here is a relaxing way to soak up the gorgeous scenery.

Legion Taxi (© 403/762-3353), or **Mountain Taxi and Tours** (© 403/762-3351). In Jasper, I recommend **Heritage Cabs** (© 780/852-5558) or **Jasper Taxi** (© 780/852-3600).

7 Planning a Backcountry Trip

If you hope to enjoy the wilderness and really leave the highway and telephone behind, consider planning an overnight trip into the backcountry. You'll achieve that sense of peace and solitude not found in busy parking lots or at popular attractions. It's hard work (but great exercise!) and takes some organizing, but it's the best way to experience the vast, natural beauty of Banff or Jasper. No RVs or cars are allowed in the backcountry.

A great planning resource is available online at the government-run Parks Canada website for each park. The *Banff Wilderness Trip Planner* is available at **www.parkscanada.gc.ca/banff**. The *Jasper Backcountry Visitors' Guide* is at **www.parkscanada.gc.ca/jasper**.

Your first task is to take a good look at a map and figure out which hiking trail best suits your abilities, time frame, and interest. Don't overestimate yourself in the wilderness. There are trips that range in length from a mere overnight jaunt to a challenging 14-day adventure. Some trails are a relatively easy stroll into a campsite, while others demand steep ascents and descents. Pick a trail you can enjoy. To help you do so, refer to the trail reviews in chapter 4 for Banff and chapter 7 for Jasper. Staff at the park information centers are also very knowledgeable about trail conditions and levels of difficulty.

Once you've selected your trail, you need to reserve your backcountry campsite well in advance (up to 3 months ahead). When you're making your reservation, the park office will ask you for a detailed outline of your trip, listing exactly which campsites you intend to stay at, on which nights. They'll issue your permit for those and only those sites—on those and only those nights! Try to follow your intended route as closely as possible. Backcountry campsites are patrolled regularly by park staff. It's their responsibility to ensure that nobody's camping where they're not supposed to

---

Tips Trail Conditions

For information on trail openings, closures, and conditions in Banff National Park, call the park's **trail report line** (© 403/760-1305). In Jasper National Park, call © 780/852-6177.

be. For more on acquiring backcountry permits, see the section "Permits" earlier in the chapter.

8 Tips for RVers

They're not for everyone, but most people who try it discover what a joy it is to travel by recreational vehicle. It affords a level of independence and comfort car travel can't. And finding a quiet campground by a river is about as close to the camping experience as you can get without giving up your pillow and mattress.

More than half of the campgrounds in Banff and Jasper national parks accommodate RVs, trailers, and camper vans, and you must stay in these designated areas. If you try to park on the side of the road, for example, you'll likely receive a knock on the door in the middle of the night from an unhappy park warden. In terms of amenities, campgrounds range from ones with showers and flush toilets to more rustic versions with outhouses and precious little else. Try to arrive at your chosen campground before 4pm to ensure that you get a spot. If it's full, you could be forced to spend the night in a nearby "overflow campground," which can look a lot like a gravel pit. See chapters 5 (for Banff) and 8 (for Jasper) for a rundown of the best campgrounds in both parks. Throughout the mountains, it's crucial that you "bear-proof" your RV at all times—keep anything that has an odor inside.

In addition to navigating around campgrounds, RVs (and their drivers) need to know how to get around town, too. In the town of Banff, there is a trailer drop-off site in the industrial area at the northeast end of Banff Avenue. You can leave your trailer here and take the car or RV itself through the streets of town. There are also a number of larger parking lots that accommodate RVs, including one near the **Mineral Springs Hospital** on Gopher Street and another one across from the post office on **Buffalo Street,** along the Bow River. In the town of Jasper, try the larger lots at the corner of **Connaught Drive and Cedar Avenue,** the lot south of the **Heritage Railway Station,** also on Connaught Drive, or the lot at the Jasper Activity Centre on Pyramid Avenue (the best bet but also the farthest).

A few roads in the parks are particularly narrow and winding and are not fit for RVs. These include **Mount Norquay Road** in Banff and **Cavell Road** in Jasper.

Many people come to the Rockies in an RV they've rented and picked up at the airport in Edmonton or Calgary. **Canadian Rockies RV Rentals** (2000 Airport Rd. NE, Calgary, AB T2E 6W5;

Backpacking for Beginners: Leave No Trace

- **Be safe:** Parks Canada recommends that you always tell someone where you are going and when you'll be back. It runs a **voluntary safety registration service,** which helps them keep track of you and locate you if you do not return by the date and time recorded. Voluntary safety registration is available for anyone, but is recommended particularly for individuals or small groups engaging in higher-risk activities such as mountaineering, river trips, or glacier travel, or who are planning to leave the designated hiking/skiing routes. It's also for solo travelers without a local contact. Although safety registration is voluntary, if you choose to use it, it becomes a binding agreement whereby you must provide your itinerary plans and report back immediately upon your return from the backcountry.

- **Cook at a distance from your campsite:** Keep everything associated with food in a localized area of your campsite, as far away from your tent as possible. Set up your cooking, eating, cleaning, and supply area at least 100m (325 ft.) from your tent. Wash and store all dishes and utensils immediately after you eat. To get rid of food smells, change out of your cooking clothes before you go to bed; otherwise, during the night you may be treated to some unwanted furry visitors looking for leftovers. You're also required to hang your food in trees overnight in storage bins provided by Parks Canada.

- **Dig a pit:** There are toilet pit facilities at all designated backcountry campsites. However, if nature calls when you're on the trail, and the nearest campsite is simply too far away, head away from the trail and put at least 50m (165 ft.) between you and any body of water. Dig a pit no larger than 15 centimeters (6 in.) in circumference. When you're done, restore the ground to how it was before you came along. Pack out your toilet paper.

- **Equip yourself properly:** You need a sleeping bag suitable for cold temperatures (I prefer one that is down-filled). Most tenters don't leave the parking lot without a sleeping pad, as well. Be sure that your pack fits you well. A professional in an outfitting store can adjust it to fit your body. That'll make the difference between an enjoyable hike and a dreadfully miserable slog.

- **Fight fire with a stove:** Before you head out, check the **fire danger reading,** posted on signs at all trail heads. If there is a fire ban in place (which usually happens at least once every summer), you can't light any fires, though you can still cook with a stove. In fact, I would encourage you to use a stove anyway, even if you do get the go-ahead to light a fire. It's less damaging to the natural environment, as it requires no wood. If you must light a fire, do so only in a designated fire pit and use the wood provided. Even though it's not prohibited, chopping your own wood is strongly discouraged. Remember that you're in a pro-tected area. Keep the fire small and be sure it is totally extinguished before you leave the campsite.

- **Leave no trace:** The motto in the backcountry is "Leave no trace." Pack out everything you pack in. Don't burn or bury anything. That goes for food wastes, unused food, and toilet paper. Heck, pack out *more* than you bring in if you see any garbage or litter on the trails. Pick up cig-arette butts and matches.

- **Plan ahead:** Reserve your backcountry site well in advance (3 months' lead time doesn't hurt). Reservations are accepted for the upcoming summer months begin-ning May 1. The booking offices open at 9am. Budget extra time during your trip for unexpected changes in weather. You may get delayed by a rainstorm that has you huddled under a rock for some time. You'll already be wet. You don't want to be late, too.

- **Respect your feet:** More than anything else, your hiking boots will make or break your hiking experience. Try to work new boots in well ahead of time by wearing them around your home. Be sure to wear socks that don't get totally waterlogged and that dry easily. I suggest a thin, synthetic inner sock and a thicker outer sock in a wool blend. Bring a few extra pairs along in your pack.

- **Stick to the trail:** Even if it seems shorter to crisscross a trail, or drier to step right around a muddy section, don't do it. Trails erode quickly.

€ **403/291-9617;** www.canadianrockiesrv.com) is the only option
if you want to pick up and drop off your RV in Banff and Jasper,
from where you could continue on by train or airport shuttle. They
have only truck/camper combos (versus larger motor home units),
at around C$155/night (US$145) in summer. Their prices are quite
budget-friendly as well. Mileage isn't included in most prices. For an
RV rental from another part of Canada or from Calgary or Edmonton, contact **CanaDream** (2510 27th St. NE, Calgary, AB T1Y
7G1; € **800/461-7368** or 403/291-1000; www.canadream.com).
Rates range from C$350 (US$327) per day to C$1,700 (US$1,590)
per week for a small RV; or from C$480 (US$449) per day to
C$2,700 (US$2,525) per week for a full-size, deluxe RV. The cost
of an RV rental is comparable to that of renting a car and staying in
a hotel.

9 Package Tours, Adventure Outings & Educational Programs

IN BANFF

The Banff Centre (107 Tunnel Mountain Dr., Banff, AB T1L 1H5;
€ **800/413-8368** or 403/762-6100; www.banffcentre.ca) is a world-
renowned school for continuing education, with sub-centers for management, the arts, and mountain culture. It offers a wide variety of
courses that range from 1 week to a few months.

The Friends of Banff (P.O. Box 2590, Banff, AB T1L 1C0;
€ **403/762-8918**; www.friendsofbanff.com), a non-profit group that
works with Parks Canada to enhance education and interpretation of
Banff National Park, leads daily interpretive hiking and walking trips
for all ages. Most of the guides are locals who know all the ins and
outs of the park and are enthusiastic to share their knowledge.

Brewster (P.O. Box 1140, Banff, AB T1L 1J3; € **877/791-5500**
or 403/762-6700; www.brewster.ca) knows Banff better than any
other tour operator and has a long history of guiding here to prove
it. It offers a large selection of sightseeing tours in both Banff and
Jasper. Taking even the 3-hour **Discover Banff with Banff Gondola
tour** with the folks at Brewster will teach you more than you'll ever
learn on your own. If you're making your way to British Columbia,
sign up for Brewster's **Rockies Discovery** 3-day, 2-night tour that
stops in Calgary, Banff, Lake Louise, Roger's Pass, and Kamloops.

Discover Banff Tours (215 Banff Ave., P.O. Box 1566, Banff, AB
T1L 1B5; € **877/565-9372** or 403/760-5007; www.bannftours.com)
leads small groups on interpretive tours of all the highlights in Banff

National Park, including the Town of Banff, Lake Louise, and Moraine Lake, as well as the Icefields Parkway. Morning and evening wildlife-viewing tours are really nice.

Yamnuska Mountain School (Suite 200, 50 Lincoln Park, Canmore, AB T1W 3E9; © 866/678-4164 or 403/678-4164; www.yamnuska.com) is a leading **mountaineering and climbing** school based in Canmore, Alberta, just outside Banff's east gate. Professional guides lead a variety of courses, from 1-day rock-climbing gigs and 1-week mountaineering courses all the way to 3-month mountain skills courses. The private guided hiking trips in Banff and Jasper are favorites. **OnTop Mountaineering** (340 Canyon Close, Canmore, AB T1W 1H4; © 800/506-7177 or 403/678-2717; www.ontopmountaineering.com) operates excellent backcountry guided trips and instructional climbing courses.

Adventures Unlimited (211 Bear St., Banff, AB T1L 1A8; © 800/644-8888 or 403/762-4554) has **fly-fishing** courses on the Bow River.

Holiday on Horseback (132 Banff Ave., P.O. Box 2280, Banff, AB T1L 1C1; © 800/661-8352 or 403/762-4551; www.horseback.com) offers wildlife adventure package trips—including a guided ride with wildlife biologists through prime grizzly bear habitat. They run the lovely and remote Sundance Lodge (see chapter 5 for information on this and other backcountry lodges).

Canadian Mountain Holidays (217 Bear St., P.O. Box 1660, Banff, AB T1L 1J6; © 800/661-0252 or 403/762-7100; www.cmhhike.com) takes hikers into the high alpine wilderness of the mountains around (but not within) the Canadian Rocky Mountain national parks via helicopter for memorable multiday trips. Participants stay in the company's luxurious (but expensive) wilderness lodges tucked deep in the mountains.

IN JASPER

The Jasper Institute (500 Connaught Dr., Jasper, AB T0E 1E0; © 780/852-4767; www.friendsofjasper.com) offers educational programs in natural history. The course syllabus varies from year to year, but the choices are always interesting and the instructors first-rate. Some recent course topics have included "The Bear Essentials," "Nature Writing," **"Warden for a Weekend," "Spring in Bloom,"** and "Nature Photography." Most courses run over a weekend. The Institute can arrange accommodations at an economical price at the Palisades Centre, Parks Canada's learning center (contact © 780/852-4767; www.friendsofjasper.com).

Sundog Tours (P.O. Box 548, Jasper, AB T0E 1E0; ℂ **888/786-3641;** www.sundogtours.com) has a slew of organized outings in Jasper, ranging from daylong wildlife tours of the Maligne Valley to guided hikes. Their 2-day Jasper Experience includes transportation from Banff.

Volunteers are always needed at the **Friends of Jasper** (which has a booth the Jasper Information Centre, 500 Connaught Dr., Jasper, AB T0E 1E0; ℂ **780/852-4767**), a non-profit association that promotes appreciation of Jasper National Park. Projects include trail rehabilitation, native species planting, and interpretive signing. Drop by the booth to see if there are any projects on the go that you can help out with for a day or two.

The **Jasper Adventure Centre** (604 Connaught Dr., Jasper, AB T0E 1E0; ℂ **800/565-7457** or 780/852-5595; www.jasper adventurecentre.com) will help you find the right guide for your mountain adventure.

10 Tips for Travelers with Disabilities

Canada's Rocky Mountain National Parks have come a long way in making this spectacular wilderness accessible to all travelers. For example, the parks are now more wheelchair-friendly than ever.

The museums and visitor centers in both townsites are all wheelchair-accessible. Most hotels now have at least one wheelchair-accessible room. The **Fairmont Jasper Park Lodge** rents out an all-terrain wheelchair (manually operated by a companion).

The **Upper Hot Springs** in Banff National Park and the Radium Hot Springs in Kootenay National Park are friendly to those with mobility restraints.

If you are planning on car camping, you'll find that campgrounds with more modern facilities tend to be more wheelchair-friendly as well, with wheelchair-accessible washrooms and (at some campgrounds) showers. In Banff National Park, head for **Tunnel Mountain, Johnston Canyon, Lake Louise,** or **Waterfowl Lakes campgrounds.** In Jasper National Park, try **Whistlers, Wapiti,** or **Wabasso campgrounds.**

Signs clearly mark which trails in the parks are paved. In Banff, try the asphalt-covered **Sundance Trail.** There is an adjustable-height viewing scope at **Bow Summit.** The Lakeside Trail at **Lake Louise** is another wheelchair-accessible trail. Wheelchair-friendly trails in Jasper include the **Clifford E. Lee Trail** at Lake Edith/Annette and the **Maligne Lake Trail,** as well as points along **Maligne Canyon,** at

---

Tips **Head to Kootenay Park**

Disabled visitors to the Canadian Rockies will find plenty of accessibility in Kootenay National Park in British Columbia, which is adjacent to Banff National Park. The park offers fascinating interpretive trails—like the Paint Pots and Maligne Canyon, and a lakeside trail at Olive Lake—that are all wheelchair-friendly.

Pyramid Island, and the interpretive loop at the **Pocahontas Coal Mine Trail.**

Disabled travelers are also discovering new ways to enjoy winter in the Canadian Rockies. Local ski areas (**Ski Banff–Lake Louise–Sunshine,** 119 Banff Ave., Banff, AB T1L 1H9; © 877/ 754-7080 or 403/762-4561; www.skibig3.com) can arrange for sit-skiing or assisted skiing lessons for blind and/or wheelchair skiers.

Pick up an *Access Guide* brochure from a park information center for more information—or better yet, ask the staff at the information centers for advice. You can also call **Voice/TTY** (press space bar) © **403/762-4256** for Banff; © **780/852-6176** for Jasper.

11 Tips for Travelers with Pets

If you cannot bear to leave Fido at home and must bring him with you, you should keep a few points in mind.

There are a few hotels in Banff and Jasper that accommodate pets, but most don't (for information on which hotels allow pets, see chapter 5 for Banff and chapter 8 for Jasper). Do not leave your pet unattended in your vehicle for any length of time—high temperatures can cause your pet to suffer from brain damage and die from heatstroke or suffocation. If you bring your dog onto a trail, make sure you've got enough water to keep your buddy hydrated. Watch for flagging energy levels. Keep your dog on a leash at all times, especially in campgrounds and on hiking trails. To wildlife like elk, wolves, bears, and cougars, your dog may look an awful lot like dinner. Avoid any areas in the parks where the potential for wildlife encounters is high (ask at an information center), and take your dog for a walk only during daylight hours. Do not leave your dog unattended outside. Unrestrained pets have been known to harass wildlife, provoke attacks, and endanger people. And please pick up after your pooch—the "leave no trace" principle applies to pets, too.

12 Tips for Travelers with Children

In Banff National Park, day care is available through the **Childcare Connection** (© 800/665-9296 or 403/761-4445), which offers private babysitting in your hotel. During the summer months, the **Town of Banff** (© 403/762-1251) offers weekday programs for kids 6 and older. The local ski hills also have established and licensed daycare facilities that will take care of your kids from just a few months to age 6 while you hit the slopes. The local **Banff YWCA** (© 403/760-3200) has a childcare registry where you can find a listing of temporary child care for visitors. In Jasper National Park, you can leave your little ones at the **Jasper Children's Center** (303 Pyramid Lake Rd., Jasper, AB T0E 1E0; © 780/852-4666).

There are many **outdoor playgrounds** in the townsites, though most of them are unsupervised. In Banff, drop your kids off at the Rotary Park, at 527 Banff Ave.; the playground at Banff Elementary School, at 327 Squirrel St.; or the **Banff Recreation Centre** (on Mount Norquay Rd., © 403/762-1235), where there is also a **skateboard park** and indoor skating rink. In Jasper, let the kids run free in **Centennial Park** (on Pyramid Lake Rd. beside the Activity Centre). The elementary school playground is across the street from Centennial Park. The **Friends of Jasper** (P.O. Box 992, Jasper, AB T0E 1E0; © 780/852-4767; www.friendsofjasper.com) loans out a "Family Hiking Kit" that includes a pack, binoculars, and a guide to a specific natural area. For some reason they have only a couple of these kits on hand, so put in your bid for one early.

Kids with imaginations (isn't that all kids?) will be happiest if they're taken to places where there is a story to be told. Historical sites fit this bill admirably. At the **Old Fort Trail** in Jasper, for example, young ones can pretend they are fur traders or railway workers.

Bike rentals and horseback riding outings are other family-friendly activities in Banff and Jasper. See chapters 4 (for Banff) and 7 (for Jasper) for more information.

Kids want to get out of the car. Pull over at all the rest sites you can to allow them to stretch, and plan picnic lunches at Lake Minnewanka in Banff and Lake Annette in Jasper.

Both Jasper and Kootenay national parks run a **Junior Naturalist Program** in the summertime. Park staff entertain and educate your kids about the natural world around them. They play games, take short hikes, and explore the wilderness. For schedules and registration, call

> ⌒(Kids) **Hiking with Kids: Let the Discovery Begin!**
>
> Getting kids to observe, count, and make lists of what they see in the mountains is a great way to introduce them to the wonders of nature. Here are a few ideas: Get them to listen quietly to the sounds of the forest or walk around a picnic area looking for tracks, scats, or other signs of animal life. Using the sensory clues around you to imagine the animal that just passed through can be just as exciting as actually seeing that animal. Or try to have them count how many different kinds of trees they can spot, looking at the needles and textures of the bark. How many different kinds of insects can they spot in a single day?

ⓒ **780/852-4767** in Jasper and ⓒ **250/347-6525** in Radium Hot Springs. Suitable for children age 8 and up. There are also family-friendly **interpretive programs** at many of the bigger campgrounds, and you don't have to be staying there to attend. Contact park information centers for schedules and locations. Suitable for children age 8 and up.

The excellent **Whyte Museum of the Canadian Rockies** (111 Bear St., Banff, AB T1L 1A3; ⓒ **403/762-2291**; www.whyte.org) has a fun "museo pack" that's loaded with activities for kids aged 6 to 12 to help them explore and learn about heritage. There is a family-friendly video area at the **Jasper–Yellowhead Museum** (400 Pyramid Lake Rd., Jasper, AB T0E 1E0; ⓒ **780/852-3013**; www.jaspermuseum.org). Great for a rainy day.

Be aware that a few hotels and lodges do not accept children (that information is included in the "Where to Stay, Camp & Eat" chapters). Others hold the door wide open to the little people. The **Fairmont Jasper Park Lodge** (P.O. Box 40, Jasper, AB T0E 1E0; ⓒ **780/852-3301**; www.fairmont.com/jasper) has a special check-in desk for kids. They receive their very own information package full of games, activities, and special events.

Camping is another great family activity. At the campgrounds, kids can meet and socialize with each other and discover the beauty of nature 24 hours a day.

13 Protecting Your Health & Safety

Don't drink the water from any streams, rivers, or lakes in Banff or Jasper national parks. A waterborne parasite called *Giardia lamblia* can cause an illness known in Canada as "beaver fever," is transmitted via infected animal feces, and can cause serious and prolonged gastrointestinal problems.

Also be on the lookout for **wood ticks**—small, flat-bodied spider-like insects that bite humans and can carry **Rocky Mountain spotted fever** and **Lyme disease** (although the latter is rare in the northern Rockies). They usually abound in dry, grassy slopes in the spring. If you're hiking through such an area, give yourself a good once-over at the end of the day. If you find a wood tick on your skin and you can't easily remove it, see a doctor. They like to burrow into your flesh and can be difficult to remove. Be careful if you try to remove the ticks yourself—try using tweezers. If in doubt, drop by the **Mineral Springs Hospital** in Banff to see a doctor (301 Lynx St., Banff, AB T0L 0C0; © **403/762-2222**). In Jasper, go to **Seton General Hospital** (518 Robson St., Jasper, AB T0E 1E0; © **780/852-3344**). There has been no evidence of West Nile virus in the Canadian Rockies.

Hiking in the mountains is so beautiful that it may make you feel lightheaded. But lightheadedness may also be a sign of **altitude sickness.** Although elevations in the Canadian Rockies aren't as high as in the Colorado and Montana Rockies, you can still feel the difference. People with severe heart or lung conditions should take note. For example, the Icefield Information Centre at the border between the parks is 2,000m (6,500 ft.) above sea level. Bring along some headache medicine and drink plenty of water.

You'll also be closer to the sun in the mountains, so wear a **sun hat** and **sunscreen.** Beyond the sun, cold, and rain are the other weather factors that could hamper your holiday. Check the latest weather forecast before heading out. Pack a rain jacket and warm clothing in your daypack. And always carry a **first-aid kit,** both in your car and in your pack. At the very least, it should include latex gloves (to prevent spreading infections), butterfly bandages, sterile gauze pads, adhesive tape, antibiotic ointment, pain relievers (for kids and adults), alcohol pads, knife, scissors, and tweezers.

In terms of personal safety in the mountains, be aware that almost any slope is a potential **avalanche** chute—and even small avalanches can be deadly. Drivers should avoid stopping in places where there are signs that read NO STOPPING, AVALANCHE AREA, and anyone venturing into the backcountry—especially in winter—should know how to recognize and travel in avalanche terrain. Call ℭ **403/762-1460** in Banff or ℭ **780/852-6176** in Jasper for the latest avalanche hazard reports from Parks Canada.

There is also a risk of getting hit by falling rock and ice or slipping into a glacier crevasse, particularly in Jasper National Park. Do not ignore the signs telling you to stay back from the **Angel Glacier** at **Mount Edith Cavell** or the **Athabasca Glacier,** both in Jasper. These can be—and have been—deadly.

14 Protecting the Environment

ECOLOGICAL INTEGRITY   You've come here to enjoy the natural beauty of the mountains. But don't be fooled into thinking that your visit won't have an impact. Every footprint leaves a mark on the health of the wilderness here.

The first national parks in Canada (which include Banff and Jasper) were established primarily as moneymaking enterprises. The parks and their spectacular natural settings were seen as lures to the rich that would increase use of the passenger trains and inspire economic development in the farthest reaches of a young, growing nation. Railways, highways, restaurants, lodges, and all the related services soon appeared in the parks. Visitors came for adventure, rest, and enjoyment of the beauty of the mountains.

Management practices and the types of tourism developments in the parks changed over time as society's understanding of and relationship with nature changed. There has always been debate over the type and level of human use that should be allowed in the national parks.

The popularity of the parks has grown as the areas of natural wilderness have diminished in the world. In response to increased user demand and other pressures on the ecosystems these parks protect, the *National Parks Act,* passed by the Canadian government in 2000, puts the protection of the natural environment first:

> *"Maintenance or restoration of ecological integrity, through the protection of natural resources and natural process, shall be the first priority . . . when considering all aspects of the management of parks."* —Canada National Parks Act, *2000.*

With more and more environmentally conscious visitors coming to Canada's national parks, business owners and commercial developers are recognizing that if we do not ensure the ecological integrity of these places, they will no longer be as attractive to visitors. Protecting the parks means keeping them wild. New understanding of ecosystem dynamics demands that we rethink patterns of human use

Tips   Wildlife Encounters: What to Do

- If you're lucky enough to see a large wild animal (elk, bighorn sheep, or bear, for example) from your car, don't destroy the moment by rolling down your window and trying to feed it.
- If you are not in a vehicle, stay calm. If a bear rears on its hind legs and waves its nose about, it's trying to identify you. Remain still and talk loudly but calmly, so the bear knows you are human and not a prey animal. A scream or sudden movement may trigger an attack. Pick up children, stay in a group, and back away slowly. Do not run.
- If you surprise a bear and it defends itself, use bear spray if you have it (bear spray is very effective if used properly). If this doesn't deter the bear, or if you have no bear spray, play dead. This lets it know you are not a threat. Lie on your stomach with your legs apart and cover the back of your head and neck with your hands. Keep your backpack on to protect you.
- To reduce your risk of running into a bear, make noise while you walk. Clap, sing, or yell to announce your presence. Travel in groups, and only in daylight hours. Minimize odors by storing your food properly and disposing of your garbage.

in the park if we want to protect the park over the long term. Parks Canada is also under increasing pressure from Canadians to be a leader in developing a culture of conservation and working to engage and educate visitors about nature.

As natural landscapes and wildlife species disappear from the earth, they become more precious. National parks have become more desirable destinations because of this fact. As a visitor, here's what you can do to help out while you're here:

- Support the many businesses in the park that have environmentally responsible practices (everything from staff and visitor education to water conservation and recycling).
- Be an environmentally responsible visitor.
- Respect wildlife; give animals the space they need.
- Stay on the main trail in high-use areas.

Having a spontaneous rendezvous with a cougar, wolf, or coyote is different from encountering a bear and requires another strategy. Frankly, your chances of seeing a cougar are extremely rare. Known as the "loners" of the wilderness, cougars are elusive—active mainly at night. They do have a tendency to follow their prey of choice (deer) into towns or campgrounds. This said, if you do see a cougar you're likely in a dangerous position.

- If a cougar approaches you, send it a clear message that you are not potential prey. Pick up small children immediately, yell loudly, and do anything you can to make yourself look and sound bigger.
- If a cougar attacks you, fight back aggressively. Do not play dead.

Wolves and coyotes are more commonly seen, but are much less aggressive than cougars. They are attracted to food first, then to small animals, and finally to small children.

- If you see a wolf or coyote, pick up small children, yell loudly at the animal to distract it, and do whatever you can to make yourself seem larger and more threatening.
- If a wolf or coyote attacks you, fight back with all your might, and again do not play dead or turn your back to the animal.

- Do not exceed the posted speed limit, and watch for wildlife along roadways.

The tourism industry has joined its clientele in adopting **environmental stewardship.** While businesses work to protect the right of park visitors to access the backcountry, many also place a high priority on visitor education, to minimize visitors' impact on the natural environment while they're there.

WILDLIFE Bighorn sheep, black and grizzly bears, coyotes, ground squirrels, elk, marmots, moose, mountain goats, wolves, and deer all live happily in the natural paradise known as the Canadian Rocky Mountains National Parks. Many biologists, park wardens, and researchers use these parks as a natural laboratory to study the patterns and health of animals lucky enough to live in a protected natural area. You may see animals with tags or collars. They're not pets—the tags belong to Parks Canada scientists, who use them to track the animals and study their habits and life cycles.

Early morning and dusk are the best times of day to see wildlife. See chapter 10 for a nature guide to the parks, with descriptions of the most commonly seen wildlife in the Canadian Rockies.

It's quite common to see wildlife along the roadside in Banff and Jasper national parks. During summer, there are often black (and, less frequently, grizzly) bears near the Trans-Canada Highway (Hwy. 1) at Lake Louise. The speed limit is usually decreased from 90kmph (56 mph) to 70kmph (43 mph) to protect drivers, passengers, and yes, bears. If you see wildlife on the road, slow down and warn other motorists by flashing your lights. If you just can't resist pulling over to watch, do so carefully and get over to the side of the road as far as you can (roads are quite narrow in some areas). Obviously, the best way to view wildlife is through binoculars or a telephoto lens. Unfortunately, some animals have become accustomed to humans and may even approach you for food. Reduce your chances of a wildlife conflict by keeping your distance from whatever wildlife you see. Keep 100m (328 ft.) or 10 bus lengths from bears, cougars, and wolves. Keep 30m (98 ft.) or 3 bus lengths from elk, sheep, goats, and deer.

Banff and Jasper are located in low river valleys—prime grazing land for **elk.** There are a lot of them; sometimes they'll even take a stroll down Patricia Street in Jasper, or chomp on a "salad bar" in a local's lovely garden. Although they may appear to be peacefully mowing someone's lawn, elk aren't as tame as they look. These are wild animals that have learned to survive in a place that's full of people. Don't disturb them. Elk are particularly dangerous during spring and fall (females calve in May and June; males are in rut during Sept and Oct).

Driving from Banff toward Lake Louise, you'll pass under two unique "wildlife overpasses." These bridges allow wildlife to cross from one side of the Trans-Canada Highway to the other without confronting traffic. The picturesque bridges are covered in natural grass and biologists say they've been embraced by elk, moose, bears, wolves, and cougars.

Parks Canada has strict laws regulating human-wildlife interaction. You could be fined for feeding, touching, enticing, disturbing, or harassing wild animals—big or small. Roadwork near Lake Louise is part of a major Government of Canada project to twin the Trans-Canada as far as the border with British Columbia, partly to prevent car accidents involving grizzly bears. Work should be finished in 2008. They're also having a fence built around the village of Lake Louise to keep humans and bears apart.

3

Exploring Banff National Park

Banff is Canada's most famous and most visited national park. A considerable part of its popularity is based on its accessibility. The park is easy to get to—the Trans-Canada Highway runs right through it and the Calgary International Airport is less than 2 hours away. Banff's backcountry is also very accessible, with many of the best wilderness trail heads a mere short car ride away from Banff Townsite. But what really sets Banff apart from other mountain areas, in my opinion, is its internationally renowned cultural scene. Excellent art galleries, fine restaurants serving a medley of cuisines, great nightlife characterized by rousing live music—they all coexist easily with the natural world, right here in the middle of a dramatic mountain park.

Those who live here know how lucky they are. Up on Tunnel Mountain, minutes from busy Banff Avenue, is **The Banff Centre,** a world-renowned arts, culture, and educational institution that hosts celebrated musicians, writers, and other artists from around the world on a regular basis. It is also the home of the **Banff Centre for Mountain Culture,** where some of the most famous mountaineers, climbers, environmentalists, and adventurers gather annually to share stories in books, film, and photography. That such first-rate cultural amenities blend with stunning mountain wilderness is remarkable in a town with a population of 7,600.

Many of the 4.3 million visitors who come to Banff each year are happy to relax during the day, window-shop, and save their energy for some late-night dining and dancing. They may take a 40-minute drive northwest to the stunning emerald waters of Lake Louise, the most photographed lake in Canada. At the other end of the spectrum are those here to embark on challenging weeklong hiking trips or mountaineering courses, where they hope to bump into barely anyone. In between are the bulk of the people who visit Banff; those who want not only to spend some time in the Town of Banff and at Lake Louise, but also to experience the peaceful wonders of the mountains that surround them. The good news is that you can do all of this here.

Banff National Park

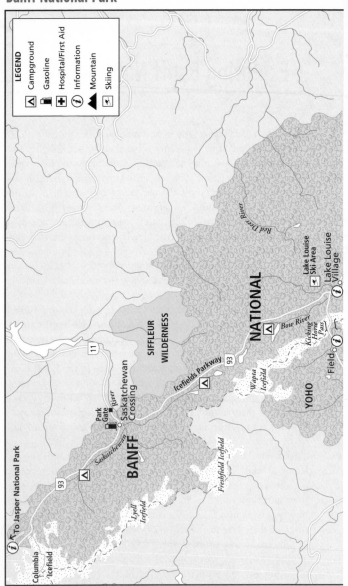

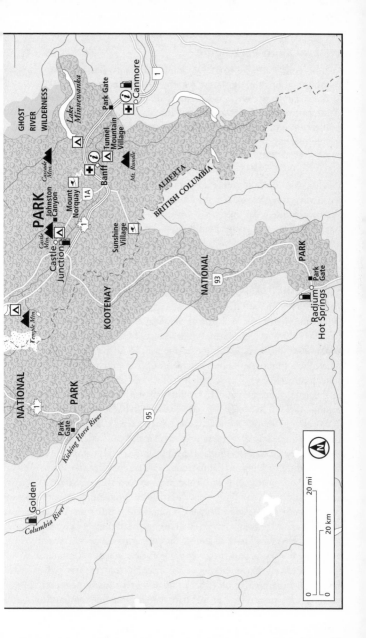

Tips Banff Park Radio

Tune your radio to 101.1 FM, Banff National Park's official radio station, for the latest weather, road, and trail conditions; any pertinent road closures or warnings; as well as interesting documentaries about the history and ecology of this stunning mountain environment. You can also tune in on the Internet at www.friendsofbanff.com.

The main communities in the park are the Town of Banff and the small village of Lake Louise, 40 minutes northwest of Banff Townsite tucked into a flat on the side of the Bow River below its famed namesake lake. The village itself has some of the best hotels in western Canada. It's a stunning area of Banff National Park, rich in human history and full of fantastic scenery.

1 Essentials

ACCESS/ENTRY POINTS   If you are arriving from the east, you'll enter Banff National Park at the main entrance, on the Trans-Canada Highway 1, 128km (80 miles) west of Calgary and just east of the Town of Banff. All visitors to the park must stop at this gate. There are a number of booths where visitors can purchase park permits. Note, however, that you cannot purchase backcountry permits at this gate. Purchase your backcountry permit before your trip by calling the Banff Park office (© **403/762-1550;** banff.vrc@pc.gc.ca).

If you live in the area and already have a pass or are driving through (for example, in a tractor-trailer headed to Golden without plans to stop in Banff National Park) you don't have to stop.

If you are arriving in Banff from the west, you'll either come through Yoho National Park (in the province of British Columbia) to Lake Louise via the Trans-Canada Highway 1, or through Kootenay National Park (also in British Columbia) to Castle Junction via the Kootenay Parkway (Hwy. 93). During the summer (late May through Sept) you'll have to stop at the park entrance booth, where you can pick up a pass, get a copy of Parks Canada's Mountain Guide, and ask any questions of the friendly staff manning the booth. If you're coming on either of these western routes in winter, you won't be greeted by a proper park gate like the one on the east side of the park. Simply follow the series of signs on the well-marked highway. A simple sign also marks the northern entrance to Banff

National Park; this time, on the side of the Icefields Parkway (the northern stretch of Hwy. 93). This is also the border between Banff and Jasper national parks. The entrance is just south of the Icefield Information Centre, 103km (64 miles) south of Jasper Townsite.

The only other entrance to Banff National Park is via Highway 11, the David Thompson Highway, which meets the Icefields Parkway (Hwy. 93) about 77km (48 miles) north of Lake Louise. The gate here is staffed in summers only (May through early Sept). You must stop here and pay the fee required by all vehicles using the Icefields Parkway (which Hwy. 11 runs into), even if you aren't planning on stopping in the park. You can also purchase a backcountry permit at this gate; however, I suggest you get this, and backcountry camping reservations, out of the way before your trip begins.

If you are coming to Banff from the northwestern United States, you have a couple of choices. You can take US Interstate Highway 15 from Montana into southern Alberta and continue north to the Trans-Canada Highway at Calgary and then west to Banff. Or you can take US interstate highways 2 and 95 from Montana into southwestern British Columbia to meet up with the Kootenay Parkway (Hwy. 93) and head north into Kootenay National Park and then east to Banff.

A note on permits: If you are a visitor entering Banff National Park at the eastern park gate on the Trans-Canada Highway 1 via Calgary (the only park entrance with an official gate), you *are* required to stop at the gate to purchase a park permit. You do not need a permit to get into the park if you are coming from the west, either on the Trans-Canada Highway 1 via Yoho National Park or the Kootenay Parkway 93 via Kootenay National Park, and you won't be penalized for not having one if you plan on driving right through. You do need one, however, if you plan to stop along the highway at any point. When you arrive in the town of Banff, visit the **Banff Information Centre** (224 Banff Ave., Banff, AB T0L 0C0; ℰ **403/762-1550**) to buy a permit, and put it in your car as soon as possible. Still, it's a good idea to pick one up beforehand, either at the **Field Information Centre** in Yoho National Park (P.O. Box 99, Field, BC V0A 1G0; ℰ **250/343-6783**) or the **Kootenay National Park Information Centre** (7556 Main St. E., Radium Hot Springs, BC V0A 1M0; ℰ **250/347-9505**). You can pick up a good road map while you're at it.

If you are coming from Jasper National Park via the Icefields Parkway (Hwy. 93), you need a permit to enter Banff, just as you need one to be in Jasper in the first place, as well as to be driving the

Numbers, Please

Size of Banff National Park: 6,641 sq. km (2,564 sq. miles)
Established: 1885
Highest elevation: Mount Forbes, 3,612m (11,850 ft.)
Naturally occurring species of mammals: 69
Roads: 320km (198 miles)
Hiking trails: 1,500km (930 miles)
Campsites: more than 2,800
Park employees: 400 in summer, 225 in winter
Visitors: 4.3 million per year
Banff Townsite year-round population: 7,600
Elevation of Banff Townsite: 1,384m (4,540 ft.)
Lake Louise year-round population: 1,500
Elevation of Lake Louise Village: 1,731m (5,678 ft.)

Icefields Parkway. Purchase one in Jasper at the **Jasper Information Centre** (500 Connaught Dr., Jasper, AB T0E 1E0; ✆ 780/852-6176; www.parkscanada.gc.ca/jasper) or at the Parks Canada information desk in the **Icefield Information Centre** (103km/64 miles south of Jasper Townsite; ✆ 780/852-6288).

Refer to chapter 2 for information about the different types of permits available, what they cost, and which one best suits your trip.

VISITOR CENTERS & INFORMATION   Banff's main **Visitor Information Centre** (224 Banff Ave., Banff, AB T0L 0C0; ✆ 403/762-1550) has information booths for Banff National Park, the Banff/Lake Louise Tourism Bureau, and the Friends of Banff. It's open year-round. The **Lake Louise Visitor Centre** (Samson Mall, P.O. Box 213, Lake Louise, AB T0L 1E0; ✆ 403/522-3833) is also open year-round and has an excellent display on the geological history of the Rockies.

SPECIAL REGULATIONS/WARNINGS   Parks Canada has a number of rules and regulations that you should be aware of. Enforced under the *National Parks Act,* many of them carry strict penalties and/or fines. It's important to comply with these rules since their general purpose is to promote the preservation of the wilderness you've come to see.

- **Area closures inside the park**   For safety and environmental reasons, certain areas in the park, including roads, wildlife corridors, and hiking trails, may be temporarily closed. Closures are marked with signs and red or yellow tape.

- **Bicycles**   Though all types of bikes are permitted on all roads and highways, off-road or mountain bikes are permitted only on certain park hiking trails. Pick up a copy of the brochure **Mountain Biking in Banff National Park** for details on trails open to mountain bikes, rules, and etiquette. You can get one at the **Banff Information Centre** (© 403/762-1550) or the **Lake Louise Visitor Centre** (© 403/522-3833).

- **Boating**   Buckling up a lifejacket and pushing off from a dock in a canoe is A-Okay. Only experienced paddlers, however, should attempt travel on mountain rivers. Motorboats are prohibited on most park waters.

- **Car camping**   Reservations can now be made ahead of time for road-accessible campgrounds, although some sites are set aside for drive-in campers without reservations. These are first-come, first-served (see chapter 2). Demand is heaviest in July and August. Some campgrounds are open year-round, but most open in early May and close in late September.

- **Climbing**   There is no specific climbing permit required in Banff National Park; however, I strongly recommend that inexperienced climbers (and sometimes even experienced climbers new to the area) hire a local guide. A certified guide can be hired through the **Association of Canadian Mountain Guides** (© 403/678-2885; www.acmg.ca). Sports shops and some hotels (like the Post Hotel and the Fairmont Chateau Lake Louise) can put you in touch with professional mountain guides. It's a good idea to register with the **Voluntary Safety Registration** before you head out on a climb.

- **Firearms**   Firearms must be disarmed and must remain in your vehicle at all times, unloaded and in a case or wrapped and securely tied so that no part of the firearm is exposed. Ammunition must be stored separately from the firearm.

- **Garbage/Littering**   You'll notice large brown garbage bins throughout Banff National Park. These are bearproof. They require a bit of extra effort to open (lift up the latch inside the handle and then lift the heavy lid), but they are a necessity. There are also blue bins for recycling cans and bottles. Littering can have a devastating impact on wildlife, by bringing animals out of their natural habitat and drastically changing their feeding patterns. You can be fined C$100 (US$93) for littering or improperly storing food or garbage. Pay special attention to this if you're doing any camping, and make sure you pack food away at night.

- **Hunting/Trapping** Hunting and trapping wildlife is prohibited in Banff National Park.
- **Motorcycles/Snowmobiles/ATVs (all-terrain vehicles)** Use of a motorized off-road vehicle is prohibited in Banff National Park.
- **Pets** Unrestrained pets may harass wildlife, provoke wildlife attacks, and endanger people. Keep your pet on a leash at all times—it's a good idea to keep them out of the backcountry, too.
- **Smoking** Smoking is prohibited in many hotels and restaurants in Banff. If you do smoke, pick up all your cigarette butts and dispose of them in the brown bearproof garbage bins distributed throughout the park.
- **Swimming** There are plenty of lakes in Banff, but only a few are actually warm enough for a dip. Although you won't be fined or charged for swimming in lakes, rivers, or creeks here, you've got to be somewhat crazy to even give it a try, given the frigid temperatures.
- **Vandalism/Defacement** Whatever you find—be it a rock, a wildflower, or a set of antlers—it belongs where it is.
- **Wildlife** It is against the law to touch, entice, disturb, or otherwise harass any wild animals—big or small.

FAST FACTS: Banff National Park

ATMs **Alberta Treasury's** Banff branch is at 317 Banff Ave., in the Town of Banff (© **403/762-8505**). In Lake Louise, there is an ATM in Samson Mall (© **403/522-3678**). The **Bank of Montreal** is at 107 Banff Ave. (© **403/762-2275**), and the **Canadian Imperial Bank of Commerce (CIBC)** is at 98 Banff Ave. (© **403/762-3317**). Exchange foreign currency at these banks or, for better rates, try the **Custom House Global Foreign Exchange**, at 211 Banff Ave. (© **403/760-6630**). The **Royal Bank,** at 117 Banff Ave., has an ATM but does not offer other banking services.

Car Trouble & Towing Services In Banff, try **Standish Towing and Recovery**, 162 Eagle Cres. (© **403/762-4869**). In Lake Louise, **Rocky Mountain Towing**, in the Lake Louise Trade Complex (© **403/522-3534**), will pick you up as far north as the Icefield Information Centre, Jasper National Park, and as far west as Yoho National Park. All of these towing services have the capacity to tow RVs. All are open 24 hours.

Drug Stores **Cascade Plaza Drugs,** lower level Cascade Plaza, 317 Banff Ave. (© **403/762-2245**), or **Gourlay's Pharmacy,** 229 Bear St. (© **403/762-2516**).

Emergencies Call © **911** for fire, ambulance, police, hospital, or Parks Canada assistance. Call © **800/332-1414** for poison control.

Gas Stations There is a long string of gas stations on Banff Avenue, including **Husky Service,** 601 Banff Ave. (© **403/762-3341**), **Banff Shell,** 230 Lynx St. (© **403/760-6675**), and **Petro-Canada,** 302 Lynx St. (© **403/762-4434**). There's a gas station about 30km (19 miles) north of Banff Townsite on the Trans-Canada Highway (Hwy. 1) at **Castle Mountain Village,** off the Trans-Canada on Highway 1A (© **403/522-2783**). In the village of Lake Louise, 30 minutes northeast of the town of Banff, fill up at **Lake Louise Esso,** 200 Village Rd. (© **403/522-3578**), or at **Lake Louise Petro-Canada,** Hector and Whitehorn roads (© **403/522-3755**). There is also a gas station at Saskatchewan Crossing, about 81km (50 miles) north of Lake Louise (© **403/761-7000**).

Grocery Stores Banff's largest grocery store is **Safeway,** 318 Marten St. (© **403/762-5378**). Locally owned **Keller Foods** has everything, 122 Bear St. (© **403/762-2140**). There's a small grocery store on Tunnel Mountain called **Chalet Grocery,** in the Douglas Fir Resort (© **403/762-5447**). In Lake Louise, head to the **Village Market,** in Samson Mall, 101 Lake Louise Dr. (© **403/522-3894**).

Laundry In the Town of Banff, try **Cascade Coin Laundry,** in the Cascade Plaza, 317 Banff Ave. (© **403/762-3444**). On Tunnel Mountain Road at the Douglas Fir Resort, **Chalet Coin Laundry** has a playground in front (© **403/762-5447**).

Medical Services Banff's **Mineral Springs Hospital** is located at 301 Lynx St. (© **403/762-2222**).

Permits Pick up your park permit at Banff's main **eastern gate,** on the Trans-Canada Highway 1 coming west from Calgary, or at the **Banff Information Centre,** 224 Banff Ave. (© **403/762-1550**), where you can also get backcountry permits and fishing permits. You can also get permits in Lake Louise at the **Lake Louise Visitor Centre,** in Samson Mall, 101 Lake Louise Dr. (© **403/522-3833**).

Photo Supplies **Banff Camera Shop,** at the corner of Banff Avenue and Buffalo Street (☏ **403/762-3562**). One-hour developing is available at the **Film Lab** at 120 Banff Ave. (☏ **403/762-2126**). In Lake Louise, **Pipestone Photo** is in Samson Mall, 101 Lake Louise Dr. (☏ **403/522-3617**).

Post Offices **Canada Post,** 204 Buffalo St. (☏ **403/762-2586**). In Lake Louise, send mail from **The Depot,** at the Samson Mall, 101 Lake Louise Dr. (☏ **403/522-3870**).

Taxis **Banff Taxi** (☏ **403/762-4444**), **Legion Taxi** (☏ **403/762-3353**), **Mountain Taxi and Tours** (☏ **403/762-3351**).

Weather Updates Call ☏ **403/762-2088** for the latest forecast. For road conditions, call **Rocky Mountain National Parks** (☏ **403/762-1450**). For avalanche reports, call **Banff National Park** (☏ **403/762-1460**).

2 Tips from Park Staff

Living in Banff means fresh air, clean water, being able to walk to work—and having a spectacular "back yard," says Banff National Park's Information Centre Supervisor Lorena Dmytriev, who came to Banff 25 years ago to learn to ski and has never left.

It's that same love of nature and adventure in the outdoors that attracts more than four million visitors a year. Banff National Park sees protecting nature as a responsibility it shares with everyone who visits, Dmytriev says. Nature is on display here and deeply influences everyone's visit.

Visitors planning their trip need to consider the climate: "Always be prepared for winter, because it can snow at elevation here any time of the year." Pack appropriate footwear and bring clothes that can be worn in layers, she suggests.

Once you're in Banff, your first stop should be the **Information Centre.** "It's really the best way to begin your trip. We've got people that can help you tailor your trip to suit you." They can also help you choose the right hikes and backpacks for the conditions and your ability. "People live in such a fast-paced world these days. We always have visitors who overcommit themselves and get in over their heads."

Dmytriev says there are hikes in Banff for everyone. Even toddlers will enjoy the interpretive walk at the **Hoodoo Trail** on Tunnel Mountain, where pavement makes it stroller-friendly. There's a very accessible (even to wheelchairs) short trail to **Stewart Canyon** at

Lake Minnewanka. Families will enjoy **Sunshine Meadows.** "The bus with White Mountain Tours makes the meadows very accessible. It's absolutely stunning up there." Hardy hikers will love the trails along the Great Divide, where the "power of being amidst the big peaks is amazing and you can see forever from the high passes."

Other summer activities she loves include cycling the Golf Course Loop below the Fairmont Banff Springs, swimming at **Johnson Lake,** and stopping for a treat at the Wild Flour Bakery on Bear Street.

Summer's glory stretches into the quieter month of September. "If you hit the weather right, you'll have plenty of sunshine in the early fall," Dmytriev says. Plus, the trails are dry and there are fewer hikers about in September. And the needles on the lovely larch tree, as well as the leaves on the aspen trees, begin to turn golden throughout the Rockies. In the winter, she loves cross-country skiing near Lake Louise. "Even if you've never skied before, cross-country isn't hard," she says.

Winter or summer, the park's **historical sites** have real charm. The cozy log teahouses behind Lake Louise, as well as rustic lodges like Storm Mountain Lodge and Num-Ti-Jah Lodge, make great destinations. "These buildings really speak to the character of Banff and its rustic beginnings. They're true classics."

Kids will find tons to enjoy in the Town of Banff, from the local playgrounds and library to the always-fascinating **Cave and Basin National Historic Site,** the birthplace of Banff National Park. "It's great any time of year, and has the most biodiversity in the entire park thanks to the lush moisture stemming from the natural springs. Even in winter, you can see fish here. And, of course, the endangered Banff Springs snails."

Wildlife roam the park in the same corridors as tourists. Dmytriev says it's important visitors understand they are in a wilderness area and to keep a good distance from any wildlife they encounter.

The new Parks Canada online campground reservation system is proving very helpful. "It takes away some stress," she says. But if you're just arriving and don't have a site booked, Dmytriev suggests calling the Banff Information Centre, which has a regularly updated list of campsite availabilities.

If you are open to something more rustic, she suggests heading north up the Icefields Parkway and camping at the more remote **Mosquito Creek** or Waterfowl Lake campgrounds. They're close to great hiking and can be used as base camps for exploring the area. "It's a primitive experience, but these are great jumping-off points to spectacular scenery and hiking."

Finds   **Top 10 Shops in Banff**

- **Banff Book and Art Den.** 94 Banff Ave.; ✆ **403/762-3919.** For guidebooks, literature, coffee-table books, and anything that's ever been written about the Canadian Rockies.
- **The Hudson's Bay Company.** 125 Banff Ave.; ✆ **403/762-5525.** A Canadian institution established in 1670, this is the place to go when you can't find what you need anywhere else. There's everything from souvenirs and electronics to clothes and cosmetics in a three-level department store.
- **Keller Foods.** 122 Bear St.; ✆ **403/762-3663.** This locally owned grocery store carries everything you need for a riverside picnic, a hiking trip, or to stock your campsite.
- **Monod's.** 129 Banff Ave.; ✆ **403/762-4571.** Banff's oldest outdoor clothing and equipment retailer. Great for skis, shoes, hiking boots, and all-weather gear.
- **Philippe of Banff.** 130 Banff Ave.; ✆ **403/760-8744.** Banff goldsmith Philippe Plourde handcrafts stunning jewelry that honors tradition yet embraces modern styles.
- **Rocks and Gems.** 137 Banff Ave.; ✆ **403/762-4331.** Carries rocks, gems, and minerals in all shapes and sizes.
- **Rude Girls.** 207 Caribou St.; ✆ **403/762-4412.** Fun and funky surf and snowboard clothing and equipment for girls of all ages.
- **Sgt. Preston's Outpost.** 128B Banff Ave.; ✆ **403/762-5335.** This store sells official products and memorabilia of the Royal Canadian Mounted Police.
- **The Spirit of Christmas.** 133 Banff Ave.; ✆ **403/762-2501.** It's a bit of a stretch, but this shop is a true year-round Christmas bonanza. It's all about joy—not to mention fabulous ornaments that make great souvenirs!
- **The Trail Rider.** 132 Banff Ave.; ✆ **403/762-4551.** Get your Albertan cowboy hats, boots, belts, shirts, and vests here.

No matter your interests, you're sure to find inspiration in the mountains of Banff National Park. Dmytriev invites you to come discover the magic of Banff, and its wide-ranging selection of amazing experiences.

3 The Highlights

Banff National Park would take a lifetime to get to know in full. You can return here year after year and continue exploring. Regardless, there are some places you simply must see, whether it's your first or fifth time in the park.

The **Town of Banff** is a destination in and of itself. It can be quite a surprise to see so many people from so many different places mingling in the shops of Banff Avenue and soaking side-by-side in the Upper Hot Springs. But the cultural appeal of Banff can outweigh the mobs. Some fine cuisine, excellent live music, and other inspiring performing arts exist in this remarkable town. Even if you disdain crowds, you should budget at least half a day to explore the town— try to see a performance at **The Banff Centre,** if you can get tickets.

Although there are many wonderful things to see and do in and around Banff Townsite, it's the many **hiking trails** that make the park what it is. Backcountry highlights include a number of outstanding hiking areas, such as Egypt Lake, Mount Assiniboine, Sunshine Meadows, Paradise Valley, Skoki Valley, and Parker Ridge. And there is some of the world's best **alpine skiing** and **snowboarding** at the park's three downhill ski resorts: Mount Norquay,

---

Moments **Arts in the National Park**

Some of The Banff Centre's most outstanding arts events include:

- **The Banff Arts Festival,** which runs from June to August and includes live outdoor theater, art displays, and jazz workshops.
- **The Banff International String Quartet Competition,** held annually in late August.
- **The Playbill Series,** which runs through the summer and includes live performances by well-known pop, jazz, and world music musicians.
- **The Banff Festival of Mountain Films,** held each November.

For tickets to any of these events, call The Banff Centre box office at ⓒ **800/413-8368** or 403/762-6301, or visit www.banffcentre.com.

Sunshine Village, and Lake Louise. See chapter 4 for reviews of hiking trails of varying difficulty throughout the park, as well as other outdoor activities.

There are also a number of attractions for those who aren't interested in too much physical exertion. If you're not much of a hiker, don't worry—there's plenty to keep you busy. To get an idea of why and how this park came to exist in the first place, don't miss the **Cave and Basin National Historic Site** in the Town of Banff. Stroll the leisurely **Discovery Trail,** just 15 minutes from the site, to see the original cave.

Enjoying a meal in one of Banff's better restaurants is a must (see "Where to Eat in Banff National Park" in chapter 5), as is taking a **picnic lunch** to **Bow Falls** or farther out of town, along the **Bow River.** You might also want to pay a visit to the Fairmont Banff Springs Hotel, the Hoodoos, and Lake Minnewanka. Be sure to bring your camera along!

Take a drive along the **Bow Valley Parkway** (Hwy. 1A) at least once while you are here to appreciate a calmer way to drive through the Rockies—it's less congested than the Trans-Canada Highway 1. Both will take you all the way to Lake Louise.

No one can go to Banff and not see placid, beautiful **Lake Louise,** and many people do just that. They drive out to the lake, get out of their car, snap some variation of what is perhaps the most

---

Fun Fact   **Banff: Where'd That Funny Name Come From?**

The Town of Banff, established in 1886, was named in honor of George Stephen, the first president of the Canadian Pacific Railway, which originally brought surveyors to the area. Stephen and CPR vice-president Donald Smith were both born in the Scottish county of Banffshire; hence the name. The town, established first as a stop on the transcontinental railroad, was originally known simply as "Siding 29," but the CPR board members in Montreal knew the name needed to be more attractive to draw tourists to the mineral hot springs and the luxury hotel they were planning. They chose well. Today, Banff is synonymous with mountain beauty and hospitality.

> ## ⟨Tips⟩ Banff Transit System: Town Traffic Made Easy
>
> Hop on one of the town's public buses, which are now running on eco-friendly biofuels. Routes run along Banff Avenue, Tunnel Mountain Road, and Spray Avenue, to the Fairmont Banff Springs Hotel. Taking the Banff Transit system saves you from spending frustrating time in your vehicle trying to figure out where to turn or looking for that elusive parking spot. You also give yourself and the environment a break. The fare is C$2 (US$1.85) for adults, C$1 (US95¢) for children ages 6 to 12. Children age 5 and under ride free. For more information call ✆ 403/762-1215.

familiar view in the Canadian Rockies, get back into their car, and drive back to their hotel. I recommend budgeting at least half a day to walk some of the **trails around the lake,** have tea in the legendary **Fairmont Chateau Lake Louise,** and make a leisurely stop at nearby **Moraine Lake.**

North of Lake Louise is the spectacular **Icefields Parkway** (Hwy. 93), which you can take farther north to **Jasper National Park.** One of the most beautiful highways in the world, this road is also a must. Budget at least a half-day to explore its wonder—you'll drive right through the kind of landscape you'd need to trek for weeks to get to anywhere else on earth. A full day will give you time to see the glaciers, walk a few short hikes, have a picnic lunch, and make it back to your hotel in Banff or Lake Louise in time for dinner.

4 Suggested Itineraries

Because there is so much to see and do in Banff National Park, try to identify your priorities before you get here. It's my hope that every visitor will enjoy a delicious meal, see at least a few bighorn sheep and maybe an elk, learn about the fascinating history of the Canadian Rockies, and manage to get out on a couple of day hikes.

IF YOU HAVE ONLY 1 OR 2 DAYS

If you have time to do only a 1- or 2-day tour of Banff, be sure to make a lodging reservation well in advance, and if you are staying in a hotel, make it in the Town of Banff. If you are camping, select either the Tunnel Mountain Campground (if you are coming from the east) or the Lake Louise Campground (if you are coming from

---

Tips **Spending time in the Chateau**

You need to make a reservation for high tea at the Fairmont Chateau Lake Louise (call ✆ **403/522-3511** to reserve). The Poppy Brasserie and the Glacier Saloon, both on the lower level, will serve people not registered at the hotel; the rest of the hotel is off-limits. If there is availability, non-registered guests may have brunch or dinner in the dining room, provided they have a reservation. For a full review of the Fairmont Chateau Lake Louise, see "Lodging in Banff National Park" in chapter 5.

---

the west). See chapter 5 for reviews of all types of accommodations in Banff, from exclusive resorts to backcountry hostels.

No matter how long you are here, your first stop should be the **Banff Information Centre** (224 Banff Ave., Banff, AB T1L 1K2; ✆ **403/762-1550;** www.parkscanada.gc.ca/banff) in the town itself. This is where you stock up on very useful maps, pick up free self-guiding tour brochures, and get any and every piece of advice you need from the knowledgeable and friendly staff of the Parks Canada, Banff/Lake Louise Tourism Bureau, and Friends of Banff desks.

If the weather is clear, take the **gondola ride** up **Sulphur Mountain** to get a good sense of where you are. From there, make a quick stop at the Fairmont Banff Springs Hotel and Bow Falls, then drive the Lake Minnewanka Loop.

In the afternoon, head out to **Lake Louise,** where you can walk the lakeshore trail or hike up to the Lake Agnes Teahouse. Drive to Moraine Lake and rent a canoe for a short paddle to see the tall rock walls of **Babel Tower,** or hike to the Moraine Lake viewpoint.

Drive back to Banff along the **Bow Valley Parkway,** looking for wildlife if you have time. Enjoy a delicious meal at one of the fine restaurants on Banff Avenue (see "Where to Eat in Banff National Park" in chapter 5) and go for a soak in the **Upper Hot Springs** before calling it a day.

If you have 2 days, spend the first day on the above excursion, but give yourself more time for walking and short hikes. Save your outing to Lake Louise for the second day. Visit the **Cave and Basin National Historic Site** and walk the trail to Sundance Canyon. Also plan for a **picnic lunch** along the route. Golfers must make time for a round at the course at the Fairmont Banff Springs Hotel, and history buffs will want to stop at the **Whyte Museum of the Canadian Rockies.**

Finds Photo Ops Galore

It seems there's an award-winning picture at every turn in Banff National Park. But a few spots that are easy to access can get help you put that once-in-a-lifetime mountain image in focus. Here's a list of the top six photo locations in Banff.

- **Surprise Corner:** At an elbow bend on the edge of Tunnel Mountain, this is the classic viewpoint for admiring the Fairmont Banff Springs Hotel in all its glory, and the majestic Bow Falls. Head up toward The Banff Centre on Buffalo Street, and keep an eye out for fellow photographers crossing the street!

- **Canada Place:** At the far end of Banff Avenue, the landscaped gardens of Canada Place provide a great perspective on the hustle and bustle, not to mention the stunning background, of Banff's main drag.

- **Vermillion Lakes:** For an angle on the sloped ridge of Mt. Rundle that can't be beat, head to these picturesque lakes. Watch for wildlife in the marshland. In the summer you can paddle into the middle of the lake for a undisturbed shot—or skate out on the frozen lakes in the winter for an icy masterpiece.

- **Corral Creek:** To combine a picnic with a photo session, pull over on the Bow Valley Parkway for a jaw-dropping view of Mt. Temple, nestled behind a lovely stream.

- **Lake Louise:** Few tourists are going to miss this one, and even though you can feel like you're competing with Hollywood paparazzi, the color of Lake Louise, with the spectacular Victoria Glacier in the distance, is certainly worthy of its spot in the photo hall of fame.

- **Peyto Lake:** With a blue deeper than the Caribbean, and steep edges of mountain all around, Peyto Lake is a must-stop on the Icefields Parkway. In July and August, wildflowers are blooming. It's well worth the short stroll.

IF YOU HAVE 3 OR MORE DAYS

Three or more days should give you enough time to see and do at least a little of everything in Banff National Park. Plan to spend at least 1 night at a hotel other than the one you'll use for a base in the Town of Banff. You may want to try a hotel in Lake Louise, or stay in one of the lodges across the provincial border in British Columbia's **Yoho National Park.** (See chapter 9, "Gateways to Banff & Jasper National Parks," for reviews of Emerald Lake Lodge and Lake O'Hara Lodge.) Also, you will not regret budgeting time to spend at least 1 night in the **backcountry.** If you can, book a site at **Egypt Lake** (one of my all-time favorite backcountry areas), a group of lakes tucked high up near the Continental Divide. You'll need a day to get there and another one to hike back out. Do a half- or full-day hike, a river float trip, or perhaps a **horseback-riding** trip. Take a drive north along the Icefields Parkway (Hwy. 93), making stops at **Bow Lake,** Bow Summit, **Peyto Lake,** and Parker Ridge before crossing into **Jasper National Park** to visit the Columbia Icefield. People who have traveled extensively often say that the road connecting Banff and Jasper national parks is the most beautiful stretch of highway in the world. (Refer to chapters 6 and 7 for things to see and do in Jasper.)

If you stop at most of the roadside viewpoints, it should take about an hour to get from Banff Townsite to Lake Louise, and

---

Banff Calendar of Events

January: Banff/Lake Louise Winter Festival and Ice Magic sculpture competition at Lake Louise

May: Slush Cup season finale at Sunshine Village

May and August: Banff Arts Festival

June: Banff World Television Festival

July 1: Canada Day parade and celebrations in Central Park

August–September: Banff International String Quartet Competition

October: Lake Louise International Food and Wine Festival

October–November: Banff Mountain Films and Book Festival

November: Winterstart Festival

December: World Cup Men's and Women's Downhill and Super G races at Lake Louise

<hr>

Moments **Stop and Look for a Grizz**

Take your time as you drive along the southern sections of the Icefields Parkway (Hwy. 93). You are passing through prime brown bear, grizzly bear, deer, and moose country. Look for wildlife along the subalpine wet meadows.

<hr>

another 2½ hours to get to the Banff–Jasper border and the Icefield Information Centre. There is a gas station, snack bar, and gift shop at **Saskatchewan Crossing,** not really a town—more like a visitor complex—about halfway up the parkway, 78km (48 miles) north of Lake Louise. It's a good place to stop, get out of the car, and stretch your legs. There are also a handful of peaceful **campgrounds** along this route. Spending a night at one of them would be a pleasant change from the large and crowded Tunnel Mountain Campground in Banff Townsite.

5 What to See & Do in Banff Townsite

Located at the confluence of the Spray and Bow rivers, and on the lower slopes of Tunnel and Sulphur mountains, Banff Townsite has a remarkable setting. To the east is the fin-tipped slope of Mount Rundle. To the northeast is the triangle-shaped Cascade Mountain.

Banff's **Information Centre** (224 Banff Ave., Banff, AB T1L 1K2; © **403/762-1550;** www.parkscanada.gc.ca/banff) has information from Parks Canada, the Friends of Banff, and the Banff/Lake Louise Tourism Bureau. This is where you can find a hotel, choose a good hike, or reserve a backcountry campsite. During the summer, there are daily movies on the park and its history.

The heart of town is a 2-block stretch of Banff Avenue, which is lined with shops and restaurants. It has recently undergone a major makeover and is more pedestrian-friendly than ever. Begin your exploring with a drive down Banff Avenue, over the Bow River bridge, and then up Spray Avenue toward the unmistakable stone towers and green roof of the **Fairmont Banff Springs Hotel,** a national landmark that Canadians cherish and protect as much as they do the Parliament Buildings in Ottawa. It's an expensive and somewhat exclusive place to stay, but a lovely building in its own right and certainly a must-see on any trip to Banff. Park your car and take a short tour of the hotel. It's a nice idea to plan to eat lunch here in one of the hotel's eight restaurants or come for a classic afternoon

The Banff Springs Hotel: Part of the Park's History

The Canadian Pacific Railway rang up massive debts while building the first trans-Canada railway in the 1880s, even though the government of Canada pitched in (saying it was doing so to promote national unity). The CPR realized it needed another venture to help offset the costs, and began exploring the idea of tourism. "Since we can't export the scenery, we'll have to import the tourists," said CPR vice-president and general manager William Van Horne at the time. In Banff, Van Horne began drawing up plans for a luxury resort and commissioned famed architect Bruce Price to design the building. Construction of the **Banff Springs Hotel** began in late 1886 and cost the CPR C$250,000. It opened June 1, 1888, to much hype across the country. Room rates for what was the largest hotel in the world at the time started at C$3.50 per night. It's because of "the Springs," as the hotel is called by locals, that the town of Banff began to grow.

Due to a number of fires and subsequent major renovations, none of the original building remains. What stands today looks truly like a castle in the mountains and is constantly being renovated and modernized. The service is outstanding, the views are excellent, the restaurants first class. The recent addition of the award-winning multi-million-dollar Willow Stream Spa has kept the place on the top of the "best hotels in the world" lists. The hotel is a national historic site with at least a handful of photo opportunities, and deserves a short tour.

tea (see "Lodging in Banff National Park" in chapter 5 for a full review of the hotel).

Tucked in behind the Fairmont Banff Springs Hotel, **Bow Falls** will let you escape the hustle and bustle of the busy Banff Townsite. The 10m (33-ft.) falls are being eroded between two rock formations. The rock on the left bank of the river is 245 million years old, while the one on the right bank is some 320 million years old. The falls roar and wash away any tension you may have picked up while trying to make your way down Banff Avenue.

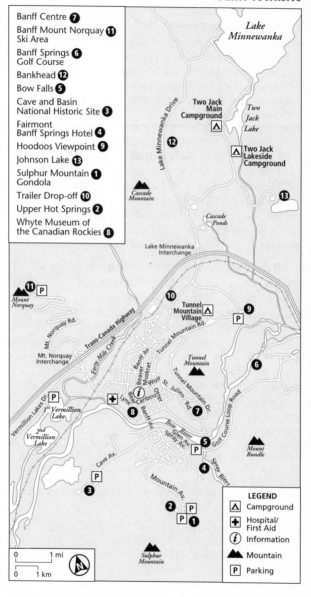

Banff Centre **7**

Banff Mount Norquay **11**
Ski Area

Banff Springs **6**
Golf Course

Bankhead **12**

Bow Falls **5**

Cave and Basin **3**
National Historic Site

Fairmont **4**
Banff Springs Hotel

Hoodoos Viewpoint **9**

Johnson Lake **13**

Sulphur Mountain **1**
Gondola

Trailer Drop-off **10**

Upper Hot Springs **2**

Whyte Museum of **8**
the Canadian Rockies

Lake Minnewanka

Two Jack Main
Campground

Two Jack Lake

Two Jack Lakeside
Campground

Cascade Mountain

Cascade Ponds

Lake Minnewanka Interchange

Mount Norquay

Mt. Norquay Rd.

Trans-Canada Highway

Mt. Norquay Interchange

Forty Mile Creek

Tunnel Mountain Village

Tunnel Mountain Rd.

Tunnel Mountain

Tunnel Mountain Dr.

Golf Course Loop Road

Vermillion Lakes Dr.

1st Vermillion Lake

2nd Vermillion Lake

Beaver Av.
Muskrat
Wolf
Otter
Lynx
Bear
Banff Av.
Caribou
St. Julien Rd.
Bow
Glen Av.
Spray Av.
River
Spray River

Cave Av.

Mountain Av.

Mount Rundle

Sulphur Mountain

0 1 mi
0 1 km

LEGEND

🔺 Campground

➕ Hospital/First Aid

ⓘ Information

🔺 Mountain

🅿 Parking

Fun Fact **A River Runs Through It**

The beautiful Bow River is the longest river in Banff National Park. From its headwaters at Bow Lake, 90km (56 miles) north of the Town of Banff, it flows south and east, passing through Banff, Canmore, and Calgary. It joins the South Saskatchewan River and eventually drains into the Atlantic Ocean, on Canada's east coast.

Or drive over to the **Fenland Trail** ⊛, which follows Forty Mile Creek for 1km (.6 mile). The trail starts just to the east of the Vermillion Lakes, off Mount Norquay Road, just south of the Trans-Canada Highway. You can also reach it by following the trail along the Bow River past Central Park, following the signs along the way. Pick up the interpretive pamphlet at the trail head in the Forty Mile Creek picnic area to learn more about the area.

Banff Gondola and Historic Weather Observatory ⊛⊛   The gondola takes you up 2,285m (7,495 ft.) to the top of **Sanson Peak** in 7 minutes flat. In summer, you can walk along a mountaintop ridge to the historic weather observatory, named for curator and meteorologist Norman Sanson. Sanson visited the ridge more than 1,000 times in the early 20th century, both to accumulate weather data and because he simply loved the place. Look for bighorn sheep, which often gather near the top. It's the easiest way to get a bird's-eye view of the peaks, and good for visitors of all ages (just keep a close eye on kids!). The trip up and down should take you 2 hours at the most. Looking for a good workout? Hike up Sulphur Mountain—and take the gondola down for free!

At the end of Mountain Rd., 2.5km (1½ miles) from Banff Ave. ⓒ **403/762-2523.** Admission C$25 (US$23) adults, C$11 (US$10) children 6–15, free for children 5 and under. June 1–Sept 2 daily 7:30am–9pm; Sept 3–Oct 14 daily 8:30am–6:30pm; Oct 15–Dec 2 daily 8:30am–4:30pm; Dec 3–Jan 8 daily 10am–4pm; Jan 9–19 closed for maintenance; Jan 20–31 daily 10am–4pm; Feb 1–Mar 31 daily 10am–5pm; Apr 1–May 31 daily 8:30am–6pm.

Banff Mountain Film Festival ⊛   Each November, the **Centre for Mountain Culture** hosts annual book, film, and photography festivals celebrating the spirit of those who live in the mountains, attracting international attention. If you're a really keen armchair adventurer it's best to buy a weekend pass, which will get you into plenty of screenings as well as to hear guest speakers and attend the awards ceremony and closing party on Sunday evening.

In The Banff Centre. St. Julien Rd. For tickets, call The Banff Centre box office at
℃ **403/762-6301**. Admission (weekend pass) C$140 (US$131) per person. Take
Banff Ave. to Buffalo St. and turn east, then up the hill and turn north on St. Julien
Rd., following the signs for The Banff Centre.

Banff Park Museum National Historic Site
Recently reopened
by Parks Canada in a lovely log building that dates to 1903, this is a
one-stop shop for learning about the natural history of the Rockies.
Birds, insects, and wildlife are the main stars here. It's a quick stop, and
particularly good if you come in time for the daily tours—starting at
3pm daily in the summertime, and on winter weekends at 2:30pm.

Banff Ave. by the Bow River Bridge. ℃ **403/762-1558**. Admission C$4 (US$3.75),
children 18 and under C$2 (US$1.85), family C$10 (US$9.35). Mid-May to Sept 30
daily 10am–6pm. Oct 1 to mid-May daily 1–5pm.

Banff Summer Arts Festivals ☆
This festival is held each sum-
mer at **The Banff Centre** ☆☆☆, itself a remarkable part of the
town's fabric. The festival showcases the best in a variety of artistic
areas—from costume design and creative writing, to drama and
opera, to jazz and classical music. If you are an arts lover, check out
the events calendar on the Centre's website (www.banffcentre.ca)
before you come and get yourself tickets to at least one show.

St. Julien Rd. The Banff Centre: ℃ **403/762-6100**. Banff Summer Arts Festival: ℃ **403/
762-6301**. Admission ranges from pay-what-you-can to C$40 (US$37) depending on
the event. May and Aug. Take Banff Ave. to Buffalo St. and turn east, then up the hill
and turn north on St. Julien Rd., following the signs for The Banff Centre.

Buffalo Nations Luxton Museum
The exhibits here tell the
story of the indigenous inhabitants of the Canadian Rockies' eastern
ranges. One of the museum's primary goals is to help visitors get to
know and understand Native people in Canada today. History and
anthropology buffs should give themselves 1 hour.

1 Birch Ave. ℃ **403/762-2388**. Admission C$8 (US$7.50) adults, C$6 (US$5.60)
seniors and students, C$2.50 (US$2.30) children 12 and under. Daily 9am–5pm. Just
across the Bow River bridge; take Banff Ave. and turn west.

Canada Place ⟨Kids⟩
If you are traveling with children, head over
to this museum for family-friendly exhibits about Canada and its
people. Surrounded by the historic Cascade Gardens; in summertime, the Siksika Nation puts up a tepee and interpretive display
about Native culture past and present.

Park Administration Building, 101 Mountain Ave., Banff, AB T1L 1K2. ℃ **403/762-
1338**. Free admission. May–Sept daily 10am–6pm. At the end of Banff Ave. across
the Bow River bridge.

Historic Banff Walk   Held daily from June through early September, this 90-minute walking tour departs from the Whyte Museum of the Canadian Rockies (see below) and meanders off the beaten path through the residential streets of Banff. Guides share stories of the colorful characters, buildings, and events that shaped Banff's history.

111 Bear St. ✆ **403/762-2291**. C$7 (US$6.50) per person. June 1–Sept 3 daily at 2:30pm.

Upper Hot Springs ✦   This is where you go to soak away your worries and take in some mountain atmosphere. The supposed curative waters of the pools have drawn visitors here for more than a century. There are lockers, swimsuit and towel rentals, and also a full-service spa (✆ **403/760-2500**). Although recently renovated, the hot springs retain their classic appearance. The views from the pool are some of the best in town. I particularly love it here on a snowy winter night—very romantic!

A Secret No Longer

Don't miss the **Cave and Basin National Historic Site** ✦✦ (end of Cave Ave.; ✆ **403/762-1566**; C$4/US$3.75 for adults, C$3.50/US$3.25 for seniors, C$2/US$1.85 for children ages 6–16, free for children under 6, C$10/US$9.30 for families).

In 1874, two Stoney Indians happened to mention the existence of some mysterious hot springs to two surveyors working for the Canadian Pacific Railway, which was being built at the time. The surveyors found the cave where the springs surfaced, and had their first hot bath in months. A few years later three brothers, also surveyors, moved in, built a cabin, and intended to stake a claim to the springs. It was only a matter of time before others heard of the springs and began dreaming of their own possibilities. Word spread to the government of Canada, which quickly stepped in and established a national park reserve in the area. Today, you can walk into the cave, smell the sulfur, peer into the cave holes, and imagine the dirty faces of the railway men who first stumbled upon tourist gold. There are a 30-minute film and a 1-hour guided tour daily in summer at 11am.

Fun Fact **Rotten Eggs**

The "rotten eggs" smell that you notice at some hot springs is partly due to sulfur, but really more a result of algae, which emits hydrogen sulfide as it metabolizes the sulfur.

At the end of Mountain Rd., 2.5km (1½ miles) from downtown Banff. ⓒ **403/762-1515.** Admission C$7.50 (US$7) adults, C$6.50 (US$6) children 17 and under, C$23 (US$22) family pass. May 17–Sept 9 daily 9am–11pm; Sept 10–May 16 Sun–Thurs 10am–10pm, Fri–Sat 10am–11pm.

Whyte Museum of the Canadian Rockies ☆☆ *Finds*   A gem for history buffs, the museum produces excellent exhibits about the human history of the Banff area. Stocked by the collections of artists Peter and Catharine Whyte, the museum has a tremendously wealthy archive of memoirs, sketches, photographs, and personal artifacts of Rocky Mountain pioneers, visionaries, and artists. Famed local guide Bruno Engler's photographs of early skiing at Sunshine Village, scholarly archives of alpinism, and the library of the **Alpine Club of Canada** are all here in this one-of-a-kind museum of mountain heritage. Give yourself a few hours to stroll the various exhibits.

111 Bear St. ⓒ **403/762-2291.** Admission C$6 (US$5.60) adults, C$3.50 (US$3.25) seniors and students, free for children 5 and under. Daily 10am–5pm. Beside the Banff Public Library across from the Banff Town Hall.

6 Driving Tours

There are a variety of driving tours you can do during your trip to Banff. On most of them, you follow the **Bow River** and the **Canadian Pacific Railway** through the Bow Valley, the most open and accessible valley in the park. If you're interested in an extended outing, try linking the Bow Valley Parkway trip to Johnston Canyon with a trip across the border into Kootenay National Park (see chapter 9), or combine the Lake Louise, Moraine Lake, and Sightseeing Gondola outings.

IN AND AROUND BANFF TOWNSITE
LAKE MINNEWANKA AND CASCADE MOUNTAIN

Head east off **Banff Avenue** on **Tunnel Mountain Road** to take a good look at the mysterious **Hoodoos.** The Tunnel Mountain Hoodoos look like they've been dropped from outer space. In fact, they are free-standing pillars made of silt, gravel, and rocks cemented together by dissolved limestone. The un-cemented particles were slowly eroded and washed away. There is a paved 500m (1,600-ft.) trail to a nice viewpoint where you can remain puzzled by the Hoodoos' appearance. Tunnel Mountain Road continues to loop around until it hooks back up with **Lake Minnewanka Road,** which passes under the Trans-Canada Highway (Hwy. 1) and goes northeast along the side of Cascade Mountain.

Pull off Lake Minnewanka Road at the **Bankhead** ✦ turnoff (there's a large sign on the right) to see the remnants of an old industrial village. Once the working center of Banff, Bankhead was a small settlement that boomed in the early 20th century. Old machinery and foundations are still in place, such as the entryway to the former church on the hill just above the parking lot and the transformer building, which features a display about coal mining. **Lake Minnewanka,** 12km (7½ miles) north of the townsite and the largest lake in Banff National Park, used to be called "The Lake of the Water Spirits" by the Stoney Nation, who apparently feared these spirits and refused to swim in or boat on the lake. Although it's too cold for a dip, boaters today have no fear. This is the only lake in Banff where motorboats are allowed. A 24km (15-mile) loop drive continues past Minnewanka, taking you past the campgrounds at Two Jack Lake, a great spot for a picnic! There are great views of the Palliser Range, behind Lake Minnewanka. You can take a **glass-enclosed boat trip** ✦ to the end of the lake (© **403/ 762-3473;** C$40/US$37 for adults, C$20/US$19 for children 5–11, free for children under 5). The 2-hour trip has good wildlife viewing opportunities. There are also guided fishing trips (© **403/ 762-3473;** 31/2-hour tours from C$275/US$257 for up to two adults, C$75/US$70 for each extra adult, C$50/US$47 for children 5–11, free for children under 5). A nice 30-minute round-trip walk along the western shore of Lake Minnewanka takes you to Stewart Canyon. Watch for bighorn sheep on the road near Two Jack Lake—and remember not to feed them. Nearby lakes are also worth a visit, including the Cascade Ponds and **Johnson Lake** ✦, a great place for a swim on a hot day.

JOHNSTON CANYON VIA THE BOW VALLEY PARKWAY

Another good day trip from Banff Townsite is northwest toward Lake Louise along the **Bow Valley Parkway 1A.** The drive takes you through rolling hillsides below towering mountains alongside the **Bow River.**

The Continental Divide

The backbone of the Americas, the Continental Divide separates the continent into two watersheds. From Canada to southern Mexico, waters on the western side of the divide all flow west to the Pacific Ocean. Waters flowing on the east side empty into Hudson Bay and the Atlantic Ocean. In the Canadian Rockies, the Continental Divide also forms the provincial border between the provinces of British Columbia to the west and Alberta to the east. There's a lovely little placard marking the border where you can see the splitting of the waters along the Continental Divide at the Alberta–British Columbia border, in Kootenay National Park.

Head out of town on **Mount Norquay Road** and take a left onto **Vermillion Lakes Drive,** just before the Trans-Canada Highway exit. Probably the remnants of one very large lake, **the Vermillion Lakes** are three separate shallow lakes (known as First Lake, Second Lake, and, you guessed it, Third Lake) formed by a meandering stream that opens up into three large ponds. They are a favorite spot for birds and other wildlife and provide a pleasant contrast to the dramatic mountain landscape that characterizes most of the park. You can make it out here in 5 minutes flat by car from downtown Banff, or make it a part of a leisurely afternoon stroll. There's a pleasant 4.5km (2¾-mile) road to drive, walk, or bike along. You can take your own version of the postcard shot of Mount Rundle from here. An excellent place for **bird-watching,** you may see osprey and bald eagles nesting at **First Lake.** Look for beavers and muskrats at Second Lake and for coyotes, wolves, and elk grazing in the wetlands.

Head left or north back on to Mount Norquay Road out of the townsite and turn left or west onto the Trans-Canada Highway (Hwy. 1). You'll meet up with the **Bow Valley Parkway** at an interchange 5km (3 miles) from town. If you have the time, I suggest driving on the Parkway, also known as the 1A, instead of the Trans-Canada. It's more leisurely and there are more chances for seeing wildlife. Built in 1920—the first road connecting Banff and Lake Louise—it still feels more like a mountain road than an expressway. Both the Bow Valley Parkway and the Trans-Canada Highway follow the **Bow River,** which looks even more like the cool, clear mountain river you were expecting when you arrived here than the river as it rages through Bow Falls. There are a number of viewpoints where you can pull off and get a good look at this beautiful river.

Heading west along the Bow Valley Parkway, it's hard to miss the turnoff for **Johnston Canyon** *★★*. In fact, it's hard to find a parking spot here, 18km (11 miles) west of Banff Townsite. An extremely popular day-use area, a **suspended walkway** takes you up Johnston Creek past two large waterfalls. The first part of the trail is on a paved surface and is a very gentle uphill climb that ends in front of the first waterfall, called the Lower Falls, which is the start of the gorge. There are interpretive signs along the way as the trail continues to climb to the Upper Falls, which are about twice the height of the Lower Falls. The trail continues 5.5km (3.4 miles) to the top of a valley, where the views are rewarding.

SUNSHINE MEADOWS

On the south side of the Trans-Canada Highway (Hwy. 1), 16km (10 miles) west of the townsite, the Sunshine Road branches into the Sunshine Range. Sunshine Meadows is a span of 14km (8¾ miles) that hugs the Continental Divide south of Banff. In the winter, it's the home of the popular **Sunshine Village ski resort.** The meadows are not accessible by car. You can either drive 15 minutes from Banff Townsite to the Sunshine Village parking lot (see below) or arrange for a bus to pick you up at your hotel or campground and drop you off. From there, you need to either hike 6km (3.7 miles) along a steep gravel road or take a second bus up a restricted-access road to get to the meadows. I recommend taking the bus for the simple reason that it's faster than walking, and will give you more time to enjoy exploring the meadows up top! Here, an abundance of wildflowers (more than 340 species) maximize their 2-month growing season by growing to short heights and short petal lengths in a spectacular display of colors. It's a magical, colorful, breath-taking place in late July and early August. To the south you can see Mount Assiniboine, the "Matterhorn of the Rockies." For information about the bus service from Banff to the Sunshine Village parking lot, call **White Mountain Adventures** at *②* **403/678-4099.** The bus ride costs C$46 (US$43) for adults and C$27 (US$25) for children 6 to 12, free for children under 3, round-trip. From the Sunshine Village parking lot to the Meadows, the cost is C$23 (US$22) for adults and C$13 (US$12) for children 3 to 12, free for under 6, round-trip. You can also sign up for guided hikes at Sunshine Meadows.

⟮Moments⟯   Castle Mountain

As you drive north along either the Trans-Canada Highway or the Bow Valley Parkway, it's impossible not to be impressed by the layer-cake-shaped **Castle Mountain**, rising out of the Bow Valley ahead on your left. At 2,766m (9,073 ft.), it dominates the eastern side of the valley. Originally named Castle Mountain in 1858 because of its fortress-like appearance, its name was changed in 1946 to Mount Eisenhower, in honor of Dwight D. Eisenhower, commander of the allied forces in World War II and later president of the United States. Eisenhower was supposed to come to a ceremony to proclaim the new name, but he apparently was detained at a golf game and failed to show up. Despite this, locals decided to name the grassy terrace on the southwest slope of the mountain "Eisenhower's Green." In 1979, the main massif was officially designated Castle Mountain, and the tower on the south end of the mountain Eisenhower Peak (or Eisenhower Tower).

Tucked in the forest below the majestic peak, the small village of **Castle Junction,** 28km (17 miles) northwest of Banff Townsite, is a good place to stop for snacks or a picnic. There is also a **gas station** (✆ **403/522-2783**).

LAKE LOUISE

Situated 56km (35 miles) northwest of the Town of Banff, Lake Louise is a famous lake (perhaps the most photographed in the country) that people all over the world associate with their image of Canada. It's also the name of the small village just below the lake. It consists of pretty much what you'd expect to see in a small village (or "hamlet," as Parks Canada refers to it): gas stations, a grocery store, post office, snack bar, restaurant, cafe, and an outdoor equipment store. And let's not forget some outstanding hotels—which, admittedly, you might not expect to find in a small village or "hamlet." Those are reviewed in chapter 5. The **Lake Louise Visitor Centre** is housed in **Samson Mall** (101 Lake Louise Dr., Lake Louise, AB T0L 1E0; ✆ **403/522-3833**). It'll take you just around 40 minutes to drive here directly from the Town of Banff on either the Trans-Canada Highway 1 or the Bow Valley Parkway 1A. You

Canada's Winter Playground

In the winter, the Lake Louise area is just as lively as it is in summer, as skiers and snowboarders from around the world come to enjoy the snow and excellent terrain at the **Lake Louise Ski and Snowboard Resort** ✮✮✮ (© **403/522-3555;** www.skilouise.com), one of the largest ski resorts in Canada. In 2005 a new four-person gondola was installed, helping skiers and snowboards get to the "Top of the World" even faster. Lake Louise hosts the fastest skiers in the world for World Cup ski races each year at the start of the season.

can park in the village and hop on a shuttle up to the lake, a great idea to avoid the traffic jams on the steep road up the hill.

It's about 8km (5 miles) or a 5-minute drive from the village to the lake itself and the often-crowded parking lot. Fed by glacial meltwater, **Lake Louise** is 2.4km (1½ miles) long, 500m (1,640 ft.) wide, and 90m (295 ft.) deep. Behind it is **Mount Victoria,** at an elevation of 3,464m (11,362 ft.), with the thick **Victoria Glacier** on its front ridge. The lake was named after Princess Louise Caroline Alberta (1849–1939), the fourth daughter of Queen Victoria and later the wife of the governor general of Canada. Don't even think about swimming in Lake Louise, though! On the hottest day of the summer the water temperature may rise only as high as 39°F (4°C). It's deep, cold, and frozen from November until June.

In summer, bus tours drop thousands of people in front of the lake each day to have their picture taken, then load them back on to the bus and head off to the next tour stop. As you might expect, the scene in the parking lot and in front of the Fairmont Chateau Lake Louise can resemble an amusement park at times. It's quite crowded. But the lake is so beautiful and pristine, you should go anyway. Parks Canada recently installed new interpretive panels at an easy-to-access lakeshore lookout just beyond the parking lot. Try to come early in the day, when the light is best for taking pictures and there's less traffic. Park your car, walk through the crowds, and try to steal some quiet time down the trails on either side of the lake (see chapter 4).

The **Fairmont Chateau Lake Louise,** which looks sometimes like a giant jail but more often a castle, dominates the lake. It's often called a "diamond in the wilderness"—certainly from the inside, it is all glitz and glamour. Expansions in 2003 (costing around C$65

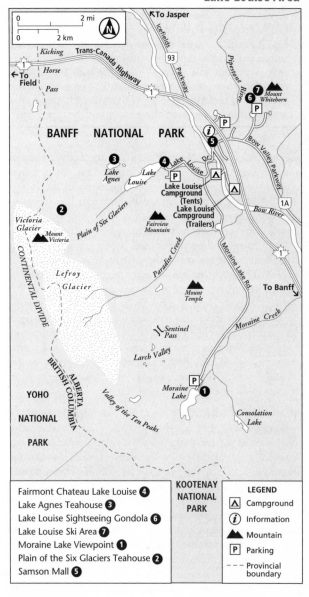

Fairmont Chateau Lake Louise **4**
Lake Agnes Teahouse **3**
Lake Louise Sightseeing Gondola **6**
Lake Louise Ski Area **7**
Moraine Lake Viewpoint **1**
Plain of the Six Glaciers Teahouse **2**
Samson Mall **5**

LEGEND

△ Campground
(i) Information
▲ Mountain
P Parking
--- Provincial boundary

Fun Fact **Why Is the Lake So Blue?**

Fine particles of glacial sediment, known as rock flour, are suspended in Lake Louise and other lakes in the area with that mysterious and beautiful turquoise hue. The particles reflect blue and green wavelengths of light because they are so small and uniform. The color of the lake is affected by the amount of light, the depth of the water, and the time of year.

---

million) include a new North Wing, a conference center, and a massive new ballroom. The Chateau's charm is in its location and its interior—so don't be dismayed by its domineering stature. It is open in a limited way to people not staying overnight. If you want to at least experience the Chateau, make a reservation for a delicious brunch buffet or afternoon tea in one of the hotel's restaurants.

The Chateau had humble enough beginnings, in the form of a cabin built on the site in 1890 by the CPR (Canadian Pacific Railway). By 1917 the cabin had burned to the ground, and a hotel with all the modern amenities of the day was erected in its place. While the Banff Springs Hotel, also run by the CPR, was to be luxurious, the CPR marketed the Chateau Lake Louise as a destination for outdoor adventurers. Mountaineers, artists, and horseback riders flooded in, giving the Chateau a level of popularity and character the Springs is still striving for. The summer staff is a cross section of Canadian youth. Ask the staff you meet where they're from— chances are it's at least a province away.

MORAINE LAKE AND VALLEY OF THE TEN PEAKS

Just south of Lake Louise is the equally stunning **Moraine Lake** and **Valley of the Ten Peaks** area. There is a rough and winding road (open only May–Oct) that takes you the 13km (7¾ miles) from Lake Louise to Moraine Lake. At the often-crowded parking lot are a lodge, a picnic area, and some interpretive exhibits. Like Lake Louise, you should try to come here early in the morning, and you can also take a shuttle from the parking lot at Samson Mall to avoid parking hassles. Some argue that Moraine Lake is even more beautiful than Lake Louise. I prefer to see them as brilliant but different. Louise is calm and symmetrical; Moraine is wild and dramatic. Ten spire-like peaks surround it, each more than 3,048m (10,000 ft.) high. You can rent canoes here (C$35/hour [US$33]), or walk an excellent interpretive trail to the Moraine Lake Rockpile for the view that used to be on the Canadian $20 bill. Moraine Lake is also the trail head for a number of the best hikes in Banff National Park (see chapter 4).

LAKE LOUISE SIGHTSEEING GONDOLA AND MOUNT TEMPLE

Up the opposite (or east) side of the valley from the village is the **Lake Louise Sightseeing Gondola** (✆ **403/522-3555;** C$24/US$22 for youth, adults, and seniors, C$12/US$11 for children ages 6–12, free for children age 5 and under). Choose between an open chair or the new enclosed gondola to take you up to the summit of **Whitehorn Mountain** at 2,088m (6,850 ft.). There are excellent views of the Bow Valley, Lake Louise, and the Continental Divide, and there are many hiking trails to explore. There's a good restaurant in the Lodge of the Ten Peaks, a stunning log cabin at the base of the mountain that's open for breakfast, lunch, and dinner.

Tips Banff on a Rainy Day

It's not that uncommon to see rain (or sometimes even snow!) fall in Banff in the middle of the summer. Here are a few ideas to help you while away a rainy day in Banff:

- Go to a movie at the **Lux Theatre,** which has daily matinees (Wolf and Bear Sts.; ✆ **403/762-8595**).
- Head over to the **Douglas Fir Resort** to play on the waterslide (Tunnel Mountain Dr.; ✆ **403/762-5591**).
- Visit the outstanding **Whyte Museum of the Canadian Rockies** (111 Bear St.; ✆ **403/762-2291**).
- Get a massage at **Willow Stream,** the award-winning spa at the **Fairmont Banff Springs Hotel.** If you're not quite into the luxury but still want to check out the Springs from the inside, C$20 (US$19) will get you into the fitness center—and the mineralized Olympic-size swimming pool—for the day.
- Do your laundry in the **Cascade Plaza** (317 Banff Ave.; ✆ **403/762-3444**).
- Read up at the **Banff Public Library** (101 Bear St.; ✆ **403/ 762-2661**).
- Have tea in the lobby of the **Fairmont Chateau Lake Louise** (111 Lake Louise Dr.; ✆ **403/522-3511**).

You can get a meal and lift-ticket package: for breakfast, C$26 (US$24) for youth, adults, and seniors and C$15 (US$14) for children 6 to 12; for lunch, C$30 (US$28) for youth, adults, and seniors and C$17 (US$16) for children 6 to 12; free for children under 6. If you're keen on learning about ecology, naturalists lead guided hikes throughout the mountain slopes. Great interactive learning experiences can be found here. Grizzly bears have been known to hang out here in the summer, so going with a guide is a wise idea.

From the gondola, it's hard to miss the massive **Mount Temple.** At an elevation of 3,543m (11,621 ft.), it dominates the northwest edge of the Valley of the Ten Peaks. Occupying 15 sq. km (9 sq. miles), it is one of the largest mountains in the Rockies and the third-highest mountain in Banff National Park.

ICEFIELDS PARKWAY

The Trans-Canada Highway (Hwy. 1) divides just north of Lake Louise. You can continue west on the Trans-Canada into British Columbia and Yoho National Park (see chapter 9), or head north on the stunning **Icefields Parkway** (Hwy. 93) toward **Jasper National Park.** If you haven't already got one, pick up a detailed map and guide to the Icefields Parkway from the Lake Louise Visitor Centre, in Lake Louise's **Samson Mall** (101 Lake Louise Dr.; ✆ **403/522-3833**).

Continuing north on the Icefields Parkway, the road steadily climbs higher and higher and the views become more and more dramatic as you make your way through three river valleys and pass beneath towering glacier-topped peaks.

The **Crowfoot Glacier** is the first of a long lineup of glaciers you'll see on the drive from Lake Louise to Jasper, on the Icefields Parkway. It's 33km (21 miles) north of the Trans-Canada Highway 1 junction at Lake Louise. There are interpretive signs posted at the roadside viewpoint. It's a good spot to contemplate the shrinking of the world's glaciers and the impacts of climate change.

Just a kilometer (½ mile) north of the Crowfoot Glacier is cool, crisp, and ice-blue **Bow Lake.** This is the third-largest lake in Banff National Park. Almost all of its water is glacier-fed. It's a nice place for a picnic. The red-roofed inn on the lake's northeast shore is Num-Ti-Jah Lodge, reviewed in chapter 5.

Continuing north on the Icefields Parkway, you'll reach the top of **Bow Pass,** also known as Bow Summit, at an elevation of 2,069m (6,786 ft.). You're at the highest point crossed by a highway that is open year-round in Canada. There is a short interpretive trail to beautifully turquoise **Peyto Lake,** named for pioneer guide Bill Peyto, who was also a warden in Banff National Park. At this point in the drive you're about 40km (25 miles) north of Lake Louise, the beginning of the Icefields Parkway. Heading north past Peyto Lake, the landscape gets bleaker and bleaker (bleaker in the beautiful sense!). You'll notice large mountains on both sides, including **Mount Chephren,** rising on the western shore of Waterfowl Lake; **Mount Wilson,** rising above the North Saskatchewan Valley; and the giant **Mount Murchison,** on the east side of the Parkway just south of where it crosses over the Saskatchewan River.

At **Saskatchewan Crossing,** on the banks of the Saskatchewan River, there is a warden station, gas station, snack bar, and gift shop at a roadside complex called "The Crossing." (This is about 77km/ 48 miles north of the Trans-Canada Hwy. 1 junction with the start of the Icefields Pkwy. 93.) It's a good place to get out and stretch your legs.

The vegetation here reflects the montane life zone—it's less barren than at Peyto Lake. Here, the North Saskatchewan River begins its journey eastward toward the foothills and plains of central Canada. Many large animals travel through the North Saskatchewan Valley into the mountains. Look for grizzly bears, coyotes, and wolves.

Just past the Saskatchewan Crossing complex, the Icefields Parkway meets up with **Highway 11,** the **David Thompson Highway,** which follows the North Saskatchewan River farther into the province of Alberta. At this point in the drive, you're 105km (65 miles) from the Trans-Canada Highway junction with the Icefields Parkway at Lake Louise.

The terrain soon begins to rise again out of the montane forest, as it follows the North Saskatchewan River to its source in the Columbia Icefield. Along the way you'll pass the **Weeping Wall,** on the east side of the highway. In summer you may see only a few drops of water wetting the ridge, but in the winter these drips and drops freeze to create a huge frozen waterfall draped in layer upon layer of ice. This is a hot spot for the technical sport of ice climbing.

The road rises steadily north from the Weeping Wall to **Parker Ridge** ⟨ϰ⟩, which provides excellent views of the **Saskatchewan Glacier** and the southeast reaches of the Columbia Icefield. This is prime hiking terrain, and the Jasper National Park border is just around the corner. See chapter 4 for information on some of the hiking trails in this part of Banff, and chapter 6 for information on visiting the Columbia Icefield.

At 2,023m (6,635 ft.), **Sunwapta Pass** is the second-highest point on the Icefields Parkway and forms the border between Banff and Jasper national parks. It's all downhill from here—108km (67 miles) north on the Icefields Parkway 93 to Jasper Townsite. This is the border between the two parks, and between the two watersheds: The North Saskatchewan River drains from here to Lake Winnipeg, Hudson Bay, and the Atlantic Ocean, while on the other side of the pass the Sunwapta River eventually makes its way to the Arctic Ocean.

7 Organized Tours

Each of these tours will help you get your bearings in the Banff area, taking you to the most popular, though often the most crowded, destinations. The good thing about this is that it lets you check some things off your list so you can spend the rest of your visit exploring on your own. Taking an organized tour is a great way to get acquainted with the park, ideal for the first day of your trip. If you're even just a little bit interested in natural history, you'll also benefit from exploring Banff with a certified local guide. Tours can be arranged through the front desk of most hotels.

The best-organized tour in the Banff area is conducted by **Discover Banff Tours** (215 Banff Ave., lower level of the Sundance Mall, P.O. Box 1566, Banff, AB T1L 1B5; ℂ **877/565-9372** or 403/760-5007; www.banfftours.com). Their **Discover Banff town and area tour** ℛℛ (3 hr., C$49/US$46 for adults, C$30/US$28 for children 6–12, free for children under 6) is very comprehensive and I highly recommend it. In 3 hours, it takes you to all the important historical sites, including the Cave and Basin National Historic Site, the Fairmont Banff Springs Hotel, and the old mine ruins at Bankhead, and introduces you to the natural world of the park at the Hoodoos, the Vermillion Lakes, and Bow Falls. All tours are in small groups led by enthusiastic and knowledgeable guides. Discover Banff Tours also offers trips to **Lake Louise and Moraine Lake** (4 hr., C$59/US$55 for adults, C$35/US$33 for children 6–12, free for children under 6) and a wonderful **Morning Wildlife Safaritour** ℛ (3 hr., C$49/US$46 for adults, C$30/US$28 for children 8–12, free for children under 6), which offers many chances to see wildlife. Their 24-passenger vans are equipped with binoculars, snacks, and drinks, and they make frequent stops for great photo opportunities or to take a closer look at something that's particularly wonderful on the day you're out. They also offer guided hikes (full-day, C$69/US$65) to different destinations each day of the week.

White Mountain Adventures (122A Eagle Cres., P.O. Box 4259, Banff, AB T1L 1E6; © **800/408-0005** or 403/760-4403; www.whitemountainadventures.com) holds guided nature walks in Sunshine Meadows, at Johnson Lake, and at the vanished town of Bankhead. Rates start at C$25 (US$23) per person, a very good deal. **Brewster's** sightseeing tours (100 Gopher St., P.O. Box 1140, Banff, AB T1L 1J3; © **877/791-5500** or 403/762-6700; www. brewster.ca) are driver-led in large tour buses and include **Lake Louise** (4 hr., C$55/US$51 for adults, C$27/US$25 for children), **Mountain Lakes and Waterfalls** (9 hr., C$100/US$93 for adults, C$50/US$47 for children 6–12, free for children under 6), and the **Columbia Icefield** (9 hr., C$134/US$125 for adults, C$67/US$63 for children 6–12, free for children under 6), including the Sno-coach outing, which takes you onto the Columbia Icefield via a massive snowmobile-like vehicle (see chapter 6).

Parks Canada offers tours of the Cave and Basin National Historic Site daily at 11am (© **403/762-1566**). The tour is free with admission to the site. Banff National Park employees lead a very interesting nature tour of the Vermillion Lakes daily at 10am. It's free, but you must pre-register for this tour at the **Banff Information Centre** (224 Banff Ave.; © **403/762-1550**). Parks Canada also offers nature walks at Lake Louise, including a Lake Louise Lakeshore Stroll, and a walk to the Plain of the Six Glaciers. You must pre-register for these free tours at the **Friends of Banff Gift Shop** in the **Lake Louise Visitor Centre** in Samson Mall (101 Lake Louise Dr.; © **403/522-3833**).

4

Hikes & Other Outdoor Pursuits in Banff National Park

Welcome to the great outdoors! Taking time to explore the mountain wilderness of Banff National Park is what draws most visitors to this park in the first place. In a world of increasing urbanization, more and more people are turning to nature to reconnect with themselves and those around them. Not only is outdoor recreation inspirational, it's good for you! And if you're conscientious about it, it can be just fine for nature as well. If you hike some of these trails, you'll likely come away with a deeper understanding of why this park is so special, and why we should continue to preserve it.

The hiking season in Banff usually gets started in early June and winds down in October. Trails on the southern slopes and at lower elevations are free of snow earlier in the season and see earlier openings. In spring, trails are often extremely wet and muddy. Widening the trail around mud in an attempt to avoid it is, however, bad for the trail, as it extends it unnecessarily. In autumn many days are sunny and warm, but the variability of the weather poses a new challenge, since snow may begin to accumulate over high passes.

1 Day Hikes

There are many unique and diverse hiking trails in Banff National Park. I've selected a group that includes the best of the best and gives you a wide variety of options for daylong outings in the park's spectacular settings. (Note that Banff National Park trail crews do regular maintenance on trails, bridges, and signs.)

BANFF TOWNSITE AREA

C-Level Cirque Past artifacts of the old **Bankhead settlement** to a panoramic view of Lake Minnewanka, and into a pocket surrounded by the high ridges of Cascade Mountain with views of Mount Rundle and the Three Sisters, this trail is a great afternoon getaway from busy Banff Avenue. The trail takes you past the ruins

Tips Hiking To-Do List

- **Select a trail:** Read through the hikes reviewed in this chapter, pick up maps and other hiking-specific trail guides, and chat with the staff at the **Banff Information Centre** (224 Banff Ave.; ✆ **403/762-1550**; www.parks canada.gc.ca/banff) or the **Lake Louise Visitor Centre** (Samson Mall, 101 Lake Louise Dr., just off the Trans-Canada Hwy.; ✆ **403/522-3833**).

- **Get a map:** The best maps are topographic ones, with a scale of 1:50,000. They'll help you find your way along the trail, as well as assist you in identifying surrounding landmarks. Maps produced by the Canadian government's National Topographic System provide a high level of detail. Gem Trek Maps, by **Gem Trek Publishing Ltd.**, produces some excellent maps of the more popular areas of Banff National Park (orders should be placed through Map Town in Calgary; ✆ **877/921-6277** or 403/266-2241; www.gemtrek.com). The maps are very accurate, colorful, and full of useful information. They're printed on waterproof, tear-resistant paper, and have three-dimensional contours. You can purchase these and other topographic maps at the **Banff Information Centre.**

- **Check the weather:** Get the up-to-date weather forecast by calling **Environment Canada** in Banff, at ✆ **403/762-2088.**

- **Check trail conditions:** Call the park office at ✆ **403/760-1305** or check the most recent trail reports posted at the **Banff Information Centre.** You can also check trail reports online, at www.parkscanada.ca/banff.

- **Bring drinking water:** To keep yourself hydrated throughout your hike, bring along at least 1 liter (2 pints) of water, 2 liters (4 pints) or more if you're going on a full-day hike.

- **Go in a group:** In general, it's safer (and usually more fun!) to hike in a group. Some areas under bear warnings require you stay with at least four people at a time for safety reasons.

- **Tell someone about it:** Let someone know where you're going and when you plan to be back.

Banff National Park Trail Heads

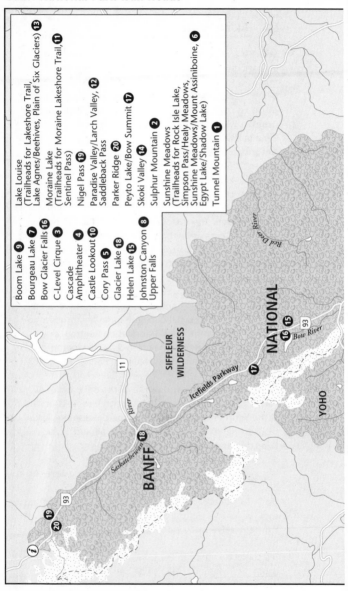

Lake Louise
(Trailheads for Lakeshore Trail,
Lake Agnes/Beehives, Plain of Six Glaciers) **13**

Moraine Lake
(Trailheads for Moraine Lakeshore Trail,
Sentinel Pass) **11**

Nigel Pass **19**

Paradise Valley/Larch Valley, **12**
Saddleback Pass

Parker Ridge **20**

Peyto Lake/Bow Summit **17**

Skoki Valley **14**

Sulphur Mountain **2**

Sunshine Meadows
(Trailheads for Rock Isle Lake,
Simpson Pass/Healy Meadows,
Sunshine Meadows/Mount Assiniboine, **6**
Egypt Lake/Shadow Lake)

Tunnel Mountain **1**

Boom Lake **9**

Bourgeau Lake **7**

Bow Glacier Falls **16**

C-Level Cirque **3**

Cascade
Amphitheater **4**

Castle Lookout **10**

Cory Pass **5**

Glacier Lake **18**

Helen Lake **15**

Johnston Canyon **8**
Upper Falls

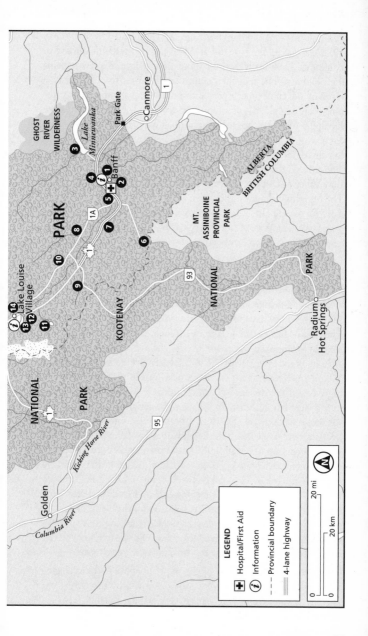

of an old mine at the Bankhead site, which operated from 1903 to 1922. At one point, as many as 2,000 people lived and worked in Bankhead. Look for fenced-off ventilation shafts and a few remaining buildings. The trail then climbs steadily west through a mixed forest of lodgepole pine, aspen, and spruce. After alighting on a stunning view of Lake Minnewanka, the trail heads back into the now subalpine forest before ending in a small cirque (like a bowl with a circular ridge surrounding it) at the highest part of the valley. Look for calypso orchids, marmots, and pika as you climb from the montane zone to the treeless alpine zone. At the top, enjoy views of the Bow Valley as far away as Canmore and the Three Sisters Mountain. The beginning elevation is 1,465m (4,805 ft.) and the elevation gain is 455m (1,490 ft.). 3.9km (2.4 miles) one-way. Moderate. Access: From the Minnewanka interchange on the Trans-Canada Hwy. 1, it's 3.5km (2¼ miles) on Minnewanka Rd. to the Upper Bankhead picnic area, on the left.

Cascade Amphitheater 🎯 *Finds*   You can't miss Cascade Mountain—the beautiful pyramid-shaped peak at the northeastern end of Banff Avenue. One of the most rewarding day hikes in the townsite area, this is a demanding outing that starts (and later finishes) at the Mount Norquay day lodge, and takes you into a high alpine cirque. The trail begins on the Cat track through the Mount Norquay ski area, following it as far as the Mystic chairlift. It then follows the edge of Forty Mile Creek and switchbacks up the side of Cascade Mountain. Keep right at all trail junctions. On your left are amazing views of the east face of Mount Louis. The trail then levels out into a large amphitheater in a hanging valley with a lush carpet of subalpine wildflowers. The amphitheater was created and enlarged by glacial erosion during the several ice ages of the past 2 million years. Farther up, the trail heads out of the flowers onto slopes this time covered with boulders from rockslides. Listen for the whistle of marmots and pikas. The trail ends at a dramatic point on the south edge of the meadows, on a small knoll of rockslide debris. The beginning elevation is 1,555m (5,100 ft.) and the elevation gain is 640m (2,100 ft.). 7.7km (4.8 miles) one-way. Strenuous. Access: Mt. Norquay ski area. Park in the lot on the left and walk through the main parking lot past the ski lodge and continue past the last chairlift, where there is a trail marker.

Cory Pass 🎯   This is one of the most strenuous and challenging hikes in Banff National Park. It's also by far the most spectacular one near the Town of Banff. The highlight for me is the 2,300m (7,544-ft.) monolithic limestone cliffs of the Sawback Range. The trail starts in a montane valley bottom and ends in a high alpine zone well above the tree line—which promises tremendous ecological diversity. Watch for bighorn sheep, deer, and elk. On the ascent, you'll pass through a pleasant aspen grove, traverse the steep side slopes of Mount Louis, and get a short break on a grassy knoll overlooking the Bow Valley. The trail then takes you up and along a forested ridge, and then down into a small and steep break in the rock. (Be careful on this part of the hike; use your hands as well as your feet.) The trail then heads back up through the trees and emerges on a long, open slope just shy of Cory Pass. Sandwiched between the tall cliffs of Mount Edith to the east and Mount Cory to the west, this pass can be a cold and windy place. From the top of the pass, take your shaking knees back down the way you came or enjoy the dramatic loop back that takes you by Edith Pass. This very challenging route will give you an idea of what it feels like to be a mountaineer. Be sure to take a good map with you on this trail. From a starting elevation of 1,435m (4,707 ft.) you gain an astonishing 915m (3,001 ft.). 5.8km (3.6 miles) one-way. Very strenuous. Access: Fireside Picnic Area at the eastern end of the Bow Valley Pkwy. 1A. Follow the access road from the parkway to the picnic area.

Sulphur Mountain   If you're generally opposed to getting to a spectacular mountain summit via a leisurely gondola ride (the Banff Gondola, in this case), hike up and enjoy a nice meal in the restaurant and then catch the gondola ride down—it's free for hikers. With 28 switchbacks, the climb up Sulphur Mountain rates moderate, but you're still climbing 655m (2,148 ft.). It's a wide trail through a shady forest. Views open up a bit when you pass a small waterfall on Sulphur's east slope. There's a small shelter along the way that marks the halfway point. From here the trail becomes steeper and starts to switchback beneath the gondola line. You know you're almost at the ridge when you see alpine larch trees and the gondola terminal. Visit the snack bar for a much-needed drink and enjoy the rewarding views! From the gondola terminal, don't miss the short walk along a boardwalk to the stone weather observatory, built in 1903, atop Sanson Peak. From a beginning elevation of 1,581m (5,186 ft.) you gain 655m (2,148 ft.). 5.5km (3.4 miles) one-way. Moderate. Access: Upper Hot Springs parking lot. Trail head is at the corner of the lot closest to the pool.

Tunnel Mountain   This is perhaps the most accessible mountain summit in Canada. Heading out just off Banff Avenue, this short, easy trail offers fantastic views of the townsite and its surroundings. One of the oldest trails in the park, this route is a daily trip for many fit locals and a great chance to reach a moderate summit. It heads

How Far (& Fast) Can I Really Go?

Hiking times depend on a hiker's experience, pace, and ability, as well as elevation gains and what the weather is up to that day. Generally, day hikers carrying only a light pack can walk from 2.5 to 3.5kmph (1.6–2.2 mph).

Hikers with some experience, carrying a loaded backpack, can cover 2.5kmph (1.6 mph), allowing for some short stops. Beginners may walk more like 1.5km (.9 mile) in an hour.

Don't judge the difficulty of a trail based on the distance alone. Some hikes are steeper than others and will take more time and require more rest stops. Noting the elevation gain will help you judge how much climbing you'll be doing.

up the western side of Tunnel Mountain from a parking lot above The Banff Centre, through a lodgepole pine forest, switchbacking to some lovely viewpoints of the town and the Vermillion Lakes. The trail passes through a Douglas fir forest before topping out on a ridge just below the summit. Enjoy views of the Spray River Valley, the tabletop ridge of Mount Rundle, and the baronial Fairmont Banff Springs Hotel. The summit itself is partially treed, so there's no chance of any panoramic views. Walk a way on either side of the summit for better views. To the west, the Town of Banff spreads out beneath you. On the eastern side, the elk on the golf course enjoy the shade of Rundle. The initial elevation is 1,416m (4,644 ft.) and the elevation gain is 260m (853 ft.). 2.3km (1.4 miles) one-way. Easy to moderate. Access: Follow Wolf St. east to St. Julien Rd. Follow St. Julien Rd. uphill to the parking lot on the left, 300m (98 ft.) from the Wolf St. junction.

BOW VALLEY PARKWAY/CASTLE JUNCTION AREA

Boom Lake 𝄐 *Kids*   A relatively gentle climb to a glacial lake surrounded by massive limestone walls, this is an undemanding hike that is a family favorite. The trail heads through an ancient subalpine forest. Give yourself extra time to linger and admire the 2.7km-long (1¾-mile) **Boom Lake,** one of the larger lakes in Banff National Park. The waters are substantially clearer than are many others so close to glaciers; scientists have discovered a marked decrease in silt in the water, evidence that the glaciers are in retreat.

Come in late spring or early summer to watch the snowpack crash into the lake and avalanches careen down nearby slopes. You may see the common loon on Boom Lake, which is also home to cutthroat trout. The tall peaks surrounding the lake include Chimney Peak, Mount Bident, and Quadra Mountain. You start out from an elevation of 1,707m (5,599 ft.) and gain 175m (574 ft.). 5.1km (3.2 miles) one-way. Easy. Access: Trail head is off Hwy. 93 S, 7km (4⅓ miles) west of Castle Junction. Parking lot is on the north side of the road.

Bourgeau Lake ⍟   It's true that the hike in is along sheltered Wolverine Creek and through a thick forest, offering no great views during the bulk of the moderately steep ascent. But the view of Bourgeau Lake at the end, tucked into an amphitheater of limestone walls and surrounded by a colorful subalpine meadow, is worth being a bit deprived on the way up. Watch for other views of the Sawback Range across the Bow Valley. As you near the top, the trail crosses the creek just below a waterfall, then starts some tough switchbacks through a series of avalanche runs to a grassy meadow. To the northwest is Mount Brett; to the southwest, Mount Bourgeau. Carved by glacial ice, this valley is typical of the Canadian Rockies: The glacier that left the lake behind in its wake is long gone. Just past the meadow, the trail climbs to the shores of icy, boulder-strewn Bourgeau Lake. Listen for marmots and pikas. The beginning elevation is 1,400m (4,595 ft.) and the elevation gain is 725m (2,380 ft.). 7.4km (4.6 miles) one-way. Moderate. Access: 13km (8 miles) west of Banff Townsite on the Trans-Canada Hwy. 1; parking lot is on the south side of the 4-lane highway, marked by a large sign.

Castle Lookout   Castle Mountain is such a beautiful ridge, no one visiting the Canadian Rockies can miss it or forget its chiseled terraces, sturdy towers, or flat top. This hike gets you close to this scenic mountain. Starting out on an old fire road, the trail takes you above the tree line up the west face of the mountain, heading across rocky, exposed slopes and flower-filled meadows to the site of a former fire lookout on Eisenhower Peak, Castle Mountain's western peak. Short but steep, the trail offers an amazing panorama of the glacier-chiseled Bow Valley and Storm Mountain, which is often surrounded by its own gnarly weather system. This trail can be very warm on a sunny day and is a great shoulder-season choice. The beginning elevation is 1,464m (4,802 ft.) and the elevation gain is 520m (1,706 ft.). 3.7km (2.3 miles) one-way. Strenuous. Access: Parking lot on the north side of the Bow Valley Pkwy. 1A, 5km (3 miles) west of Castle Junction.

Johnston Canyon Upper Falls ✦ *Kids*   Although it's one of the busiest in Banff, this trail is pleasant and cool, and the canyon is deep and easy to admire. Many hundreds of people visit the Lower Falls; very few hike above to see no fewer than seven gorgeous waterfalls—take a fun side trip through a wet tunnel and get a close-up look at the Upper Falls, twice the size of the lower ones. This trail begins on a wide, paved, shaded path. The canyon on the east side is an eyeful. Continue along a suspended walkway bolted to the side of the cliff partway up the canyon wall. Pass under an overhanging cliff of solid limestone to the Lower Falls, swirling in a green pool beside a copper-colored wall. Head across the bridge, go through a tiny, dark rock passage and continue past small Twin Falls, then come back to the main trail and head up to the Upper Falls. There are two viewpoints: Reach the bottom of the falls by a boardwalk and the top of the falls by hiking up a short, steep trail to a platform hanging out over the gorge, above the falls. Keep to the right for the best views. Head out in the early morning or late afternoon to avoid the crowds. The beginning elevation is 1,430m (4,690 ft.) and the elevation gain is 120m (394 ft.). 2.7km (1.7 miles) one-way. Easy. Access: Trans-Canada Hwy. 1 west to the Bow Valley Pkwy. 1A. 18km (11 miles) west to the Johnston Canyon parking lot.

SUNSHINE MEADOWS AREA ✦✦

Famous for its beautiful alpine meadows brilliant with wildflowers, Sunshine Meadows is a large (15km/9.3-mile) section of the Continental Divide that is unusually lush and rolling, with incredibly high viewpoints. Moist, warm weather systems from the Pacific Ocean often get trapped here, and the result is heavy precipitation, gorgeous rock gardens, and such an abundance of wildflowers that you could spend an entire day counting the many species (some of which are found only here). The elevation averages 2,225m (7,298 ft.). Most of the trails are rolling, so they're never too steep.

GETTING THERE   Sunshine Meadows is located high in an alpine bowl that is also the site of the **Sunshine Village ski resort.** To get there, you can either hike up a somewhat drab fire road for a few hours, or (a much better idea) take a shuttle to the Sunshine Village day lodge. This leaves you more time to explore the high alpine meadows. **White Mountain Adventures** (© **800/408-0005** or 403/678-4099; www. whitemountainadventures.com) runs a shuttle service to the area.

Rock Isle Lake   This hike leads you to the other side of the Continental Divide, into British Columbia's Mount Assiniboine Provincial Park. Rock Lake is particularly lovely in the calm early morning, when it mirrors the surrounding scenery, and the view stretches off into British Columbia's mountains. A favorite of artists and photographers. The beginning elevation is 2,200m (7,216 ft.) and the elevation gain is 105m (344 ft.). 2.5km (1.6 miles) one-way. Easy. Access: From Sunshine Village, southeast on a gravel road to the trail head.

Simpson Pass/Healy Meadows This route is not too steep, and is worth an afternoon outing for rewarding views of Wawa Ridge, Mount Assiniboine, and the Monarch, a massive pyramid-shaped peak. It's a wildflower-lover's dream, a favorite of Banff's old outfitters and pioneers, including Jim Brewster and "Wild Bill" Peyto, two of Banff's original mountain guides. The beginning elevation is 2,200m (7,216 ft.) and the elevation gain is 160m (525 ft.). 7.6km (4.7 miles) one-way. Moderate. Access: From Sunshine Village, down the hill from the day lodge at the base of the Wawa Ridge ski lift on the left (west) side.

LAKE LOUISE/MORAINE LAKE AREA

Lake Agnes/Beehives ⊛ Nestled in a picturesque hanging valley above Lake Louise, Lake Agnes has been a favorite of visitors to the lake for more than a century. The first half-hour of the hike takes you up a steep climb to **Mirror Lake,** surrounded by Engelmann spruce trees and subalpine firs. Take the trail to the north to get to Lake Agnes, and be thankful for the stairway that takes you up along rockslides below the Big Beehive. There are great views of the Bow Valley and wonderful history to be had at the **Lake Agnes Teahouse** ⊛ on the shore of the lake, which serves freshly baked scones and tea throughout the summer. From the teahouse, take the trail to the north shore of the lake to connect with the **Big Beehive,** one of the best viewpoints in Banff National Park. Perched nearly a kilometer above the shimmering, turquoise waters of Lake Louise, there are spectacular views of mounts Temple, Fairview, and Lefroy, as well as the slopes of the Lake Louise ski area, across the valley. All trails to the top are steep; stick to the north-facing ridge for the most gradual climb. You start out at an elevation of 1,735m (5,691 ft.) and gain 400m (1,312 ft.). 5.1km (3.2 miles) one-way. Moderate. Access: Lake Louise shoreline trail, in front of the Fairmont Chateau Lake Louise.

Lakeshore Trail *Kids* A broad, flat trail that lets you take in all the views of the peaks surrounding Lake Louise, this may be the most well-trodden trail in Banff National Park. This gentle stroll will take you away from the crowds gathered on the lawns of the Fairmont Chateau Lake Louise. The trail leads around the north shore of the lake to the base of **Mount Victoria** and the shimmering **Victoria Glacier.** To the

---

Tips **Lock Your Car**

When you leave the parking lot for a hike in the backcountry, should you carry all your valuables with you? Unfortunately, thefts are increasingly common in trail head parking lots. Therefore, take whatever you can with you on your hike; namely, your wallet, money, and keys, preferably in a water-proof zip-lock bag that you keep in the top of your backpack or in your jacket pocket. If you have to leave valuables in your vehicle, lock them in the trunk.

---

immediate east is Fairview Mountain; to the north, the Beehives. The formal gardens of the Chateau blend in nicely with the daisies, asters, and other wildflowers lining the path. Kids will enjoy the different varieties. The turquoise color of the lake, caused by suspended rock flour from the Victoria Glacier, appears to change every time you look at it. The path begins to thin out as you reach the northwestern shore of the finger-shaped lake. Spend time watching rock climbers tackle quartzite cliffs, where glacial streams crisscross their way into the silt-filled waters of the lake. There are many benches along the trail where you can sit and marvel at Lake Louise's color and beauty. Come early in the morning to beat the crowds. The light is also more photo-friendly at this time of day. There is no elevation gain. 1.9km (1.2 miles) one-way. Easy. Access: Fairmont Chateau Lake Louise.

Moraine Lakeshore Trail   Moraine Lake is a popular destination, but luckily this trail, along the western shore of the lake, is still peaceful and pleasant, giving you a chance to soak up the serenity of the area. Surrounded by the imposing **Valley of the Ten Peaks** ⍟, Moraine Lake is dramatic indeed. The trail passes through a mellow forest and is often lined with pretty wildflowers. The lake's color appears to change with each new view—from turquoise, to teal blue, to emerald green. The trail passes through a thick forest before ending at Wenkchemna Creek, draining the Wenkchemna glacier above. The best views are at the start of the trail, but for a spectacular view of Moraine Lake at the end of the hike head 5 minutes up to the **Moraine Lake Viewpoint,** at the south end of the parking lot, following the sign to Consolation Lakes. There is no elevation gain. 1.2km (.7 mile) one-way. Easy. Access: Moraine Lake parking lot.

Paradise Valley/Larch Valley ⍟   A rewarding and challenging full-day hike, this trail starts out in a lovely forest and crosses Paradise

Creek numerous times. Starting in Paradise Valley, you'll hike below mounts Temple and Lefroy. It's a tough but rewarding climb up to the top of **Sentinel Pass.** This trail takes in Lake Annette, Horseshoe Meadows, and the waterfall series known as both the "Giant Steps" and the "Giant's Staircase"—all of them highlights. You then hike down into the Larch Valley, scattered with both lush alpine forests and wide-open meadows. One of only a few areas in the park where larches predominate, it is particularly lovely in the fall, when the larches turn a magnificent gold. Mount Fay is the large peak that towers above the **Valley of the Ten Peaks** 𝕲 below. Listen for pikas and marmots on the high passes. Since the trail ends at a different parking lot from where it begins (it finishes up at the Moraine Lake parking lot), you'll need to organize a shuttle back to your car or ask one of the other cars heading down the road for a lift. If you've got two vehicles, drive ahead and leave one at the Moraine Lake parking lot, then come back to the trail head at the Paradise Valley lot and leave the other vehicle there. Because of bear activity in the area during some summers, Parks Canada may ask you to hike this trail in a group of six or more. The beginning elevation is 1,720m (5,642 ft.) and the elevation gain is 880m (2,886 ft.). 17km (10.5 miles) one-way. Strenuous. Access: Follow Moraine Lake Rd. for 2.5km (1½ miles) south and park in the Paradise Valley lot, on the right side of the road.

Plain of the Six Glaciers 𝕲   This trail takes you through post-card-worthy scenery as it makes its way around Lake Louise and below mounts Victoria and Lefroy. The trail follows the Lake Louise Lakeshore trail (reviewed above) to the western end of the lake and then climbs through forests of spruce, pine, and larch. It empties into a harsh glacier- and avalanche-scoured terrain before climbing into a lush meadow, above. Here you might like to stop at the **Plain of the Six Glaciers Teahouse,** a charming establishment built in the 1920s by the Canadian Pacific Railway. Take a break and enjoy one of their tea scones baked in a wood-burning oven—a summer favorite. The food is packed in and out by horse and all the cooking is done just as it was when the teahouse was first built. It's a real window onto mountain life as it was.

You can continue another kilometer (.6 mile) to the top of the trail, at the summit of a small moraine. The views here will astound you: From left to right (southeast to southwest) the glaciers are Aberdeen, Upper Lefroy, Lower Lefroy, Upper Victoria, Lower Victoria, and Pope's. On a clear day, you can make out **Abbot Hut,** located on a pass between mounts Victoria and Lefroy. It was named after Phillip Abbot, who died attempting to climb Mount Lefroy in 1896. You start at an elevation of 1,735m (5,691 ft.) and gain 365m (1,197 ft.). 5.3km (3.3 miles) one-way. Moderate. Access: Follow Lake Louise Shoreline trail in front of Fairmont Chateau Lake Louise hotel.

Saddleback Pass   The shining star of this hike is the colossal 3,543m (11,620-ft.) **Mount Temple.** The trail takes you to a stupendous view of Temple from a pass between Saddle and Fairview mountains. Heading out along the lower slopes of Mount Fairview, the trail soon starts switchbacking steeply through an Engelmann spruce forest, until it reaches flower-filled **Saddleback Meadow.** Stick to the northeast side of the larch-abundant meadow to avoid snow patches below the pass. Though Mount Temple appears to be attached to Saddle Mountain, its base is in fact quite a way away, in Paradise Valley. This trail does hook up with the **Paradise Valley/Larch Valley trail** at a junction less than half a kilometer (.3 mile) into the hike. The beginning elevation is 1,735m (5,691 ft.) and the elevation gain is a healthy 595m (1,952 ft.). 3.7km (2.3 miles) one-way to pass. Moderate to strenuous. Access: Viewpoint near the boathouse on the south shore of Lake Louise.

Sentinel Pass ⊛   Sentinel Pass is a must for fit hikers looking for a challenge. The trail makes its way through the high meadows above Moraine Lake for views of the **Valley of the Ten Peaks** ⊛. Take the trail switchbacking from the back of the meadow up a steep slope between Pinnacle Mountain and Mount Temple. At 2,611m (8,564 ft.), this rugged, primal pass is the highest point reached by a major trail in the Canadian Rocky Mountain National Parks. From the pass, most people choose to return along the same trail, although you can continue on into **Paradise Valley.** If you decide to take the alternative route into Paradise Valley, you need to arrange a shuttle back to your car at the Moraine Lake trail head. Call for a trail report before you head out (© **403/762-1305**) to make sure there is no snow on the pass. The beginning elevation is 1,887m (6,189 ft.) and the elevation gain is 725m (2,378 ft.). 5.8km (3.4 miles) one-way. Challenging. Access: Moraine Lake Lodge parking lot.

ICEFIELDS PARKWAY AREA

Bow Glacier Falls   Although Bow Glacier has retreated, it left behind a majestic 120m (394-ft.) waterfall that simply hints at the massive icefield above it. The trail is broad and scenic alongside the flats skirting **Bow Lake,** a Rocky Mountain gem. At the western shore of the lake there are views of the stunning Crowfoot and Bow glaciers, nestled into the ridges of the Waputik Range, which strad-dles the Continental Divide. Only 100 years ago, the Bow Glacier extended to cover the entire Bow Valley. There is a deep canyon in the hillside, by the gravel flats at the western end of the lake, cut by a glacier-draining creek. Peer over the canyon edge to see the stream raging through narrow cracks and under a natural bridge created when a huge rock fell across the gorge. The trail takes a short but steep climb up to a vast moraine covered in gravel and glacial debris. It ends here, although you can follow a series of rock cairns leading up to the Bow Glacier Falls themselves. The beginning elevation is 1,960m (6,429 ft.) and the elevation gain is a mere 95m (310 ft.). 4.7km (2.9 miles) one-way. Easy. Access: Take Icefields Pkwy. 93 to Num-Ti-Jah Lodge (36km/23 miles north of the Lake Louise junction). Trail head parking lot is on the left side of the lodge road opposite the washrooms.

Helen Lake   With tall peaks, alpine meadows, lakes, and wide views, this trail is diverse enough to draw you enthusiastically around every corner to see something new. This is a relatively quick and pain-free way to access the high alpine environment. It reaches the tree line 3km (1.9 miles) in, after passing through a dense forest of spruce and fir. The trail then reaches a ridge, makes a big turn northward, and then descends into a cirque, where Helen Lake lies peacefully. The lakeside meadows draw friendly hoary marmots. Check out the view of the Crowfoot Glacier. Not a good option on a rainy or windy day because the trail runs along a high ridge and is very exposed to the elements. The beginning elevation is 1,950m (6,396 ft.) and the elevation gain is 455m (1,492 ft.). 6km (3.7 miles) one-way. Moderate. Access: Take Icefields Pkwy. 93 to the Crowfoot Glacier View-point (33km/21 miles north of the Lake Louise junction). Trail head is across the highway from the viewpoint.

Nigel Pass ⊛   On this rewarding hike that tops out on a rocky 2,195m (7,200-ft.) ridge that marks the boundary between Banff and Jasper national parks, you'll have views of the **Columbia Icefield** to the west and the remote corners of the **Brazeau Valley** to the east. The trail follows open avalanche paths up the east side of the Brazeau Valley and continues steeply past **Camp Parker,** an old campsite used by native trappers and later by early mountaineers. The climb continues at a moderate rate through a sparse forest and then becomes quite steep for the last kilometer (.6 mile) or so, up to the pass. The views are even more outstanding to the east of the pass, where you can scramble over rocks to catch sight of the Brazeau River and the waterfall along the rocky north wall of Nigel Pass. To the southwest are **Parker Ridge** ⟡⟡ and **Mount Athabasca.** The beginning elevation is 1,860m (6,101 ft.) and the elevation gain is 365m (1,197 ft.). 7.2km (4.5 miles) one-way. Moderate. Access: Take Icefields Pkwy. 93 to the trail head, 2.5km (1½ miles) north of the "Big Bend" switchback (114km/70 miles north of the Lake Louise junction) or 8.5km (5½ miles) south of the Banff–Jasper boundary. Parking lot is on northeast side of the highway.

Parker Ridge ⟡⟡⟡   The best short day hike in the Icefields Parkway area, this high and open route takes you deep into the heart of the unforgiving alpine zone. Heading out just 4km (2.5 miles) south of Sunwapta Pass (the border between Banff and Jasper national parks), the trail quickly rises through an open meadow and a sparse forest of subalpine fir. In summer—which can last only a few weeks up here—the meadows turn a brilliant red with heather. Scattered throughout are white mountain avens and blue alpine forget-me-nots. The trail then leaves the forest behind and enters the harsh alpine zone. It passes a few boulder-strewn slopes covered in the remains from rockslides, then takes one last switchback to the crest of the ridge. Once you reach the summit, enjoy views of the **Saskatchewan Glacier** (the glacier that reaches the farthest out into a valley in the Columbia Icefield) below you, and **Castleguard Mountain** in the distance. This is the northernmost hike in Banff National Park. You begin at an elevation of 2,000m (6,560 ft.) and gain 250m (820 ft.). 2.7km (1.7 miles) one-way. Moderate. Access: Parking lot on the west side of the Icefields Pkwy. 93, 4km (2½ miles) south of the Banff–Jasper park boundary.

Peyto Lake/Bow Summit   Named after early Banff guide Bill Peyto, this lake is a gem. It's also the most popular short hike along the Icefields Parkway. Escape the crowds by continuing on to the Bow Summit lookout; then hike down to the lake for an almost bird's-eye view of the Bow River's source. When you start out, make a note of where the trees are growing and where they aren't—the tree

---

⟨ *Tips* **An Extra Arm**

Don't hesitate to pick up some hiking poles at an outdoor equipment store in Banff or Lake Louise. They will provide you with a fifth limb for stream crossings and very valuable support for both your knees and back. Hey, hiking poles make life easier! Pick a pair up at **Mountain Magic Equipment** (224 Bear St.; ⟨ **403/762-2591**).

(Tips) Crossing Streams

There are three kinds of stream crossings in the Canadian Rockies. The first is known as a **rock-hop,** where just the soles of your boots may get wet. Then there is a **boulder-hop,** where the surface of your boots may get wet. A **ford** is a crossing through deep water, where your boots will be entirely submerged. The keys to successful crossing are balance and route selection. Decide which part of the stream you are going to cross before you get started—preferably a narrow, shallow section. Take your time making your way across (it's not a race), and provide a hand to others in your group once you are safely on the other side.

line appears to be uniform. But as you approach the lake, you'll notice that the line is in fact quite gradual and varied. This trail takes you through what is known as the **transition zone;** what begins as a thick forest soon becomes a stunted one, getting sparser and sparser until you come to an area where there isn't a single tree growing. The trail to the Peyto Lake viewpoint has interpretive signs that will help you identify the different kinds of trees. From the first viewpoint, Peyto Lake is far below you, with **Peyto Glacier,** the **Mistaya Valley,** and the **North Saskatchewan River** visible in the distance. Continue another kilometer (.6 mile) and marvel at the remarkable plants that somehow survive in this harsh landscape—where snow often falls year-round. It can be cold up here, so dress warmly. The beginning elevation is 2,085m (6,839 ft.) and the elevation gain is 230m (754 ft.). 3.1km (1.9 miles) one-way. Easy. Access: Take Icefields Pkwy. 93 to Bow Summit (41km/26 miles north of the Lake Louise junction). Follow the viewpoint access road off the west side of the parkway and turn right at the fork into the Bow Summit parking lot.

2 Exploring the Backcountry

Backpacking is the ultimate Rocky Mountain experience. It's a challenging undertaking—most people just starting to backpack will find the routes in Banff National Park demanding, because of the mountainous terrain. And, oh yes, you must be very well organized.

Start getting organized by reserving your backcountry campsite ahead of time. Contact the **Banff Information Centre** (224 Banff Ave., Banff, AB T1L 1K2; ✆ **403/762-1550;** www.parkscanada. gc.ca/banff) or the **Lake Louise Visitor Centre** (in the Samson

Mall, 101 Lake Louise Dr., Lake Louise, AB T0L 1E0; © **403/
522-3833**). The folks at the information center can also bring you
up to speed on trail conditions, bear warnings, and the weather forecast.

How long should you hike for? The longer you can spend in the
backcountry, the more relaxing and exciting the trip. However, most
visitors to the park don't have weeks to spend. So I suggest a 2- or
3-night trip.

The backpacking trips listed in this section are the best Banff has
to offer. You can do a trip in one of two ways. You can either walk
straight from the trail head to the end, stopping occasionally to
enjoy the view and to pitch a tent at night. This option is for those
who are on a time budget. The other, more leisurely option—which
does require more time but is, I think, well worth it—is to set up
camp at a campsite that you'll use as a base from which to do side
trips. They can range from half- to full-day excursions, and give you
a better opportunity to drink in all that the area offers.

WHEN TO GO   The peak hiking season is from late June to mid-
September. It can be busy during these months, so be sure to reserve
your campsite well ahead of time. July is prime wildflower season
and the days are very long (it stays light until well after 9pm).
August is a very sunny month.

Plan to get out on the trail in the morning, ideally before 9am, to
get a head start. If you aren't able to reach the trail head until after
lunch, alter your plans accordingly and make sure there is a campsite within 10km (6¼ miles) of the trail head that you can reach by
nightfall.

WHAT TO BRING   Having the right equipment is crucial to any
activity in the outdoors.

Backpack   Select a pack made of coated **ripstop nylon,** which will
be both lightweight and waterproof. Make sure the zippers and buck-
les are in good shape. If you are planning on doing day hikes, you'll
need to bring along a smaller backpack. A good size is 30 to 35 liters
(8–9 gal.). For an overnight pack, you'll need something capable of
carrying 60 to 80 liters (16–20 gal.), with an internal or external
frame, an adjustable shoulder strap, compression straps, one or two
easily accessible outer compartments, and comfortable padding,
especially around the hips. Packs should be adjusted to fit your body.
Most of the weight will be carried on your hip belt. Before your trip,
wear the pack around your house or take it to the grocery store to get
used to it and to make sure it's the right one for you.

Clothing   It's hard to have fun if you're too cold, too hot, or too wet. Layering your clothing is the key to staying warm (or cool) and, most importantly, dry. The layering technique allows you to adapt your clothing to the environment. Start with an inner layer (or underwear) that will keep sweat away from your skin and pass it on to a next layer where it will evaporate. Synthetics like polypropylene and polyester are best. Chose synthetic pile or fleece for the mid-layer (and have a vest or pullover as an additional mid-layer). Top it off with a shell garment that will keep wind, rain, and snow at bay. Look for a waterproof/ breathable jacket (the same type of pants are also very handy). Don't forget a sun hat, a winter hat, gloves, and at least one change of clothes.

First-aid kit   This should contain latex gloves (to prevent spreading infections), butterfly bandages, sterile gauze pads, adhesive tape, antibiotic ointment, pain relievers, alcohol pads, a knife, scissors, and tweezers.

Flashlight   Even though dusk comes late in the Rockies, and chances are you'll be ready to hit the sack early, a flashlight is a must. I suggest bringing one that you can wear on your head like a miner's lantern, keeping your hands free. Keep extra flashlight batteries in the first-aid kit.

Insulated sleeping mat   This is the key to a good night's sleep in the backcountry. Inflatable mats are more comfortable (but also more expensive) than foam ones.

Matches   Bring two cigarette lighters (put them in two different places) and waterproof, strike-anywhere matches.

Pots and utensils   Bring two stainless steel cooking pots. One should fit inside the other for more compact carrying. Use one for boiling water and the other for cooking. You'll also need a potholder, pocketknife, wooden spoon, plastic bowl, and insulated travel mugs.

Repair kit   It should contain a needle and thread, a length of duct tape, a length of fiberglass tape, a 3-millimeter (.1-in.) cord, light-gauge wire, adhesive nylon patches, and a spare bootlace.

Sleeping bag   Even in the heart of summer, nights can be quite cool in Banff. Choose a three-season synthetic bag or a down-filled summer bag. Keep your bag in a large plastic bag inside your pack so it stays as dry as possible.

Stove and fuel   Don't leave for the backcountry without a stove. You need one firstly because fires are often not permitted in high-use areas, and secondly because they cook your food quickly and

---

Tips **What Food to Bring to the Backcountry**

Do bring good food that packs well and gives you energy: cheese, chocolate (yes, chocolate!), dried fruit, dried grains and cereals, fresh fruit and vegetables (but be sure you eat them early on in the trip), granola bars, hot and cold instant drink mixes, instant soups and sauces, mixed nuts, pasta, peanut butter, pita bread, tea.

Don't bring bad food that is highly perishable and attracts wildlife: fresh, dried, or canned meat or fish; any food with a powerful scent.

---

efficiently—which is key to keeping you warm and happy on the trail. Both **MSR** and **Coleman** have excellent, lightweight stoves designed especially for backcountry use. They burn **white gas** (also known as naphtha or Coleman fuel), which can be bought in gas stations and outdoor shops in Banff and Lake Louise. You'll need a 623-gram (22-oz.) fuel canister to provide two people with three meals a day for 3 days, but bring along extra fuel if you can.

Tent   Choose a free-standing tent that does not need to be tied to trees. A tent in a light color is also a good idea, since it will keep heat out while letting daylight in, which will keep you smiling on a cloudy or rainy day. Make sure it's the right size for your party (one-, two-, or four-person), lightweight, and easy to assemble. It should have a large fly.

BEFORE YOU GO   Once you have chosen your trail and reserved your backcountry campsite, double-check trail conditions (© **403/ 760-1305**) and the weather forecast (© **403/762-2088**) before heading out.

BACKCOUNTRY TRAILS

Egypt Lake/Shadow Lake ★★   This is the most popular backpacking area in Banff National Park. To make things easier, Egypt Lake and the nearby lakes (including Scarab, Sphinx, Mummy, and Pharaoh) have come to be known as the Egypt Lakes. However, there is in fact only one true lake named Egypt! Also known as "Lakes and Larches," this route incorporates the Egypt Lakes and **Shadow Lake** area into a multiday exploration of Banff's highest-elevation hiking routes. With a series of passes along the Continental Divide, encompassing cliffs, meadows, and tarn, this trail takes you through some quintessential Canadian Rockies landscape.

Although many begin this trail at the northern trail head and head south, I prefer to do the opposite, taking advantage of the shuttle up to Sunshine Meadows that leaves from the base of the Sunshine Village ski area. Taking the shuttle eases some of the overall ascent and leaves more time to explore the high lakes. Start the first day with a trip over **Healy Pass.** Head to Egypt Lake (the real one) and set up camp. On Day 2, plan for a couple of excellent halfday hikes: around Egypt Lake to **Mummy Lake,** and to **Ball Pass** in the afternoon. On Day 3, make your way to the **Shadow Lake Campground,** enjoying the rise over **Whistling Pass,** where, from 2,300m (7,544 ft.), you'll soak up views of the entire eastern slope of the Canadian Rockies. Take a side trip to visit glacier-carved Scarab Lake, and make a return visit to Mummy Lake. Spend a fourth and perhaps fifth day exploring the Shadow Lake area, relaxing and taking tea at the Shadow Lake Lodge (tea served daily 11am–5pm). Hike out the next day via Gibbons Pass to **Twin Lakes** and shuttle back to your vehicle at Sunshine Village.

If you have only 2 nights, skip Ball Pass. If you have only 1 night, hike from Sunshine to Egypt Lake and then out Redearth Creek via Pharaoh Creek (it's downhill all the way!). The beginning elevation is 1,570m (5,150 ft.) and the elevation gained is 790m (2,591 ft.). 40.4km (25 miles) one-way. Moderate. Access: From Banff Townsite, take Trans-Canada Hwy. 1 west to Sunshine Rd. (8.3km/5 miles). Take Sunshine Rd. south to the Sunshine Village ski area (9km/5½ miles). Walk or take the shuttle up to Sunshine Village.

Glacier Lake *(Kids) (Finds)* This overnight trip isn't too strenuous and gets you into the **Icefields Parkway backcountry** ⚐. It's a nice outing for families, since the hike is quite flat and the elevation is relatively low. The trail starts on an old roadbed through a lodgepole pine forest, then drops down to a narrow bridge over the North Saskatchewan River. You then climb above the river, and the trail flattens out again to a wide-open bluff with views of Howse Pass before joining Howse River and climbing gradually up to Glacier Lake, one of the largest lakes in the backcountry. There is a lovely campsite on the western edge of the lake. Snow clears early from this trail and is also late in arriving, so its season lasts a bit longer than most of the other trails in the park. You should be able to hike it by late spring well into early fall. The beginning elevation is 1,450m (4,756 ft.) and you gain 210m (689 ft.) over the course of the trip. 8.9km (5.5 miles) one-way. Easy. Access: West side of the Icefields Pkwy. 93, 1.2km (¾ mile) north of the junction with Hwy. 11, near Saskatchewan Crossing.

Skoki Valley ⚐ Tucked in behind the Lake Louise ski area, this trail takes you to the heights of the **Slate Range** into an area loaded with human history. You can make it a 2- or 3-night trip. The trail starts at Fish Creek and heads 4km (2.5 miles) up the Lake Louise ski area's limited-access maintenance road. It climbs over Boulder Pass and carries on alongside **Ptarmigan Lake,** then drops to Baker Lake, where you can camp for your first night. On your second day the trail takes you around **Fossil Mountain** and past historical **Skoki Lodge** to **Merlin Meadows** ⚐, which is a great place to camp on your second night (and your third, if you choose to extend the trip). You complete the loop with a climb up **Deception Pass,** after which the route rejoins the access trail at Ptarmigan Lake, taking you back past the Lake Louise ski area to the parking lot at Fish Creek. The beginning elevation is 1,555m (5,100 ft.) and the elevation gain is 1,136m (3,726 ft.). 34km (21 miles) round-trip. Moderate to challenging. Access: Lake Louise ski area. From the Trans-Canada Hwy. 1 interchange at Lake Louise, take Whitehorn Rd. northeast toward the ski hill. Turn right onto Fish Creek Rd. and continue 1km (½ mile) to the parking lot.

Sunshine Meadows/Mount Assiniboine ⚐ Showcasing the spectacularly colorful Sunshine Meadows and Mount Assiniboine region, this route covers high alpine terrain, crosses dramatic passes, and runs alongside picturesque lakes. Park your vehicle at the Sunshine Village ski area parking lot. From there, you can either walk or take the shuttle up to Sunshine Meadows and the trail head. I suggest you take the shuttle—save your energy for the hike itself!

Starting from Sunshine Meadows, hike to **Howard Douglas Lake** and spend your first night at a beautiful campsite by the lake. On Day 2, head over Citadel Pass all the way to the **Lake Magog Campground,** which is in an ideal spot to admire Mount Assiniboine (the highest mountain in Banff National Park, also known as the "Matterhorn of the Rockies"). You might want to spend your second night in the same spot and make a day trip to the Nub, also known as **Nub Peak,** a nice climb on an exposed ridge. Come back to your campsite at the Lake Magog Campground via Elizabeth and Cerulean lakes, making a loop to rejoin the main trail. On the next day, it's a gentle rise to the top of Wonder Pass and then a series of zigzags down overlooking Gloria Lake. You can make it all the way from Lake Magog to the trail's end in a single day (27km, or 17 miles) if you want, since the route is flat once you reach Marvel Lake and Bryant Creek, near the end of the route. But be warned—if you do, you'll be hurrying through some of the best scenery in the Canadian

Rockies. If you've got one more night, reserve a site at the **Marvel Lake Campground.** Exit at the Mount Shark parking lot, in Kananaskis Country. Since this trail is one-way, you'll need to arrange transportation from the end of the route back to your car at the Sunshine Village ski area parking lot. You begin the hike at an elevation of 1,570m (5,150 ft.) and gain 655m (2,148 ft.). 62.2km (38.6 miles) one-way. Moderate to strenuous. Access: From Banff Townsite, take Trans-Canada Hwy. 1 8.3km (5 miles) west to Sunshine Rd. Take Sunshine Rd. 9km (5½ miles) south to Sunshine Village ski area parking lot. Walk or take the shuttle up to Sunshine Meadows at Sunshine Village.

3 Other Activities

Hiking may be the most popular outdoor activity in Banff National Park, but it's far from the only one. There are a variety of other outdoor activities in the park—enough of a variety to keep you busy doing something new on each day of your trip.

ROAD BIKING & MOUNTAIN BIKING

With more than 190km (118 miles) of mountain-bike trails and numerous options for road biking, Banff is a friendly place for two wheels. Bike season runs from May to October. Note that not all hiking trails are open to bikers.

You can rent both road and mountain bikes in Banff National Park at **BacTrax Bike Rentals** (225 Bear St.; © **403/762-8177**). The rental rates run from C$9 to C$13 (US$8–US$12) per hour, and C$32 to C$44 (US$30–US$41) per day. Guided tours of the Vermillion Lakes and Sundance Canyon leave daily. In addition to renting regular-size bikes for adult riders, **Adventures Unlimited** (211 Bear St.; © **403/762-4554**) rents kids' bikes, trailers, and strollers, too. Rates are C$9 to C$12 (US$8–US$11) per hour, or C$30 to C$38 (US$28–US$36) per day. In Lake Louise, rent bikes at **Wilson Mountain Sports** (Samson Mall; © **403/522-3636**). Rates are C$17 (US$16) per hour, or C$41 (US$38) per day.

ROAD BIKING   Many people choose to see the beauty of the Canadian Rockies by bike. You can plan your route to coincide with campgrounds or hostels each night. Biking the **Icefields Parkway** (Hwy. 93) from Banff to Jasper National Park is very popular, and takes 3 to 4 days. If you're looking at taking a slightly more relaxed trip, here are a couple of suggestions. One trip is from the Trans-Canada Highway 1/Kootenay Parkway 93 junction below Castle Mountain, in Banff National Park, heading west through Kootenay

---

(*Tips* **Share the Trail**

Bike trails in Banff National Park are also hiking and horse-back-riding trails. Expect to encounter people using the trail in other ways. Ride in control and always be prepared to stop. Slow down when you come upon a hiker. A friendly greeting will make them aware of your presence. Bikes can spook horses. When passing a horse, let the rider know you are coming. If a horse approaches you, move to the side of the trail, stop your bike, and let the horse pass. If you have a chance to stop and chat a little, ask the rider about the trail conditions ahead.

National Park and into the town of Radium Hot Springs, British Columbia, following the Kootenay Parkway Highway 93 South. Another option is to start out in Lake Louise and bike through Yoho National Park into the town of Golden, British Columbia, along the Trans-Canada Highway 1.

Some other good routes around the Banff Townsite area include the **Lake Minnewanka Loop,** the **Banff Springs Golf Course drive,** and the **Vermillion Lakes.** When you head out from the townsite, take the **Bow Valley Parkway** (Hwy. 93A). There's much less traffic than on the Trans-Canada Highway (Hwy. 1). If you're up at Lake Louise, try the old **Great Divide Road,** which leads into Yoho National Park—a quiet ride through mountain scenery.

MOUNTAIN BIKING   Mountain biking is permitted on only a select few of the trails in Banff National Park. You are subject to fines if you are caught biking on hiking-only trails. Taking a bike off the road and into the backcountry can mean facing a lot of technical obstacles, like roots, boulders, rocks, creeks, and steep hills. So, when you select a trail, be conservative. Start out with short, easy trails and work your way up to more challenging ones. Wear a helmet and bring plenty of water and snacks, as well as extra clothing, since mountain weather is nothing if not mercurial—often changing at the drop of a hat. Always tell someone where you are going and when you'll be back. Travel in groups; it's safer and more fun.

In the Banff Townsite area, the best ride for beginners and families is the 12.5km (7.8-mile) **Spray River Loop.** Those in search of a more challenging ride should try the 14km (8.7-mile) **Rundle Riverside Trail.** Near Lake Louise, families with kids will enjoy the relatively flat but very scenic 7.1km (4.4-mile) **Bow River Loop,** which leaves from the Lake Louise Campground. There are interpretive signs along the trail. The most exciting, technically challenging ride in the area is the 10km (6.2-mile) **Moraine Lake Highline Trail** ⊛, a single-track route along the shoulder of the majestic Mount Temple that descends into the Moraine Lake basin.

Mountain bikers looking for downhill or free-riding trails should consider heading to Kicking Horse Mountain Resort in Golden, BC (see chapter 9). There are also world-class mountain bike trails at the Canmore Nordic Centre, just east of Banff, which regularly hosts races on the World Cup of Mountain Bike tour.

CANOEING

Around Banff Townsite, launch your canoe at **Two Jack Lake** or **Johnson Lake,** both off Lake Minnewanka Drive. There are boathouses where you can rent canoes at both **Moraine Lake** and **Lake Louise.** The **Moraine Lake Lodge's boathouse** (14km/8¾ miles south of Lake Louise on Moraine Lake Rd.; ✆ **403/522-3733**) rents canoes for C$35 (US$33) per hour. The **Fairmont Chateau Lake Louise** (111 Lake Louise Dr.; ✆ **403/522-3511**) rents canoes for C$35 (US$33) per hour. In the Town of Banff, rent a canoe at the **Bow River Canoe Rentals** (end of Wolf St.; ✆ **403/762-3632**) for C$22 (US$21) per hour or C$48 (US$45) per day.

CLIMBING

Climbing has a long history in Banff National Park, from the early days of the Swiss guides who led Victorian travelers up the high peaks, to modern-day climbers who guide themselves up a different climb every weekend. Visitors to Banff who've taken the time and energy to learn the ropes enjoy this highly technical sport. There are no specific regulations governing climbing or mountaineering in Banff National Park; however, Parks Canada does suggest you contact the **Banff Warden's office** (in Banff ✆ **403/762-1470;** in Lake Louise ✆ **403/ 522-1220**) for more information before you head out.

There are a number of excellent rock-climbing locations in Banff, including the Tower of Babel, at **Moraine Lake,** and "Back of the Lake," at **Lake Louise.** Just to the east, the town of Canmore has some great sport climbing spots at Grassi Lakes and Cougar Creek Canyon. Books that can help you select a route include *Sport Climbs in the Canadian Rockies* by John Martin and Jon Jones (Calgary: Rocky Mountain Books); *Bow Valley Rock* by Chris Perry and Joe Josephson (Calgary: Rocky Mountain Books); and *Selected Alpine*

Climbs in the Canadian Rockies by Sean Dougherty (Calgary: Rocky Mountain Books). Classic mountain climbs include mounts Athabasca and Assiniboine—both are for experienced climbers only.

For advice on planning a climbing trip, contact the **Alpine Club of Canada** (Indian Flats Rd., P.O. Box 8040, Canmore, AB T1W 2T8; ✆ **403/678-3200;** www.alpineclubofcanada.ca) or the **Association of Canadian Mountain Guides** (P.O. Box 8341, Canmore, AB T1W 2V1; ✆ **403/678-2885;** www.acmg.ca).

For private lessons and guiding, contact Canada's premiere mountaineering school, **Yamnuska Inc.** (Suite 200, Summit Centre, 50 Lincoln Park, Canmore, AB T1W 1N8; ✆ **403/678-4164;** www.yamnuska.com). Private climbing guides charge a base rate of C$380 (US$355) for one person, C$210 (US$196) for two. Rates drop for groups up to four people. Another good idea for would-be climbers is to stop by to chat with the experts at **Mountain Magic Equipment** (224 Bear St., Banff, AB T0C 1C0; ✆ **403/762-2591;** www.mountainmagic.com). They know the climbing routes in the area better than anyone.

FISHING

You need a permit to fish in Banff National Park. Pick one up at the **Banff Information Centre** in Banff Townsite (224 Banff Ave.; ✆ **403/762-1550**) or at **Standish Home Hardware** (223 Bear St.; ✆ **403/762-2080**). You can also get one at the **Lake Louise Visitor Centre** (Samson Mall, 101 Lake Louise Dr.; ✆ **403/522-3833**), or at the boathouse at Lake Minnewanka (take Banff Ave. north under the Trans-Canada Hwy. bridge and continue on to Lake Minnewanka, following the signs). National Park fishing permits cost C$8 (US$7.50) for a 7-day period. An annual permit costs C$25 (US$23). Pick up a copy of the brochure *Fishing Regulations* at the Banff Information Centre or the Lake Louise Visitor Centre to find out what species of fish are biting and which areas are open, when.

Vermillion, Johnson, and Two Jack lakes, just outside the Town of Banff, are very popular fishing spots, so not surprisingly there aren't too many fish left. **Lake Minnewanka** does have some big fish—if you can find them. Rainbow trout and lake trout as big as 18 kilograms (40 lb.) have been caught there in the past. Another good location is **Upper Cascade River at Stewart Canyon,** where it flows into Lake Minnewanka. Here you'll potentially hook brook trout, rainbow trout, and cutthroat. Don't even bother trying to fish at Lake Louise—again, there are none left. However, there is still a possibility that you'll catch something at **Moraine Lake.** The **Bow**

River is one of the world's finest fly-fishing rivers and is the only area in Banff National Park open year-round.

For guided fishing trips, try **Hawgwild Flyfishing Guides** (P.O. Box 2534, Banff, AB T1L 1C3; ✆ **403/760-2446;** www.flyfishing banff.com), with guide "Big" Jim Dykstra. Dykstra is a fly maker and rod builder who will customize your outing. Rates range from C$404 (US$378) for two anglers for a half-day, to C$479 (US$448) for two anglers for a full day. He guarantees you'll catch something, or else you get your money back. **Banff Fishing Unlimited** (P.O. Box 8281, Canmore, AB T1W 2V1; ✆ **403/762-4936;** www.banff-fishing.com) specializes in year-round fly-fishing, spin casting, and trophy lake trout fishing. Their guides know all the secrets. **Alpine Anglers** (P.O. Box 2440, Banff, AB T1L 1C2; ✆ **403/762-8223;** www.alpineanglers.com) offers top-notch instruction in the mild sensibilities of fly-fishing on the pristine, turquoise waters of the Bow River.

GOLFING

The **Fairmont Banff Springs Hotel's** ★★ 27-hole Stanley Thompson Course is world-famous (405 Spray Ave.; ✆ **403/762-6801**). Recently upgraded, the course has three tee-offs and an amazingly scenic location along the **Spray and Bow rivers,** beneath **Mount Rundle.** It's expensive but legendary, and open to the public (you don't have to be a guest at the hotel to play a round). Course fees range between C$125 (US$117) in May and October and C$200 (US$187) from June through September, including cart. There's also a 9-hole course. Watch for geese and elk on your drives! To the east and west of Banff are some other fabulous golf courses. See chapter 9 for golfing in the gateways.

HORSEBACK RIDING

Riding a horse in the Canadian Rockies is as logical as riding a camel in the Sahara Desert. Saddling up not only lets you explore the cowboy heritage of the Rockies, it also lets you wind your way into parts of the Banff backcountry you might not otherwise have seen. Having said this, only a select few trails in Banff National Park are able to accommodate horses, so I recommend taking a trip organized by a local outfitter. They'll show you a good ol' time, while keeping you on course!

Timberline Tours (P.O. Box 14, Lake Louise, AB T0L 1E0; ✆ **403/522-3743;** www.timberlinetours.ca) leads scenic trips at Bow Lake, in Lake Louise. A half-day outing is between C$55 and

Saddle Up & Head High

If you're not sure about long days of hiking and carrying your own packs but you still want to explore the back-country of Banff, consider an overnight horseback trip. From early May to late October, trail rides range from 1 night to 1 week. Some outfitters combine guided trail rides with stays at rustic but comfortable backcountry lodges, while others include overnights in wilderness tents situated in truly spectacular settings. The nights are crystal clear and naturally silent. Food is often cowboy-style, casual and hearty. This is one of the best ways to see the back corners of Banff—with considerably less effort than backpacking. For trips from 2 to 4 days ranging from C$434 (US$405) to C$863 (US$806), try **Holiday on Horseback** (132 Banff Ave.; ✆ **403/762-4551** or **800/661-8352;** www.horseback.com). Starting at the Lake Louise Corral, **Timberline Tours** (P.O. Box 14, Lake Louise, AB T0L 1E0; ✆ **403/522-3743;** www.timberlinetours.ca) has overnight trips starting at C$330 (US$308) per person.

C$105 (US$51–US$98), while an overnight trip is C$330 (US$308). **Brewster's Lake Louise Stables** (208 Caribou St., Banff, AB T1L 1A5; ✆ **403/762-5454;** www.brewsteradventures.com) has a variety of tours in the Lake Louise area, including a lovely half-day ride to the Plain of the Six Glaciers that costs C$115 (US$107). They also offer a spectacular **all-day ride** ✪ featuring **Paradise Valley,** the **Giant Steps,** and **Lake Annette.** The cost is C$250 (US$234), and includes lunch. **Overnight pack trips** start at C$420 (US$392), with accommodations provided at Brewster's Kananaskis Guest Ranch. **Holiday on Horseback** (132 Banff Ave., Banff, AB T0L 0C0; ✆ **800/661-8352** or 403/762-4551; www. horseback.com) has a corral at the Fairmont Banff Springs Hotel, where they run 1-hour tours along the Spray River (C$36/US$34). They have another corral at Martin Stables (located on the banks of the Bow River across from Banff Townsite), where short 1- to 3-hour trips head into the Sundance Range (C$65–C$88/ US$61–US$82). They also organize wonderfully fun **wilderness cookouts** ✪✪, which include a Mountain Morning breakfast ride

(C$92/US$86) and an Evening Trailride steak fry, where they serve a large Western barbecue dinner (C$92/US$86).

4 Winter Sports & Activities

Famous for its crisp blue skies, winter in the Canadian Rockies is just as beautiful as summer. In fact, many people swear that winter is an even better time to visit. The streets of Banff bustle with skiers and snowboarders, as folks celebrate the snow that makes so many winter sports and activities possible. For those not hindered by the cold, skiing in Banff is a one-of-a-kind experience.

From cozy nights by the fire to fondue dinners, there's plenty to keep you warm! For a great winter evening, head out for a sleigh ride with **Holiday on Horseback** (132 Banff Ave.; ✆ **403/762-4551**). A private sleigh ride (C$149/US$139) is the ultimate in romance.

To catch some of the world's best ice hockey players in action, **Banff Adventures Unlimited** (✆ **403/762-4554;** www.banffadventures. com) offers a tour to the **NHL's Calgary Flames** home games. Pure Canadiana! To get up close and personal with ice, sign up for the **Johnston Canyon Icewalk** from **Discover Banff Tours** (✆ **877/565-9372** or 403/762-7768; www.discoverbanff.com). You'll strap on some crampons and follow frozen trails in a winter wonderland.

You can rent cross-country and downhill skis and equipment, as well as snowboarding equipment, at a number of places in Banff and Lake Louise, including rental shops at all three downhill ski resorts listed farther on in this section. In Banff Townsite, try **Ski Stop** (203A Bear St.; ✆ **403/762-1650**). It has a second location, in the conference center at the **Fairmont Banff Springs Hotel** (405 Spray Ave.; ✆ **403/762-5333**). In Lake Louise, rent skis, snowshoes, and snowboards at **Wilson Mountain Sports** (Samson Mall, 101 Lake Louise Dr.; ✆ **403/522-3636**). There are numerous shops that specialize in winter gear, where you can get your skis tuned and your snowboard bindings adjusted. Try **Ultimate Ski and Ride** (206 Banff Ave.; ✆ **403/762-0547**) or **Monod Sports** (129 Banff Ave.; ✆ **403/762-4571**). Average daily rental rates are between C$33 (US$31) and C$44 (US$41) for downhill skis and snowboards (depending on the level of equipment performance you want) and around C$18 (US$17) for cross-country.

CROSS-COUNTRY SKIING

A wonderful way to explore the park in winter, cross-country skiing promises great exercise, views—and solitude, if you're seeking it.

Tips Winter Driving

There are beautiful winter days in Banff when there isn't a cloud in the sky and the roads are clear and clean. Then there are days when you can't see your hand in front of your face because it's snowing so hard. You need to adjust your driving in winter. Roads may be closed at any point if driving conditions are very poor. Here are a few general rules to keep you safe on winter roads:

- Slow down if the road is snow-covered or if visibility is poor.
- Watch out for slippery **black ice,** which is hard to spot on asphalt. You'll often hit it on bridges and near water.
- Turn off your **cruise control.** Driving with it on makes it more difficult to react to changing road conditions and unexpected slippery spots.
- Make sure you have the proper tires. By law, your car must be equipped with snow tires, all-season radial tires, or chains to travel on all roads in Banff National Park, with the exception of the Trans-Canada Highway 1.
- Be wary of wildlife grazing near the shoulder. In fact, since there is less traffic, there are often more animals near the road.
- Carry a shovel, flashlight, blanket, and water, plus extra food and warm clothing in your car. You can't rely on your cellphone in case of an emergency, since reception is good only in and around the Town of Banff and the village of Lake Louise.

For a recorded report on road conditions in Banff National Park, call ℂ **403/762-1450.**

There are more than 80km (50 miles) of managed trails in Banff National Park, many of them within a half-hour drive of Banff Townsite. The cross-country ski season runs from December to March.

Some of the best ski trails in the park head out from the town of Banff, including the novice loop at the **Banff Springs Golf Course,** the **Cave and Basin River Trail,** the **Spray River Loop** ⊛, and the **Cascade Fireroad.** There is excellent skiing at **Boom Lake,** a little farther away from the townsite. The **Shoreline Trail** at Lake Louise is groomed for skiing in winter and there are track-set trails along the **Moraine Lake Road.** In nearby Canmore is the Canmore Nordic Centre, one of North America's top Nordic skiing venues and host to the 1988 Winter Olympics (see chapter 9).

DOG SLEDDING

Just over the border from Banff National Park, another classic winter tradition draws tourists from around the world for dog-sledding. Friendly huskies mush across frozen lakes for an adventure that is exhilarating. Try **Snowy Owl Sled Dog Tours** (104–602 Bow Valley Trail, Canmore, AB T1W 2T8; © **888/311-6874;** www.snowy owltours.com), where 2-hour trips cost C$127 (US$119) for adults and C$85 (US$79) for children under 9, and full-day tours cost C$525 (US$490) for adults and C$325 (US$304) for children under 9. At Lake Louise, **Kingmik Dog Sled Tours** (© **877/ 919-7779** or 403/763-8887; www.kingmikdogsledtours.com) has smaller and more personal tours on trails that run along the Great Divide.

DOWNHILL SKIING & SNOWBOARDING

As Canada's oldest and one of its most celebrated ski destinations, there is excellent skiing and snowboarding to be had at Banff's three ski resorts. Each has a unique character and offers something different to skier and snowboarder alike, and all are great for families. I recommend visiting them each for at least a day.

Banff Mount Norquay (at the end of Mount Norquay Dr., P.O. Box 1520, Banff, AB T1L 1B4; © **403/762-4421;** www. banffnorquay.com) is the locals' favorite because it's intimate and close. Less than 15 minutes from Banff Avenue, you can likely see your hotel from the chairlift here. Runs are generally quite steep. Economically smart **ski-by-the-hour** deals mean you don't have to spend the entire day here to feel like you're getting your money's worth. Full-day lift tickets are C$49 (US$46) for adults, C$39 (US$36) for students and seniors, C$17 (US$16) for children ages 6 to 12, and free for children under 6. Ski-by-the-hour tickets cost C$29 (US$27) for 2 hours, C$32 (US$30) for 3 hours, and C$41 (US$38) for 4 hours for adults; C$25 (US$23) for 2 hours, C$30 (US$28) for 3 hours, and C$35 (US$32) for 4 hours for students and seniors; and C$11 (US$10) for 2 hours, C$13 (US$12) for 3 hours, C$15 (US$14) for 4 hours for children ages 6 to 12. Children age 5 and under ski for free. Farther north, the **Lake Louise Ski and Snowboard Resort** ⊀ (follow Whitehorn Rd. off the Trans-Canada

A Word of Caution: You Are in Avalanche Country

The Canadian Rockies is avalanche country. An extremely powerful wave of snow and ice that cracks off a mountain slope in the middle of winter, an avalanche can destroy everything in its path. It is extremely challenging to predict when an avalanche might occur, and even more challenging to escape if you are caught in one. Drivers should avoid stopping in areas where Parks Canada has posted an AVALANCHE ZONE sign. Parks Canada updates avalanche forecasts regularly throughout the winter. In Banff, call ℂ 403/ 762-1460.

Hwy. 1 at the Lake Louise exit; ℂ **800/258-7669** or 403/522-3555; www.skilouise.com) has views that will have you picking your jaw up off the glistening powder snow. Easy to access and full of varied terrain, folks remain loyal to Louise. Beginners will find a friendly ski and snowboard school, as well as some lovely green runs to get started. Head straight to the top of the new **Grizzly Express Gondola** for more advanced blue runs. **Larch** is a great place for intermediates. Advanced skiers should take to the **Top of the World "Six-Pack" Chair** then the **Summit Platter** and go nuts in powder bowls like **West Bowl** and **Boomerang.** For snowboarders, there is a terrain park with jumps, obstacles, and railings. When you're ready for a break, head over to the **Lodge of the Ten Peaks,** one of the largest log cabins in Canada, with two restaurants, two bars, a rental shop, and a beautiful stone fireplace at its center. Cozy and rustic **Temple Lodge,** tucked in behind the resort below Whitehorn Mountain, is a good lunch restaurant. Full-day lift tickets are C$69 (US$65) for adults, C$55 (US$51) for seniors, C$48 (US$45) for youth 13 to 18, and C$22 (US$21) for children ages 6 to 12. Children under age 6 ski for free. Prices go up about $5 per day during the Christmas–to–New Year and Easter holidays. **Sunshine Village** ⊛ (8km/5 miles west of Banff Townsite at the end of Sunshine Rd.; ℂ **800/661-1676** or 403/762-6500; www.skibanff.com) is tucked high in the alpine zone in a series of scenic bowls centered around a "village" with a hotel, day lodge, ski school, and gondola station. Sunshine's newest terrain, **Goat's Eye Mountain,** is great for advanced skiers. And only experts need attempt the aptly named **Delirium Dive.** Advanced snowboarders will find a lot of flat terrain at Sunshine, but the terrain park has grown steadily over the years and is a fun spot for catching some air. There is often fresh snow daily at Sunshine—it's the rare ski resort that doesn't make any snow. When it's clear, you can see the spectacular peaks of the **Continental Divide,** including **Mount Assiniboine,** the "Matterhorn of the Rockies." Full-day lift tickets cost C$70 (US$65) for adults, C$57 (US$53) for seniors, C$50 (US$47) for youth, and C$24 (US$22) for children ages 6 to 12. Children under age 6 ski for free.

It's possible to visit all three Banff ski resorts, thanks to the innovative **ski packages** 🌟 offered by the **Ski Banff–Lake Louise–Sunshine** partnership (119 Banff Ave., Banff, AB T1L 1H9; © **877/754-7080** or 403/762-4561; http://www.skibig3.com). Packages include hotel and lift tickets at each of the three resorts. The price for adults ranges from C$301 (US$281) for 3 days to C$1,021 (US$954) for 5 days. No student rates. It's a great deal and an excellent way to sample Banff's outstanding skiing.

ICE-SKATING

There are a number of places where you can skate outdoors under the winter sky. It's an exhilarating activity that's popular with families. Try the Vermillion Lakes, just outside the Town of Banff, in the early winter before the snow starts to pile up. At the **Fairmont Chateau Lake Louise,** there is an **outdoor rink** 🌟🌟 on the lake with a spectacular ice castle built right on top. It's a very scenic and romantic place to skate.

5

Where to Stay, Camp & Eat in Banff National Park

Once you've decided to come to Banff National Park, the next step is to decide where you want to stay. The earlier you do this, the better your chances are of getting the kind of accommodations you want, whether it's a resort, a hotel, a cabin, a campsite, or an economical hostel. Most of the hotels in the park are located right in or very close to Banff Townsite. They are extremely busy during the summer season, from mid-June to early September. Almost all of the rest of the hotels are located in the village of Lake Louise. There are very few lodging possibilities elsewhere in the park; two of the best (Storm Mountain Lodge and Num-Ti-Jah Lodge) are reviewed here. If you're going to base your visit in the Town of Banff, try to spend at least 1 night of your trip away from the townsite; head to one of the excellent lodges in Lake Louise.

Campgrounds in Banff also fill up fast. Parks Canada's new campground reservation system has helped ease the pressure and allows you to book a campsite well in advance. But as certain campsites are very popular, it's a good idea to reserve early at www.pccamping.ca or by calling © 877/737-3783.

1 Lodging in Banff National Park

Hotel rooms in Banff aren't cheap. And despite the long strip of hotels, lodges, and the like that line Banff Avenue, there are remarkably few vacancies in summer. So book ahead. For help selecting a hotel and making a reservation, contact the **Banff/Lake Louise Tourism Bureau** (224 Banff Ave., P.O. Box 1298, Banff, AB T1L 1B3; © **403/762-8421;** www.banfflakelouise.com). Part of the **Banff Information Centre,** they have an up-to-the-minute list of hotel vacancies in the park. You might also try **Banff Lake Louise Central Reservations** (© **877/542-2633** or 403/277-7669; www.banffreservations.com). They work with 75 area hotels and are knowledgeable enough to help you make the best choice. A C$50

(US$47) deposit is required. **Banff Accommodation Reservations** (© **877/226-3348** or 403/762-0260; www.banffinfo.com) offers a similar service.

IN AND AROUND BANFF TOWNSITE
EXPENSIVE
Buffalo Mountain Lodge ⊀   Perched on Tunnel Mountain just outside Banff Townsite, this is a first-class mountain lodge that has a cozy feel. With peeled log frames, fieldstone fireplaces, and log furniture, there's an overall subdued decor that's straight out of an L.L. Bean catalog. The gorgeous stainless-steel outdoor hot tub is reportedly the largest in Canada. The first buildings were built in the 1980s, with new wings added on since. The guest rooms in these newer wings have wood-burning fireplaces and private balconies. Guest room nos. 900 through 1100 are the farthest removed from Tunnel Mountain and, therefore, the most private. They look out onto a peaceful forest. My favorite guest rooms are nos. 1100 through 1200, also on the west side of the property. They have great views of **Mount Rundle** and the **Bow Valley.** Request an upper-level guest room with a climbing stone fireplace and high, open ceilings with wooden beams.

Beds are dressed with feather duvets over flannel sheets. Amid dark green tiles, premium room bathrooms have heated slate floors, claw-foot tubs, and open glass stand-up showers. All of the guest rooms now have fireplaces. Suites with kitchenettes are also available. This hotel is an excellent choice, particularly if you want to be away from the bustle of Banff Avenue but still close enough to walk into town.

700 Tunnel Mountain Rd., Banff, AB T1L 1B3. © **800/661-1367** or 403/410-7417. Fax 403/410-7406. www.crmr.com. 108 units. May–Oct C$189–C$259 (US$177–US$242); Nov–Apr C$159–C$249 (US$149–US$233). Extra person C$25 (US$23). Children 12 and under stay free in parent's room. AE, MC, V. **Amenities:** 2 restaurants; lounge; Jacuzzi; activities desk; ski storage; babysitting; laundry service; Internet. *In room:* TV/VCR, Internet, coffeemaker, hair dryer, iron.

Fairmont Banff Springs Hotel   The *Titanic* of the Canadian Rockies, this is one of the most famous buildings in Canada. It's because of this spectacular and legendary hotel that Banff came to exist in the first place. Built in 1883, "the Springs" certainly stands out, not just because it looks like a baronial Scottish castle in the mountains, but also because of the steady stream of tourist traffic heading to the hotel. Wandering through the halls, you'll likely bump into shutter-happy tourists who have no intention of actually staying at the hotel—they're just dropping in for a rushed tour and a photo op. If you *are* a guest at the hotel it makes for quite a bit of distraction, and can keep you from really relaxing. (The hotel has moved the bus tour drop-off out of the main lobby to make the area more friendly to real guests.)

But, undeniably, the Springs is a sight to behold. The turrets, green roof, and thick stone walls are unique enough, but what really impresses is the hotel's public space: grand halls and lounge areas, stairwells and sitting areas, each with a unique (though sometimes bizarre) design and function. The guest rooms here have long had a reputation for being quite stuffy and cramped, and uncomfortably warm in summer. All the rooms in the main building have been renovated in the last few years to address this problem, and the guest rooms are now brighter, cooler (thanks to air-conditioning), and cleaner, although they are essentially the same size. Even though they *feel* bigger, this still isn't a place to come after a great hike or ski to stretch out. Guest rooms are tastefully designed, with antique furniture and photos of the hotel's early days. Bathrooms are small but very clean. Besides the basic Fairmont rooms, there are a slew of suites (ask for one in the **Tudor House** for more privacy). What is phenomenal about the Springs is what lies *outside* the guest rooms: incredible amenities, including the decadent **Willow Stream Spa,** a bowling center, horse stables, and eight restaurants. Enhancements seem to never stop, with the old adage "If you can't get bigger, get better" directing plans. If you love history and grand elegance, this is the spot for you.

I don't think the Springs is overrated, but I do think it's over-the-top. The best way to shave some dollars is via the hotel's many packages, from bed-and-breakfast to skiing. It's worth the price to stay here if you want a big hotel with all the amenities you could ever dream of, but spending more for a deluxe room or suite should be left to those with overflowing coffers. If you're here to visit the park and enjoy the outdoors, save your money and stay elsewhere.

405 Spray Ave., Banff, AB T1L 1J4. 🄲 **800/441-1414** or 403/762-2211. Fax 403/762-5755. www.fairmont.com/banffsprings. 778 units. Rates vary based on desired views, dates, and availability. Oct–May starting from C$329 (US$308); June–Sept starting from C$459 (US$429). Meal, ski, and special occasion packages available. Children under 18 stay free in parent's room. AE, DC, DISC, MC, V. Valet parking C$26 (US$24) per day. **Amenities:** 8 restaurants; 3 lounges; pub; indoor and outdoor heated pools; 27-hole golf course on property; 5 outdoor tennis courts; spa; gym; activities desk; ski desk; ski storage; riding stables; 5-pin bowling; concierge; business center; shops; salon; 24-hr. room service; parking; babysitting; laundry service. *In room:* TV w/movies and video games, minibar, Internet, hair dryer, iron.

Rimrock Resort Hotel   With a view any hotel owner would kill for, the Rimrock, perched on the edge of **Sulphur Mountain,** has tastefully integrated its stunning natural setting with a very fine lodging experience. Though it can't claim the historical appeal of the Fairmont Banff Springs, this is one very classy resort nevertheless. What it *can* claim over the Springs is peace and quiet—high on most vacationers' lists. It's also smaller than the Springs, and much more manageable. A giant marble fireplace, cherry oak walls, leather chairs, and big windows offering views you can't get even in the penthouses of other local hotels grace the lobby. Guests are now charged $5 to use the expansive gym; the pool, sauna, and steam room are included. In the winter, there's an outdoor ice rink with a fire pit. Hot chocolate and cider are served.

The guest rooms are airy and a good size. Many have been upgraded, so there are more upper-category options. They all have a clean and crisp feel to them, with new linens and more king-size beds. All are decorated in the same deep colors and run at a base price; you just pay more for a better view. Request a guest room on the east wing for the choicest views. Suites with panoramic mountain views are also available. Bathrooms have cream-colored walls and large tubs. Worth mentioning is their turndown service, which features handmade chocolates by renowned chocolatier and Banff local Bernard Callebaut.

The Rimrock has luxury, harmony, and natural beauty all rolled into one. With a whiff of an old boys' club, it's a good choice for families who aren't on a tight budget, and for those looking for some inspiring (but pampered) time with nature. The view is outstanding and the atmosphere is very classy, but still welcoming. The Rimrock offers a complimentary shuttle to downtown Banff.

Mountain Ave., P.O. Box 1110, Banff, AB T1L 1J2. ⓒ **800/661-1587** or 403/762-3356. Fax 403/762-4132. www.rimrockresort.com. 346 units. June 1–Oct 6 C$418–C$560 (US$391–US$524); Oct 7–Dec 22 C$278–C$360 (US$260–US$337); Dec 23–Jan 1 C$358–C$480 (US$335–US$449); Jan 2–May 30 C$278–C$360 (US$260–US$337). Extra person C$25 (US$23). Suites start at C$510 (US$477) and go up to C$1,220 (US$1,141). Children 18 and under stay free in parent's room. AE, DISC, MC, V. **Amenities:** 2 restaurants; 2 lounges; cafe; large indoor saltwater pool; squash court; health club and spa; 24-hr. room service; parking. *In room:* A/C, TV w/movies, minibar, coffeemaker, safe, wireless Internet, hair dryer, iron.

MODERATE
Buffaloberry Bed and Breakfast *(Finds*   Staying at the newest little inn in town gives you a taste of what it's like to live in Banff. Combining modern technology with a classic design, the unpretentious

owners have reflected their own personal style and love of the outdoors in a building nestled in one of downtown Banff's quieter areas. It may be the best sleep in town, thanks to soundproof rooms, blackout curtains, solid-core doors, and luxurious natural linens. Bathrooms are spacious. The Olds Room is my favorite, thanks to lovely local furniture and nice views. Each room has its own heat control. Breakfasts include homemade pastries and friendly service, and make a great time to get tips from the owners to plan your day. The vibe here is comfortable and relaxing, and it's a nice place to make new friends.

417 Marten St., P.O. Box 5443, Banff, AB T1L 1G5. ⓒ **403/762-3750.** Fax 403/762-3752. www.buffaloberry.com. 4 units. May 20–Sept 30 and Christmas to New Year's C$325 (US$304); Oct 1–May 19 C$235 (US$220). MC, V. No children under 10 allowed. **Amenities:** Library; game room; patio. *In room:* TV.

Bumper's Inn   Not quite cheap enough to be considered inexpensive, Bumpers is still a great bargain. It's neither swanky nor swish. Instead, it's simple, clean, and friendly. There's a bit of a '70s vibe lingering about. Most of the rooms have two double beds; some have only one queen-size bed. Balconies look out over a quiet courtyard or a thick forest, 1 block from the action on Banff Avenue. Next door is their family-friendly restaurant, also named Bumper's, where the slogan is "If you haven't been to Bumper's, you haven't been to Banff." For those looking for a simple place to rest their head after a day exploring the mountains, and for those on a budget, Bumper's is a fine choice.

603 Banff Ave., P.O. Box 1328, Banff, AB T1L 1B3. ⓒ **800/661-3518** or 403/762-3386. www.bumpersinn.com. 39 units. Jan 1–May 31 and Oct 1–Dec 23 C$65–C$85 (US$61–US$79); June 1–Sept 30 C$125–C$135 (US$117–US$126); Dec 25–31 C$100–C$135 (US$93–US$126). Children under 12 stay free in parent's room. AE, MC, V. **Amenities:** Restaurant; parking. *In room:* TV, hair dryer.

Fox Hotel & Suites   Banff's newest hotel is a smart option. Opened in June 2007, this is the only place in downtown Banff with kitchenettes, something that will please those coming for longer stays or those who like to do breakfast their own way. The rooms are mainly suites with a small fridge, sink, microwave, and toaster—enough for breakfasts and lunches, and only the most simple of dinners. The suites have either one or two bedrooms, and some have a loft-style second floor with great mountain views. The style is "mountain chic," more contemporary than most hotels in town. There are four buildings set around a courtyard with a stunning hot pool in the middle that's themed after the Cave and Basin

National Historic Site. With a modern feel, the Fox will give you a taste of what it's like to have your own condo in the Rockies.

46 Banff Ave., Banff, AB T1L 1B1. ⓒ **800/661-8310** or 403/760-8500. www.bestof banff.com/fox. 117 rooms. June 8–Oct 7 and Dec 21–Jan 6 C$249–C$649 (US$233– US$607); Oct 8–Dec 20, Jan 6–Feb 7, and Apr 6–May 7 C$149–C$324 (US$139– US$303); Feb 8–Apr 6 C$174–C$549 (US$163–US$513). Extra person C$20 (US$19). Children 16 and under stay free in parent's room. AE, DISC, MC, V. **Amenities:** Restaurant; hot pools; gym; shuttle service. *In room:* A/C, kitchenette, Internet, coffeemaker, hair dryer.

Ptarmigan Inn *(Value)*   With quite reasonable rates, enough class to make it special, and an excellent location (just a block from the heart of town), this inn is a good midrange choice. Built in the 1980s, the inn was recently renovated and now has a more casual and modern style. Only a few of the guest rooms actually front onto the busy main drag of Banff Avenue, so most are very quiet. The quietest of all are the 19 rooms that overlook the atrium. They're also the least expensive, since they have no view of the mountains (or of anything at all, really, except some empty chairs and the neighboring room's curtains). If you're willing to do without a view from your hotel room (remember that you'll be surrounded by the mountains the minute you step outside), and can squish into somewhat cramped bathrooms, you'll be able to save some money on this hotel.

The guest rooms are cozy, with down comforters and pine furniture. Families will enjoy the double rooms with the bathroom in the middle, separating the two sleeping areas. Premium guest rooms have better views, larger bathrooms, and a sitting area.

337 Banff Ave., Banff, AB T1L 1B7. ⓒ **800/661-8310** or 403/762-2207. Fax 403/ 760-8287. www.bestofbanff.com/bpi. 134 units. June 10–Oct 9 C$229 (US$214) standard room; C$244 (US$228) superior room; C$279 (US$261) premium room. Oct 10–Dec 19 C$129 (US$121) standard room; C$144 (US$135) superior room; C$199 (US$186) premium room. Dec 20–Jan 3 C$185 (US$173) standard room; C$204 (US$191) superior room; C$279 (US$261) premium room. Jan 3–Feb 10 C$129 (US$121) standard room; C$154 (US$144) superior room; C$249 (US$233) premium room. Feb 11–June 9 C$159 (US$149) standard room; C$174 (US$163) superior room; C$239 (US$224) premium room. Extra person C$15 (US$14). Children 16 and under stay free in parent's room. AE, DISC, MC, V. **Amenities:** Restaurant; lounge; Jacuzzi; sauna; bike and ski storage; meeting facilities; limited room service; laundry service. *In room:* TV, coffeemaker, hair dryer, irons in premium rooms.

Storm Mountain Lodge *(Finds)*   Halfway between Banff and Lake Louise (or 20 min. from either one), this collection of rustic cabins, originally built in the 1920s and carefully restored by new owners, is situated with gorgeous views of its namesake peak and nearby Castle Mountain. The heritage rooms offer a simple yet elegant style, and

Hostelling: Is it for You?

If you are looking for a social, economical way to experience the less-populated areas of Banff and Jasper national parks, think about booking a bunk at one of the dozen hostels in the area. The non-profit organization **Hostelling International** runs them all.

Hostels are particularly popular with groups and with younger people, but are open to travelers of all ages. They generally have dormitory-style guest rooms with anywhere from 10 to 30 bunk beds to a room. Some dormitories are male or female only, while others are coed. All hostels in the area have at least one well-equipped communal kitchen. The Banff and Lake Louise International Hostels also have good and affordable restaurants on-site. Some have family rooms. Bring food from town and a sleeping bag, and be prepared to give up some privacy. Hostels, however, are loads of fun. You'll likely meet new hiking partners, not to mention nab one of the cheapest beds in the Canadian Rockies!

Annual memberships to **Hostelling International** cost C$35 (US$33) for adults. Membership is free for children under age 18. Get a membership at any of the hostels or online at www.hihostels.ca.

For more information on hostels in Banff National Park, call ✆ **403/762-4122.** For hostels in Jasper National Park, call ✆ **780/852-3215.** You can also log on to www.hihostels.ca/Alberta.

Alpine Club of Canada also runs a number of very rustic backcountry hostels (all are at least 4 hr. hiking from the nearest road). You don't have to be a member to stay, but you do need a reservation. ACC memberships cost C$21 (US$20) for adults and C$11 (US$10) for children under age 17. Call the ACC at ✆ **403/678-3200** or visit them online at www.alpineclubofcanada.ca.

the forested property means plenty of privacy. It's quiet and charming. Cabin nos. 11 and 14 have the best views; cabin nos. 9 and 10 are farthest from the road and are the quietest. The restaurant specializes in Canadian cuisine and is worth the drive on its own, and the breakfasts are delightful. Big bathtubs, crackling fireplaces, comfy beds—it's your own Rocky Mountain getaway. With great chances for wildlife watching and hiking right outside your door, this is a lovely way to blend activity with relaxation.

On Hwy. 93 just west of Castle Junction. P.O. Box 3249, Banff, AB T1L 1C8. ℂ **403/762-4155.** Fax 403/762-4151. www.stormmountainlodge.com. 16 units. June 11–Oct 9 and Dec 21–Jan 2 C$229 (US$214) double; C$219 (US$205) pine cabin with kitchenette; C$269 (US$252) log cabin with kitchenette. Dec 8–June 14 C$150–C$168 (US$140–US$157) double; C$140–C$159 (US$131–US$149) log cabin with kitchenette; C$169–C$199 (US$158–US$186) log cabin with kitchenette. C$20 (US$19) extra person. Closed Oct 9–Nov 9. Rates include breakfast. Children under 8 stay free in parent's room. MC, V. **Amenities:** Restaurant; concierge; hiking and cross-country ski trails. *In room:* Coffee, iron, hair dryer, no phone, no TV.

INEXPENSIVE

Banff Alpine Centre and Hostel   This well-known establishment is beloved by travelers and backpackers around the world. It's a fun place to stay, and is very reasonably priced. Dorm rooms sleep 4 to 6 people, and there are quite a few private rooms available also. The atmosphere here is casual yet full of energy, as so many of the guests are keen outdoor types. There's a new pub downstairs. A good option for younger travelers and active families.

801 Hidden Ridge Way, Banff, AB T1L 1B3. At Tunnel Mountain Dr. ℂ **403/762-4123.** Fax 403/762-3441. www.hihostels.ca/alberta. 52 units, which accommodate between 2 and 6 people. 216 beds total. C$30 (US$28) per person for Hostelling International members; C$33 (US$31) per person for nonmembers. Private rooms for 2 from C$87 (US$81) for Hostelling International members; C$94 (US$88) for nonmembers. Children under 12 stay half-price with parents. MC, V. **Amenities:** Restaurant; kitchen; coin-op washers and dryers; wireless Internet. *In room:* No phone.

IN LAKE LOUISE

Fairmont Chateau Lake Louise ✿✿   The Chateau Lake Louise is a public landmark that continues to be selected among the best hotels in North America. Standing all by itself, right on the shore of Lake Louise, the Chateau is an elegant, Bavarian-style hotel, not in the least bit stuffy like its sister the Banff Springs.

Originally built in the 1890s, the hotel has seen many renovations. It's difficult to spot what is new and what is old, though—it all blends together in a style that can only be characterized as "Canadian Rockies meets the Swiss Alps." It reminds me of that childhood story, *Heidi.* Swiss elements are everywhere: from alpine flowers adorning the hotel walls to photographs of the Swiss guides who were the first employees of the hotel. There's even a man in lederhosen playing an alphorn who greets you as you step outside the hotel toward the lake.

The guest rooms, while quite modest in size, are nevertheless very elegant, warm, and comfortable, with pine and oak furniture, walls done in soft tones, and luxurious feather duvets. Each guest room has a different heritage photo of a local pioneer and a botany sketch—unique touches. Having said this, there is a large variety in size and decor, depending on which of the three wings you stay in. The guest rooms in the **Painter Wing** are generally the oldest and most unique. Those in the middle wing have the best views of the lake, and are my favorite. The Fairmont rooms, scattered throughout the three wings, are the standard doubles. The newly renovated rooms on the Fairmont Floor offer top-notch concierge services and pampering. All bathrooms are well-appointed and have marble-finished vanities. Guests shouldn't miss the heritage tours of the Chateau, held daily at 4pm. There are more stories tucked into the corners of this hotel than you'd ever spot on your own. The new Temple Wing has plenty of meeting spaces, another restaurant, and more rooms.

There is a wealth of activities at the hotel, and it's an excellent base for day hikes, canoe outings, biking, and horseback riding, not to mention downhill and cross-country skiing in the winter (see "Winter Sports & Activities" in chapter 4). Don't miss outings with the Chateau's own heritage guides. It's a lovely place in winter, complete with an outdoor skating rink and ice sculptures. With 500 rooms, it can feel a bit impersonal and formal. I wouldn't call the place charming since it's so large, but it is a fabled and magical hotel.

111 Lake Louise Dr., Lake Louise, AB T0L 1E0. (*C*) **800/441-1414** or 403/522-3511. Fax 403/522-3834. www.fairmont.com/lakelouise. 550 units. Rates vary based on desired views, dates, and availability. Meal, ski, family, and special occasion packages available. C$279 (US$261) and way up for standard room; C$429 (US$401) and way up for deluxe standard room; C$529 (US$495) and way up for junior suite with mountain view; C$629 (US$588) and way up for junior suite with lake view; C$529 (US$495) and up for Fairmont Gold Concierge floor. Suites C$679 (US$635) and way up. Children under 18 stay free in parent's room. AE, DC, DISC, MC, V. **Amenities:** 6 restaurants; 2 lounges; small indoor heated pool; spa; bike, ski, and canoe rentals; ski storage; activities desk; business center; shops; salon; 24-hr. room service. *In room:* TV, minibar, coffeemaker, hair dryer, iron.

Lake Louise Hostel and Canadian Alpine Centre *(Value* Perhaps the best hostel I've come across, this is a wonderful gathering place, not to mention the only reasonably priced lodging alternative in Lake Louise. Jointly owned by Hostelling International and the Alpine Club of Canada, it's great for people on a budget, or outdoor enthusiasts hoping to mingle with like-minded travelers. Guest rooms range from small dormitories with two bunk beds to larger

guest rooms that sleep up to six. Simple communal bathrooms and showers are down the hall.

203 Village Rd., P.O. Box 115, Lake Louise, AB T0L 1E0. ☎ **403/522-2201**. Fax 403/522-2253. www.hostellingintl.ca/alberta. 45 units, 164 beds total. C$34 (US$32) for Hostelling International members; C$38 (US$36) for nonmembers. Private rooms from C$99 (US$93) for members; C$106 (US$99) for nonmembers. Ski packages available. MC, V. **Amenities:** Restaurant; lounge; coin-op washers and dryers; wireless Internet; ski and luggage storage; library. *In room:* No phone.

Num-Ti-Jah Lodge ⟨ (Finds) This rustic and secluded lodge on the shores of **Bow Lake** sports the most scenic location of any lodging in Banff National Park. Built in 1937 by trapper and guide Jimmy Simpson, the building is pretty much as it was then, with every detail preserved. (Simpson, who left England and came to Canada at age 19, became a legendary, eccentric, and much-admired Banff pioneer.)

There's nothing overly fancy here, just simple comforts, an incredible view, and the pleasure of being a half-hour's drive from the next-closest lodge. The stairs creak as you climb them and the walls are thin; guest rooms are furnished in a modest style and the light flickers a bit when you switch it on. Bathrooms in all guest rooms are clean, though quite basic and small, with stand-up showers. All-inclusive packages take away any worrying about meals. The restaurant serves simple but hearty food at a reasonable price, and the setting is full of rustic mountain ambience. A world-class location for ski touring, Num-Ti-Jah is at its best in winter. Drawing an outdoor-loving crowd of people who aren't necessarily looking for luxury amenities, guests here prefer a lodge with heaps of character and history. Sometimes that just leaves you imagining the possibilities an upgrade could do, but to love Num-Ti-Jah is to love it as it is. It's one of the few secluded lodges in Banff National Park even though it's located right off the Icefields Parkway. For that benefit alone, it gets my vote.

P.O. Box 39, Lake Louise, AB T0L 1E0. 40km (25 miles) north of Lake Louise on the Icefields Pkwy. Hwy. 93. ☎ **403/522-2167**. Fax 403/522-2425. www.num-ti-jah.com. 25 units. June 15–Sept 15 C$200 (US$187) 2 singles with shared bathroom; C$230 (US$215) queen with mountain view; C$310 (US$290) double with lake view. Sept 16–Oct 7, Dec 1–20, and Jan 2–June 14 C$110 (US$103) 2 singles with shared bathroom; C$130 (US$122) queen with mountain view; C$160 (US$150) double with lake view. Dec 21–Jan 1 C$130 (US$122) 2 singles with shared bathroom; C$170 (US$159) queen with mountain view; C$205 (US$192) double with lake view. Extra person C$15 (US$14). Children 17 and under C$15 (US$14). AE, MC, V. Closed 2nd Mon in Oct (Canadian Thanksgiving) to Dec 1. **Amenities:** Restaurant; lounge; sauna; cross-country ski and snowshoe rentals; outdoor skating rink in winter; horseback riding tours. *In room:* No phone.

Post Hotel 🐾🐾   A quintessential mountain inn, the Post Hotel combines beautiful guest rooms and excellent service in a location imbued with a peaceful, relaxing atmosphere. Tucked quietly along the banks of the Pipestone River in the heart of the Lake Louise village, this hotel is the only real alternative to the Fairmont Chateau Lake Louise in terms of quality and class. Then again, it's really in a category of its own: an exquisite mountain inn. With one-fifth the number of rooms as the Chateau, it's more intimate, charming, and personal. A member of the prestigious Relais & Château organization of global fine inns, the Post Hotel is a subtle blend of Swiss and Canadian mountain styles. Built in the 1940s as a backcountry lodge, the hotel was bought in the 1970s by Swiss brothers George and Andre Schwartz, who renovated and expanded it in the 1980s. With its rustic pine and timber construction and dramatic red roof, it's elegant and modern at the same time. Guest rooms are simple but luxurious, with wood-burning fieldstone fireplaces, balconies, down quilts, and heated slate floors in the bathrooms. The Temple Mountain Spa is the best in Lake Louise, and the old owners' cabin has been renovated into a new cabin that accommodates a larger group. Tea is served every afternoon in the lobby. The European-influenced food and wine (including an astounding wine cellar with more than 2,000 labels) further exemplify the luxury, class, and creativity here. There's quite an adult feel to this hotel. Guests stay quiet, keep to themselves although there are many public spaces to enjoy, and generally behave themselves. For that reason, I'm not so sure it would be a great match for young children. Older kids will probably do just fine, however. There are two riverside log cabins that sleep a family of four.

200 Pipestone, P.O. Box 69, Lake Louise, AB T0L 1E0. ℂ **800/661-1586** or 403/522-3989. Fax 403/522-3966. www.posthotel.com. 92 units, 5 cabins. May 19–June 14 C$245 (US$229) and up double room. June 17–Aug 28 C$335 (US$313) and up double room. Aug 29–Sept 25 C$275 (US$257) and up double room. Sept 26–Oct 15 C$225 (US$210) and up double room. Nov 22–Dec 20, Jan 6–Feb 7, and Mar 30–May 15 C$275 (US$257) and up double room. Dec 21–Jan 5 and Feb 8–Mar 29 C$315 (US$295) and up double room. Riverside cabins C$295–C$1,400 (US$276–US$1,309). Children 18 and under stay free in parent's room. AE, MC, V. Closed for renovations every Oct–Nov. **Amenities:** Dining room; piano lounge; pub; heated indoor pool; exercise room; spa; Jacuzzi; steam room; limited room service; library; cigar room; outdoor skating rink in winter. *In room:* TV/VCR, hair dryer, iron, safe, coffeemaker.

2 Frontcountry Camping in Banff National Park

Whether it's hooking up the electricity and plumbing in your RV, opening up your tent-trailer, or just pitching your tent, the accessibility and ease of drive-in (frontcountry) campgrounds will make

Regular vs. Self-Registering Campgrounds

There are now three kinds of registration methods for frontcountry campgrounds in Banff and Jasper national parks.

In 2006, Parks Canada introduced a new reservation system that allows campers to reserve a site in advance via a website (www.pccamping.ca) or via telephone (© 877/737-3783). There is a C$11 (US$10) fee to make a reservation, but it can provide peace of mind after a long day's drive or hike. You cannot select a specific site within a campground. In Banff National Park, the campgrounds for which you can make an online site reservation are Tunnel Mountain and Lake Louise Trailer.

The second method is the regular registration method, which applies to campsites that are set aside for first-come, first-served campers who prefer not to reserve ahead of time. You register with a Parks Canada attendant at the campground when you first arrive (there's usually a building staffed 24 hr. a day).

The third method is to self-register, and it applies to many of the more remote campgrounds in both parks. Unlike the more accessible campgrounds, there's no building at the entrance to these campgrounds. It's sort of a "self-serve" approach. You simply drive in to the campground and find an empty campsite. There's a small kiosk near the entrance, which will take your money (it doesn't accept credit or debit cards, and it doesn't give change). Put your money in one of the envelopes provided and drop it in the slot, remembering to tear off the end of the envelope and mark the date that you're staying until on it. Take it back to your campsite and fasten it to the sign with your site's number on it. A Parks Canada staff member making daily rounds will pick it up first thing in the morning.

you a happy camper. There is a wide variety of campgrounds in Banff National Park, and you can now reserve a spot online at www.pccamping.ca or via telephone at © 877/737-3783. There are very few last-minute spots available; you must plan ahead, especially if you want to be near the Town of Banff. Refer to the table later in this section for a quick comparison of Banff campgrounds and the amenities they offer.

A note on campground rates: Rates quoted are per site, and are applicable for single occupancy up to six people. Therefore, a family of four will pay the same rate as a couple or a person traveling alone. If you're in an RV, I suggest you stick to the campgrounds that have hookup facilities, although RVs are welcome to park for the night at many of the outlying campgrounds that do not have hookups. Prices will continue to rise annually to meet Banff National Park plans to upgrade most facilities, including washrooms, showers, and general campground maintenance.

BANFF TOWNSITE AREA

Castle Mountain Campground This is a small, remote campground located on the Bow Valley Parkway (Hwy. 1A). It's quite rustic, with very few amenities at the campground itself, but the shop at **Castle Mountain Village** is just a short walk away. It's also very scenic, and a good base for exploring the trails below the fabled walls of Castle Mountain. A good family campground.

34km (19 miles) west of Banff Townsite on the Bow Valley Pkwy. Hwy. 1A. 43 sites. No RV hookups. C$21 (US$20). Open May 18–Sept 4.

Johnston Canyon Campground This is a tranquil campground nestled in a pleasant forest less than 20 minutes from Banff Townsite. The nicest of the sites back onto **Johnston Creek.**

25km (16 miles) west of Banff Townsite on the Bow Valley Pkwy. Hwy. 1A. 132 sites. No RV hookups. C$26 (US$24). Open June 1–Sept 18.

Tunnel Mountain Village Campground This is Banff's biggest campground, and it's also the closest one to the townsite, within walking distance of Banff Avenue. It's scenically located on the ridge of Tunnel Mountain and is quite spacious for a campground, with more than 1,000 sites. It's divided into three sections: a mixed tent and RV camp 2.5km (1½ miles) east of town; an RV mecca 4km (2½ miles) east of town; and a trailer- and tenter-friendly section to the east of the RV area. RVers will love this place; tenters wanting to walk to Banff Avenue will like it, too. But anyone looking for the peace and quiet of the mountains should head elsewhere.

4km (2½ miles) east of Banff Townsite on Tunnel Mountain Rd. Tunnel Mountain Village I: 618 sites. No RV hookups. C$26 (US$24). Open May 4–Oct 1. Tunnel Mountain Village II: 188 sites. Electrical hookups only. C$30 (US$28). Open year-round. Tunnel Mountain Trailer Court: 321 sites. Full hookups. C$34 (US$32). Open May 4–Oct 1.

Banff National Park Frontcountry Campgrounds

Campground	Total Sites	RV Hookups	Dump Station	Flush Toilets	Drinking Water	Showers	Firepits/ Grills	Laundry	Public Phones	Self-Register	Fees	Open
Banff Townsite Area												
Castle Mountain Campground	43	No	No	Yes	Yes	No	Yes	No	No	No	C$21 (US$20)	May 18–Sept 4
Johnston Canyon Campground	132	No	Yes	Yes	Yes	Yes	Yes	No	No	Yes	C$26 (US$24)	June 1–Sept 18
Tunnel Mountain Village I	618	No	Yes	Yes	Yes	Yes	Yes	No	Yes	No	C$26 (US$24)	May 4–Oct 1
Tunnel Mountain Village II	188	189 (electrical hookups only)	Yes	Yes	Yes	Yes	Yes	No	Yes	No	C$30 (US$28)	Year-round
Tunnel Mountain Trailer Court	321	322	Yes	Yes	Yes	Yes	Yes	No	Yes	No	C$36 (US$34)	May 4–Oct 1
Two Jack Main Campground	380	No (but RV-friendly)	Yes	Yes	Yes	No	Yes	No	No	No	C$21 (US$20)	May 18–Sept 18
Two Jack Lakeside Campground	74	No	No	Yes	Yes	Yes	Yes	No	No	No	C$26 (US$24)	May 18–Sept 18
Lake Louise Area												
Lake Louise Trailer Campground	189 (30 in winter)	189 (electrical hookups only) (30 in winter)	Yes	Yes	Yes	Yes	Yes	No	Yes	No	C$30 (US$28)	Year-round
Lake Louise Tent Campground	210	No	Yes	Yes	Yes	Yes	Yes	No	No	No	C$26 (US$24)	May 11–Oct 1
Protection Mountain Campground	89	No	No	Yes	Yes	No	Yes	No	No	Yes	C$21 (US$20)	June 22–Sept 3
North of Lake Louise												
Mosquito Creek Campground	32	No	No	No	Yes	No	Yes	No	No	No	C$15 (US$14)	Year-round
Waterfowl Lakes Campground	116	No	Yes	Yes	Yes	No	Yes	No	No	No	C$21 (US$20)	June 15–Sept 9

Two Jack Campground   The main area here is just off the road in a densely wooded forest 13km (8 miles) northeast of Banff Townsite, on the Minnewanka Loop. It's quite private, although there are no great views. The small lakeshore area at **Lakeside** is very popular and is the most scenic and peaceful campground near the Town of Banff.

12km (8 miles) from Banff Townsite on Minnewanka Loop Rd. Two Jack Main: 380 sites. RV-friendly but no RV hookups. C$21 (US$20). Open May 18–Sept 4. Two Jack Lakeside: 74 sites. No RV hookups. C$26 (US$24). Open May 18–Sept 18.

LAKE LOUISE AREA

Lake Louise Campground   This campground is not actually on the shore of Lake Louise. It's downhill from the Fairmont Chateau Lake Louise, away from the lake. The tent and the trailer areas are separated. The tent area is in the trees near the river. The trailer area is more open and closer to the highway and railway line. It's a 10-minute walk to Lake Louise village. Less hectic and congested than the Tunnel Mountain campgrounds near the Town of Banff, this is a great campground for relaxing.

58km (36 miles) northwest of Banff Townsite on the Trans-Canada Hwy. 1. Exit at Lake Louise and turn left after passing under the railway bridge onto Fairview Rd. Lake Louise Tent: 210 sites. No RV hookups. C$26 (US$24). Open May 11–Oct. 1. Lake Louise Trailer: 189 sites. Electrical hookups only. C$30 (US$28). Open year-round.

Protection Mountain Campground   This scenic campground is nicely situated between Banff and Lake Louise, making it an excellent base for exploring all corners of Banff National Park. It's rustic with few amenities, though. A good choice for tenters and trailers but not ideal if you're traveling by RV.

48km (25 miles) west of Banff Townsite on the Bow Valley Pkwy. Hwy. 1A. 10km (6 miles) west of Castle Junction. 89 sites. No RV hookups. C$21 (US$20). Open June 22–Sept 3.

NORTH OF LAKE LOUISE

Mosquito Creek Campground   Twenty-four kilometers (15 miles) north of Lake Louise on the Icefields Parkway, this campground has two distinct areas: one a gravelly field, the other a wooded space. Stick to the field if you can. With no showers, sinks, or flush toilets, prepare to rough it out here.

24km (15 miles) north of Lake Louise on the Icefields Pkwy. Hwy. 93. 32 sites. No RV hookups. C$15 (US$14). Open year-round.

Waterfowl Lake Campground *(Finds)*   This lovely campground, 58km (36 miles) north of Lake Louise, is right by a stream and the large Waterfowl Lake. It's my favorite in the park because of the scenery and peacefulness. There is an open area on the lakeshore for relaxing or playing games, plus amazing views of the surrounding mountains and glaciers. This is a wonderful spot to do some canoeing and exploring.

57km (36 miles) north of Lake Louise on the Icefields Pkwy. Hwy. 93. 116 sites. No RV hookups. C$21 (US$20). Open June 15–Sept 9.

3 Backcountry Camping & Lodging in Banff National Park

Spending a night in Banff's backcountry makes for a particularly special experience. For those with a keen interest in roughing it, choose a backcountry hike from "Exploring the Backcountry" in chapter 4, and refer to the information below on booking a campsite. There are also a handful of backcountry lodges and rustic backcountry hostels to choose from.

BACKCOUNTRY CAMPING

Backcountry camping in Banff National Park is permitted in designated campsites. You must reserve your campsite before you hit the trail. Of the 53 designated backcountry campsites, some are only an hour or two from a trail head, while others are as much as a full day's hike (20km/12.4 miles) into the wilderness. You can access a handful of backcountry campsites from the Town of Banff via the **Spray Valley Trail.** If you drive half an hour from town, you can access other backcountry sites, like Egypt Lake, Shadow Lake, and Fish Lakes. For others, it's a 2-hour drive northwest of the townsite along the **Icefields Parkway** (Hwy. 93). There are even campsites along the shores of **Lake Minnewanka,** northeast of the townsite, which are accessible only by canoe. Some campsites are legendary among hikers all over the world and get booked up as soon as Banff National Park turns on its **backcountry reservation line** on May 1 (© **403/762-1550**). A backcountry campsite costs C$10 (US$9.35) per person per night and there is a C$12 (US$11) reservation fee. You can not reserve backcountry sites online.

BACKCOUNTRY HOSTELS

Hostelling International (HI) runs a small group of backcountry hostels in Banff National Park. All are highway accessible. Although quite rustic, each of them is a special place full of visitors relishing their time in the mountains. They're a good choice for larger groups or if you're looking for hiking and backpacking companions. Hostels are also a great place for learning, since fellow guests are often very keen on sharing their knowledge about the mountains and leaving the hustle and bustle of the Town of Banff behind them. Reservations are recommended, particularly in the summer months. Each has a shared kitchen and most have only outdoor plumbing (that means no showers or bathtubs!). You can make a reservation (recommended) by calling Hostelling International, at © **403/670-7580,** or by logging on to www.hihostels.ca/alberta. None of the hostels listed below have direct phones.

Open year-round, the **Castle Mountain Shelter,** on the Bow Valley Parkway (Hwy. 1A) 1.5km (1 mile) east of the Trans-Canada Highway (Hwy. 1) and Highway 93 junction, is in a scenic area with several hiking and cross-country ski trails nearby. It's also well situated for downhill skiing, since it's within 20 minutes of all three area ski resorts: Mount Norquay, Sunshine Village, and Lake Louise. Rates are C$23 (US$22) per person per night for Hostelling International members, C$27 (US$25) per person per night for nonmembers. Just 26km (16 miles) north of Lake Louise on the Icefields Parkway 93 is the **Mosquito Creek Hostel,** also run by Hostelling International. This one is a group of peaceful, rustic cabins; a sauna and fireplace are on hand to keep you toasty warm in winter. Rates are C$23 (US$22) per person per night for HI members, C$27 (US$25) per person per night for nonmembers. There are private rooms available.

There is one more Hostelling International hostel in the northern reaches of Banff National Park. The **Rampart Creek Hostel,** 95km (59 miles) north of Lake Louise, also on the Icefields Parkway 93, is popular with rock and ice climbers. Many cyclists heading from Lake Louise to Jasper also stop here for the night. Rates are C$23 (US$22) per person per night for HI members and C$27 (US$25) per person per night for nonmembers.

BACKCOUNTRY HUTS

It's a distinct challenge to get to one of the eight **Alpine Club of Canada (ACC) huts** in Banff National Park, but that's surely part of the appeal. When you do make it, you are deeply rewarded and will enjoy a wonderful, peaceful overnight high in the mountains. Strategically located in some of the most spectacular mountain settings, the huts are often used by hikers on long traverses, by mountaineers as a base for a summit push, or by ACC members on a course. Almost all are a good full-day hike or ski into the backcountry. **Bow Hut,** the easiest one to access, is 6 hours from the trail head at Bow Lake, on the Icefields Parkway. Some of the "huts" are cabins, others look more like shacks. Most have no electricity or running water, so it's best to prepare for a stay at one of them in much the same way you would prepare for a camping trip. If you aren't a member of the ACC, rates range from C$18 to C$32 (US$17–US$30) per person per night. Rates for members are substantially lower. For more information on backcountry huts, or on an ACC membership, contact the **Alpine Club of Canada** at ✆ **403/678-3200** or at www.alpine clubofcanada.ca.

BACKCOUNTRY LODGES

There are three privately run backcountry lodges in Banff National Park. All are rustic but remarkably pricey considering the amenities they offer. Most don't have electricity, telephones, or running water. But the atmosphere is rejuvenating and the peace is, well, unparalleled. **Brewster's Shadow Lake Lodge** (✆ **866/762-0114;** www. shadowlakelodge.com), on the shore of Shadow Lake in the **Egypt Lakes area,** is open during the summer for hikers and mountain bikers and in winter for cross-country skiers. Its log cabins are heated, its beds cozy with feather down comforters. There are new heated washrooms with running water, showers, and solar-powered lighting—this is backcountry luxury! Built in 1928, it's a true retreat, great for groups of friends or for romantic getaways. Rates are C$185 (US$173) per person per night based on double occupancy, C$200 (US$187) per person per night single occupancy, and C$155 (US$145) per extra person in each cabin, with reduced rates for additional nights. Children's rates available (but not published). Meals are included. There is a 2-night minimum stay.

Built nearly a century ago as one of Canada's first ski resorts, **Skoki Lodge** (✆ **800/258-7669;** www.skokilodge.com) now welcomes only cross-country skiers and hikers. Located in a gorgeous valley behind the **Lake Louise ski area,** it's an 11km (6.8-mile) hike in to reach the rustic lodge, with awesome landscape and colorful wildflowers filling up the view. Amenities include a glorious wood-fired sauna and gourmet meals served buffet-style. Candles and kerosene lamps light up the lodge at night, making for· an eerily beautiful scene. Rooms range from private cabins to lodge rooms. Rates start at C$159 (US$149) per person. There is a 2-night minimum stay.

Open in summer for horseback tours and in winter for cross-country skiers, **Sundance Lodge** (✆ **800/661-8352;** www.xcski sundance.com) is a heritage building deep in the woods, but only a

16km (10-mile) ski from the Town of Banff. It's a great choice for families looking for a true wilderness experience, albeit one with hot showers and fresh-cooked meals. Rates are C$150 (US$140) per person for the first night, with lower rates for additional nights (there are no special children's' rates, but children are welcome). During summer, the lodge operates with **Holiday on Horseback** (✆ 800/661-8352; www.horseback.com), offering multiday expeditions leaving Banff regularly. A 2-day pack trip to the lodge costs C$434 (US$406) during May, June, September, and October; C$491 (US$459) during July and August.

4 Where to Eat in Banff National Park

There are some outstanding restaurants in Banff, many of which are also very expensive. Don't be afraid to branch out of your hotel to roam the streets of town looking for what you want. You'll love the fresh, creative, and well-prepared food, but it will take up a large chunk of your budget. To avoid spending a fortune on food, try keeping your lunches light—pick up sandwich fixings at the grocery store and have a picnic. Also, note that all restaurants in Banff National Park are now smoke-free.

IN BANFF TOWNSITE

Athena's (Kids) PIZZA   Affordable and fun, Athena's has the best pizza in Banff and is a family favorite. It's a very simple setting, with rose-colored plastic tablecloths, bright lights, and mountain landscapes on the wall. There are 16 different options for pizzas, including vegetarian and the loaded house special, with pepperoni, bacon, olives, and shrimp. Other options include classic spaghetti and fish and chips. Kid-size portions are available. Located upstairs in the Swiss-styled Clock Tower Mall on Banff Avenue, they also offer free (and fast) delivery.

110 Banff Ave. ✆ 403/762-4022. Main courses C$8–C$19 (US$7.50–US$18). MC, V. Sun–Thurs noon–11pm; Fri–Sat noon–midnight.

The Bison Mountain Bistro ✦ CANADIAN   The menu at this impressive and thoughtful new restaurant proclaims itself "Rocky Mountain comfort food." The food and the atmosphere are elegantly rustic and perfectly suited for Banff. Vaulted fir ceilings and enormous windows play off the mountain views. The chef has designed a menu that is regional and seasonal, with staples like braised lamb shank, seared scallops, grilled bison rib steak, or daily game—each paired with fresh and creative vegetables, accents, and garnishes. Everything except the pickles and mayonnaise is made from scratch. For dessert, try the lavender s'more or the white chocolate and coconut-lemon tart. The weekend brunch is worth driving in from Calgary for, and the outdoor patio is the nicest in town. Downstairs is a deli and sandwich shop.

Bison Courtyard, 211 Bear St. *C* 403/762-5550. Reservations recommended on weekends. Main courses C$15–C$35. AE, MC, V. Mon–Fri 11am–11pm; Sat 10am–11pm; Sun 10am–10pm.

Bow Valley Grill CANADIAN   With fine and fresh seasonal cuisine and views of the Fairholme Mountain Range from inside the swanky Fairmont Banff Springs Hotel, this isn't so much an over-the-top splurge as it is a memorable dining experience. The open-concept design keeps this restaurant from feeling too formal—you can keep an eye on the chefs at the grill. Specializing in rotisserie-grilled meats, in the summer it hasabulous market-style dinner buffets and in the winter an ambitious a la carte menu. During summer the restaurant offers tours of the hotel to diners who indulge in a huge lunch buffet. Fish lovers will enjoy the Bow River trout, pan-fried with lemon, herb butter, and new potatoes. The Alberta AAA prime rib is slowly roasted in its natural juices and served with a trusty baked potato. The progressive wine menu is presented in an easy-to-select fashion, well categorized and with full descriptions. Saturday and Sunday brunch buffets let you sample a little of everything.

In the Fairmont Banff Springs Hotel. 405 Spray Ave. *C* 403/762-6860. Reservations recommended June–Aug daily and on weekends during the rest of the year. Breakfast buffet C$27 (US$25); main courses C$24–C$39 (US$22–US$36). AE, DC, DISC, MC, V. Daily breakfast 6:30–11:30am; lunch 11:30am–2pm; dinner 6–9pm.

Cilantro Mountain Café CALIFORNIAN   This cozy cafe is excellent for casual summer dining. The California-style cuisine includes salads, pasta, chicken, and seafood. Pizzas from the applewood-fired oven are the best item on the menu, with deep crusts and creative ingredients. The rustic decor includes peeled logs and wood paneling. The patio is a lovely place on a warm afternoon.

In the Buffalo Mountain Lodge. 700 Tunnel Mountain Rd. *C* 403/760-4488. Reservations recommended on weekends. Main courses C$14–C$28 (US$13–US$26). AE, MC, V. June 7–Sept 9 daily 5–10pm; Dec 19–June 5 Wed–Sun 5–10pm. Closed Sept 10–Dec 13.

Coyotes Grill SOUTHWESTERN   A local favorite, a reservation may come in handy since this place is almost always busy. With a fresh, healthy menu, it's a happening place where Santa Fe meets the Canadian Rockies. The atmosphere is fun and relaxed, made

---

Tips **Wanted: A Cheap Lunch and a Coffee Break**

Even in pricey Banff, a filling yet reasonably priced lunch can be had. Try the **Cascade Mall Food Court** (downstairs at 317 Banff Ave.). You'll find a dozen different counters serving everything from sushi and pizza to curries. You can buy lunch for under five dollars!

Banff has no shortage of coffeehouses. Head to **Evelyn's Coffee House** ✪ (201 Banff Ave.; ✆ **403-762-0332**) for the best java in town. If it's crowded, sneak around to **Evelyn's Too** (229 Bear St.; ✆ **403/762-0330**). **Jump Start** (206 Buffalo St.; ✆ **403/762-0332**), near the post office, is great for lattes, sundaes, and filling lunches. Banff's newest java joint is also an artisan bakery. **Wild Flour Bakery** (211 Bear St.; ✆ **403/ 760-5074**) is in the new Bison Courtyard.

---

more so by the open kitchen. Expect lots of corn and chile peppers on the menu. The breakfast menu, with French toast stuffed with cream cheese and fresh fruit and topped with maple syrup, may be the best in town. For lunch, the sweet potato and corn chowder is a good choice, as is the blue-corn-crusted chicken. Corn-crusted pizza is a specialty: The barbecue chicken pizza is delicious. New World wines are featured. Servers know their menu well and are comfortable making recommendations to suit your tastes.

206 Caribou St. (west of Banff Ave.). ✆ 403/762-3963. Reservations recommended June–Aug daily and on weekends during the rest of the year. Breakfast C$7–C$12 (US$6.50–US$11); lunch items C$8–C$15 (US$7.50–US$14); main dinner courses C$16–C$28 (US$15–US$26). AE, MC, V. Daily 7:30am–11pm.

Maple Leaf Grille and Lounge ✪ CANADIAN This stylish restaurant has a charm reminiscent of Canada's early days. You are greeted by a giant birchbark canoe mounted over the expansive staircase leading to the second-floor dining area. The food is fresh and regional, tying together tastes from coast to coast in a smart and sophisticated way. There's a hefty selection of starters, including PEI mussels and a wild game platter. For dinner, Canadian classics include Rocky Mountain Rainbow trout, elk, venison, and lake duck. Try the grilled Atlantic salmon with a wasabi ginger glaze. There's a stunning bison tenderloin, wrapped in bacon and blue cheese. The wine and dessert menus are also noteworthy. Although casual in atmosphere, the food is decidedly upscale. It's relaxing and yet indulgent, a great place to sample Canada's best.

137 Banff Ave. © **403/760-7680.** Reservations recommended June–Aug daily and on weekends during the rest of the year. Main courses C$21–C$42 (US$20–US$39). AE, DISC, MC, V. Daily 10am–2am.

Melissa's Restaurant and Bar *Kids* STEAKHOUSE   Melissa's has been in business since 1928, making it a true local landmark and a great choice for all ages. The food is simple and fresh. Of course, the highlights of the menu are the steaks, including T-bone, rib-eye, filets, strips, ham steak, and AAA sirloins. You choose the cut and the sauce (from a selection of peppercorn, mushroom, hollandaise, or béarnaise). Your steak is accompanied by a salad and fries, baked potatoes, or rice and served with a slice of Melissa's own multigrain bread and the vegetable of the day. There's also Melissa's Canadian mountain stew to warm you up on a chilly day, deep dish pizzas, and handmade gourmet burgers, not to mention one of the best breakfast menus in town. There's a kids' menu and a heated patio. Bring your appetite.

218 Lynx St. Across from the Banff Park Lodge. © **403/762-5511.** Breakfast C$6–C$9 (US$5.60–US$8.40); main courses C$9–C$26 (US$8.40–US$24). DC, MC, V. Daily 7am–10pm.

Saltlik STEAKHOUSE   The steakhouse concept isn't new to Banff, but the Saltlik is different: Choose a cut of AAA Black Angus then add a marinade like chipotle barbecue or citrus rosemary. The steak—fast-cooked in a 1,200°F (650°C) infrared oven—is truly delicious. Other options, like the flame rotisserie chicken and pan-seared halibut, are also excellent. I've heard the calamari described as "spectacular." With a boast-worthy wine cellar and a swanky atmosphere, this is perhaps Banff's most chic and urban spot. Downstairs, a lounge features live jazz and a huge fireplace.

221 Bear St. © **403/762-2467.** Reservations accepted for groups of 8 or more. Main courses C$17–C$36 (US$16–US$34). AE, MC, V. Daily noon–1am.

Sukiyaki House JAPANESE   Of the handful of sushi restaurants in Banff, this is the best: a fun, traditional Japanese atmosphere that can accommodate larger groups. The sushi is fresh and well-prepared, the atmosphere is relaxing and tasteful, and the prices are reasonable, given the attentive and professional service. The Love Boat—a wooden board filled with a wide variety of sushi, including sashimi and maki, plus vegetable tempura—easily feeds two hungry hikers. It comes with miso soup and rice. If you're not too keen on raw fish, the salmon teriyaki is a nice option.

For the Sweet Tooth

Banff has some excellent chocolate and candy shops. For some of the best truffles in Canada, made using a four-generations-old Belgian technique, visit **Chocolaterie Bernard Callebaut** (111 Banff Ave.; ✆ **403/762-4106**). **The Fudgery** (215 Banff Ave.; ✆ **403/762-3003**) makes candy while you watch and often has a bowl by the cashier with free samples.

---

211 Banff Ave. 2nd floor Park Ave. Mall. ✆ **403/762-2002**. Reservations recommended for parties of 5 or more and on weekends. Main courses C$8–C$26 (US$7.50–US$24). AE, MC, V. Daily noon–10pm.

Typhoon ASIAN   Like a tropical island amid a sea of ranches, Typhoon is what every other place in Banff isn't—creative, vibrant, and multi-ethnic. The menu is Pan-Asian, with everything from curry to sushi, and features lots of cilantro, peanuts, ginger, curry, coconut, and chile. For lunch, try the dreamy Naanwich. For dinner, the daily curries are outstanding. Drop by in the evening for a martini, a selection from the varied appetizer menu, and the funky atmosphere. For some privacy, reserve the secluded room in the back corner.

211 Caribou St. ✆ **403/762-2000**. Reservations recommended for parties of 5 or more and on weekends. Entrees C$16–C$24 (US$15–US$22). AE, MC, V. Daily 11:30am–11pm.

Wild Flour Bakery CAFE/BAKERY   Lovers of artisan breads and sweets linger at this friendly new cafe on Bear Street. Baked goods are natural, organic, and back-to-basics. They have great éclairs, granola bars, brioche cinnamon buns, and walnut rye brownies. The blueberry scones are local faves. Organic Kicking Horse coffee comes as espresso, lattes, or americanos. For lunch or a heartier snack, try the prosciutto and provolone grilled panini or the daily soup (on Sat it's curried pumpkin and carrot).

Bison Courtyard, 101–211 Bear St. ✆ **403/760-5074**. Lunches C$4–C$9 (US$3.70–US$8.40). MC, V. Daily 7am–7pm.

IN LAKE LOUISE

Bill Peyto's Café ★ *Value* *Kids* CAFE   Located inside the Lake Louise Hostel and Alpine Centre, the food here is healthy, creative, and very reasonably priced for most budgets. The timber-framed room with stone fireplace makes for a relaxed, friendly atmosphere. Service is fast. Try the bison burgers, the chicken pesto burger, or the macaroni and cheese. There's also a kids' menu.

In the Lake Louise Hostel and Alpine Centre. 203 Village Rd. ℭ 403/522-2200. Breakfast C$4–C$9 (US$3.70–US$8.40); lunch and dinner main courses C$9–C$15 (US$8.40–US$14). MC, V. Daily 7am–9pm.

Laggan's Mountain Bakery and Deli DELI/BAKERY   A mainstay in Lake Louise for nearly a century, this is the spot to stop for takeout coffee or to load up on sandwiches and treats before hitting the hiking trail. It's a deli, so you order over-the-counter and then take a seat if you want to stay, or take your order to go. The quiches and the tofu vegetarian rolls are affordable and delicious. Sandwiches are made on Laggan's homemade breads (try the seed bread; it's delicious). There's often a lineup out the door here, but you can beat the crowds if you enter via the alternate door on the left side and skip to the often-missed second cashier.

101 Lake Louise Dr. In Samson Mall. ℭ 403/522-2017. Breakfast, lunch, and dinner items C$4–C$7 (US$3.70–US$6.50). No credit cards. Summer daily 6am–8pm; winter daily 6am–6pm.

The Station Restaurant at Lake Louise CONTEMPORARY CANADIAN   Built in 1909, The Station is the oldest building in Lake Louise. No longer a functioning railway station, today the restaurant has glowing fires and fine food to draw visitors in. The menu was revamped in 2007, with a new focus on fresh ingredients and inspired combinations of retro classics with modern twists. Start with a healthy watermelon salad with feta and blood orange olive oil. The lunch menu includes organic bison burgers and haddock 'n'chips. For dinner, there is grilled pork in Okanagan cider, or AAA Alberta beef tenderloin with caramelized shallot confit. In the summer, the vintage railway cars are often open for dining, and barbecues are held in The Station garden. If you're driving out to Lake Louise from Banff Townsite, consider stopping here for lunch. Although memories of its past evoke a time of formal elegance, The Station today is casual and intimate, well-matched to its surroundings.

200 Sentinel Rd. 1st right past Samson Mall off the Trans-Canada Hwy. 1. ℭ 403/522-2600. Reservations recommended June–Aug daily and on weekends during the rest of the year. Lunch items C$7–C$15 (US$6.50–US$14); main dinner courses C$17–C$37 (US$16–US$35). AE, MC, V. Winter 5–9pm daily; summer 11:30am–9:30pm daily. Closed 6 weeks before Christmas.

Walliser Stube ⚘ FONDUE   Come and dine at the Fairmont Chateau Lake Louise and you'll discover that Swiss food doesn't merely consist of potatoes, cheese, and cream. This restaurant features lighter versions of traditional Alpine dishes. The fondues include bourguignon (beef in canola oil), Swiss cheese (baguette in a mix of Emmental Gruyère cheese, white wine, and kirsch liquor), and Bacchus (veal medallions in a white-wine broth). The service is impeccable, and the atmosphere, with the views of Lake Louise out the window, very indulgent and romantic. A true treat.

In the Fairmont Chateau Lake Louise. 111 Lake Louise Dr. ✆ 403/522-1817. Reservations recommended June–Aug daily and on weekends during the rest of the year. Main courses C$27–C$44 (US$25–US$41). AE, DC, DISC, MC, V. Daily 6–9pm.

5 Banff After Dark

Banff's nightlife is as legendary as its mineral springs or cowboy pioneers. Most hotels have lounges and bars where skiers gather in winter for the famous "après-ski" experience—which consists of sharing stories about your adventures on the snowy slopes and showing off your goggle tan! Try to schedule at least 1 night to peruse the local bar scene. For a town the size of Banff, it's hip and diverse. There is regular live music and a variety of beers and spirits on tap. Banff at night is a great place for people-watching, too.

Wild Bill's Legendary Saloon (201 Banff Ave., upstairs; ✆ **403/762-0333**) is the local cowboy hangout. What can I say? Head here if you want to drink beer and do some line dancing. Besides virtual golf and pool, **The Banff Rose and Crown** (202 Banff Ave., upstairs; ✆ **403/762-2121**) has a spacious rooftop patio and a long list of beers on tap. There is often live music. The locals you meet at **Tommy's Neighbourhood Pub** ✦ (120 Banff Ave.; ✆ **403/762-8888**) are happy to share stories of what it's like to live in such a storied town. This is a friendly place where you can actually have a conversation without yelling. **Saint James's Gate** ✦ (205 Wolf St.; ✆ **403/762-9355**) will take you away to the Emerald Isle and make selecting a draft just about the toughest challenge in Banff—there are 33 beers on tap, as well as 50 single-malt scotches and 10 Irish whiskeys. Live music is almost always Celtic, and a blast! For later-night dancing, head to the funky techno atmosphere of the **Aurora Nightclub** (110 Banff Ave., downstairs; ✆ **403/760-5300**) around midnight. There's a cigar room and a martini bar. Or join the young crowd in the basement at **Hoodoo Lounge** (137 Banff Ave.; ✆ **403/760-8636**) for top-20 dance tunes.

6

Exploring Jasper National Park

Jasper National Park, the largest of the national parks in the Canadian Rockies, encompasses an area north of Banff National Park that measures 10,878 sq. km (4,200 sq. miles). The park has several unique lodging options and a wide variety of natural attractions. Less crowded and touristy than Banff, the Town of Jasper, in the center of the park, has a feel quite unique to its counterpart to the south. This is a deliberate move on the part of park management, as well as property- and store-owners in Jasper. They like differentiating their park from Banff in this way—and they intend to keep it like that.

Many people visit Jasper in conjunction with a stop in Banff. If you've already visited Banff, you'll find Jasper much more low-key, down-to-earth, and tranquil. There is a distinct lack of swanky shops and techno-pumping nightclubs (okay, there *is* one nightclub). In Jasper, many more people take to the woods.

Visitors come to Jasper to see wildlife, forests, and mountain lakes. There are more than 1,200km (740 miles) of hiking and walking trails—including some short but sweet trails around the Town of Jasper itself. For close to 10 years Jasper residents, the Town of Jasper, and Parks Canada have been teaming up to increase signage on these trails in an effort to encourage people to get out of their cars and visit the wilderness, if only for an hour or two. The park trails are very well marked as a result. Refer to "Day Hikes" and "Exploring the Backcountry" in chapter 7 for more on individual hiking trails in the park.

Jasper National Park was designated a park reserve by the Canadian government in 1907. But its earliest days, and its namesake, date back more than a century before. Fur traders first explored the Jasper park area in the early 1800s. Trappers harvested furs from beavers, wolves, bears, and other animals. Fur traders built an outpost along a route through the mountains to the Athabasca Pass, the

Jasper National Park

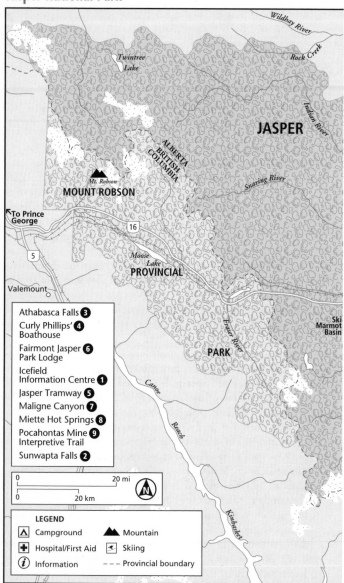

Wildhay River

Rock Creek

Twintree Lake

JASPER

Indian River

ALBERTA
BRITISH COLUMBIA

Mt. Robson

MOUNT ROBSON

Snaring River

To Prince George

16

5

Moose Lake

PROVINCIAL

Valemount

Fraser River

Ski Marmot Basin

PARK

Canoe

Reach

Kinbasket

Athabasca Falls ❸
Curly Phillips' ❹
Boathouse
Fairmont Jasper ❻
Park Lodge
Icefield
Information Centre ❶
Jasper Tramway ❺
Maligne Canyon ❼
Miette Hot Springs ❽
Pocahontas Mine ❾
Interpretive Trail
Sunwapta Falls ❷

0		20 mi
0	20 km	

LEGEND

◭ Campground   ▲ Mountain

✚ Hospital/First Aid   ⛷ Skiing

ⓘ Information   --- Provincial boundary

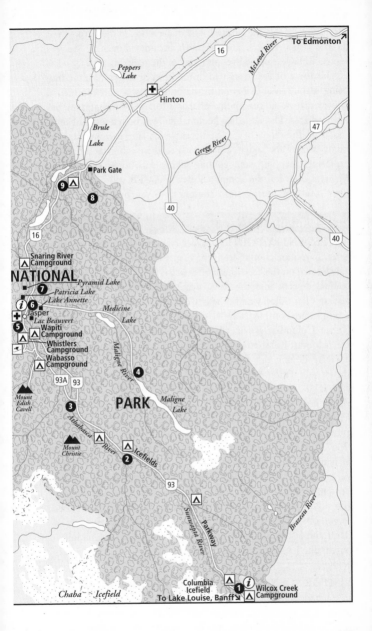

shortest route over the Rockies. The trader who ran the outpost was named Jasper Hawes, and the post became known as "Jasper's House." Hawes's name lives on today in the park's name.

The Town of Jasper, located in the heart of the park, came into being mainly in anticipation of the building of a transcontinental railway that would run up the Athabasca Valley and through the Yellowhead Pass. The Canadian National Railway built a series of small cabins on the shores of Lac Beauvert, which later became the Fairmont Jasper Park Lodge. Outfitters used these cabins as a base for exploring, mapping, and guiding hiking and horseback tours to Maligne Lake and the Tonquin Valley. The CPR still runs through town, shuttling tourists from Edmonton to Vancouver daily.

1 Essentials

ACCESS/ENTRY POINTS Jasper National Park has three park gates. If you are coming from the east, you'll enter the park at the gate located on the Yellowhead Highway (Hwy. 16). There is a long, gradual descent into the Athabasca Valley toward the park gate, 325km (202 miles) west of the city of Edmonton. The western gate is also located on Highway 16, a few kilometers from the Alberta–British Columbia provincial border, where Jasper National Park meets Mount Robson Provincial Park. You'll come through this gate if you're driving east from British Columbia. Prince George, the closest population center, is 382km (237 miles) northwest of the gate. If you are approaching from the south, you can access the park via the Icefields Parkway (Hwy. 93), which connects Banff and Jasper national parks. This third "gate," however, is not an official park entrance. If you're coming north from Banff in the summer months (May–Oct), you are required to stop at another gate, one leading out of Banff, just north of Lake Louise, and show your park permit to Parks Canada staff. (You need one to drive the Icefields Pkwy.) You can purchase one at the gate. In the off season (mid-Oct to May) you still need a permit to drive the parkway but the kiosk is closed, so you can just drive on through. See the map "Highway Access to Banff and Jasper National Parks" in chapter 2. For information on purchasing park permits, see the section "Entrance/Camping Fees" below.

VISITOR CENTERS & INFORMATION The recently redesigned **Jasper National Park Information Centre** (500 Connaught Dr., Jasper, AB T0E 1E0; © **780/852-6176**) is a good first stop to get your park bearings. Here, you can also get information

Numbers, Please

Size of Jasper National Park: 10,878 sq. km (4,200 sq. miles)
Established: 1907
Highest elevation: Mount Columbia 3,747m (12,290 ft.)
Naturally occurring species of mammals: 69
Roads: 396km (245 miles)
Hiking trails: More than 1,200km (740 miles)
Campsites: 1,772
Park employees: 380 in summer, 185 in winter
Visitors: 1.6 to 2 million per year
Jasper Townsite year-round population: 5,000
Elevation of Townsite: 1,067m (3,500 ft.)

from the Friends of Jasper, Parks Canada, and Jasper Tourism and Commerce, all of which have booths at the information center. **Jasper Tourism and Commerce** can tell you about hotel, restaurant, and outfitting options in the park (© **780/852-3858**).

Parks Canada staff host a second information desk during the summer season (May 1–Oct 15) at the Icefield Information Centre, 103km (64 miles) south of Jasper Townsite on the Icefields Parkway (Hwy. 93). Stop here on your way between Banff and Jasper national parks to learn about the Icefields area (© **780/852-6288**).

ENTRANCE/CAMPING FEES   All vehicles driving in a national park require a park pass. The fees support the maintenance of scenic drives, trails, picnic areas, information services, and interpretive displays and tours. A **National Park Day Pass,** which is valid from the date of issue until 4pm the following day, costs C$10 (US$9.30) for adults, C$7.50 (US$7) for seniors, and C$4.50 (US$4.20) for children 6 to 12; children under 6 are free. If you are a group of two to seven it's more economical to buy a group pass, which costs C$18 (US$17) for up to seven adults and/or children. Prices are the same during both the high-traffic (May–Oct) and low-traffic (mid-Oct to May) seasons. Purchase your pass at the Jasper Information Centre (500 Connaught Dr., Jasper, AB T0E 1E0; © **780/852-6176**). You can also purchase a pass at an information center in neighboring Banff National Park. If you're going to stay in Jasper National Park for more than a few days, and in fact plan to visit several national parks over the course of your trip, consider purchasing an **Annual Pass.** It's good for 1 year from the month of purchase and includes a passbook with more than C$100 (US$93) worth of discounts for camping and other attractions in Jasper and Banff national parks, as well as 27 other national parks in western Canada. Individually, adults pay C$62 (US$58), seniors pay C$54 (US$51), and children 6 to 12 pay C$32 (US$30), younger than 6 are free. The group/family pass rates are a better deal: The pass costs C$124 (US$116).

Although it's hardly necessary to be so organized, you can purchase both a National Park Day Pass and an Annual National Pass before you arrive at the park. Call **Parks Canada** at © **800/748-7275** or e-mail natlparks-ab@pch.gc.ca (there is no online payment system). These passes are for sale at all park gates and information centers.

The new online campground reservation system has changed things dramatically in Jasper. There's no rush for the best, or the last, spot at some of the very popular frontcountry (road-accessible) campgrounds like Whistlers, Pocahontas, Wapiti, and Wabasso. For C$12 (US$11) plus the cost of the site, you can make your reservation by visiting www.pccamping.ca or calling © **877/737-3783.** A number of sites are always set aside for drive-in campers, and they are still available on the old first-come, first-served basis. Single-night fees per site (accommodating up to two tents and six people) range from C$14 (US$13) at more primitive campgrounds to C$36 (US$34) at Whistlers—Jasper's largest and best-equipped campground.

If you're headed away from the road and into the backcountry, you are required to get a permit and reserve a campsite in advance, in addition to your National Park Day Pass or an Annual National Pass. Call the Jasper National Park's **backcountry campsite booking office** at © **780/852-6176.** Permits are C$10 (US$9.30) per person. You cannot reserve a specific site ahead of time. Instead, you select a site along a specific trail. Some sites along popular hiking trails book up months ahead of time (especially in the summer), so I suggest you book as early as possible. The booking office opens for the season on May 1. Once you get to Jasper, you can pick up your permit at the **Jasper National Park Information Centre** (500 Connaught Dr., Jasper, AB T0E 1E0; © **780/852-6176**), and you can also pick it up at the Banff National Park Information Centre (224 Banff Ave., Banff, AB T0L 0C0; © **403/762-1550**). You need to pick it up within 24 hours of departing for your backcountry trip.

SPECIAL REGULATIONS/WARNINGS   Parks Canada has a number of rules and regulations whose purpose is to preserve the wilderness you've come to see.

- **Area closures inside the park**   For safety and environmental reasons, certain areas in the park, including roads, wildlife corridors, and hiking trails, may be temporarily closed. Closures are marked with signs and red or yellow tape.
- **Bicycles**   Though all types of bikes are permitted on all roads and highways, off-road or mountain bikes are permitted only on certain park hiking trails. Pick up a copy of the brochure **Mountain Biking in Jasper National Park** for details on trails open to mountain bikes, rules, and etiquette. Get one at the **Jasper National Park Information Centre** (✆ **780/852-6176**).
- **Boating**   Buckling up a lifejacket and pushing off from a dock in a canoe is A-Okay. Travel on mountain rivers, however, should be attempted only by experienced paddlers. Motorboats are prohibited in the park.
- **Car camping**   Frontcountry (road-accessible) campgrounds are first-come, first-served. Demand is heaviest in July and August. No reservations are accepted, so plan to arrive at your chosen campground before 4pm. Some campgrounds are open year-round, but most open in early May and close in late September.
- **Climbing**   There is no specific climbing permit required in Jasper National Park; however, I strongly recommend that inexperienced climbers (and sometimes even experienced climbers new to the area) hire a local guide. It's a good idea to register with the **Voluntary Registration Service** before you head out on a climb.
- **Firearms**   Firearms must be disarmed and must remain in your vehicle at all times, unloaded and in a case or wrapped and securely tied so that no part of the firearm is exposed. Ammunition must be stored separately from the firearm.
- **Garbage/Littering**   You'll notice large brown garbage bins throughout Jasper National Park. These are bearproof. They require a bit of extra effort to open (lift up the latch inside the handle and then lift the heavy lid), but they are a necessity. There are also blue bins for recycling cans and bottles. Littering can have a devastating impact on wildlife, by bringing animals out of their natural habitat and drastically changing their

feeding patterns. You can be fined C$100 (US$93) for littering or improperly storing food or garbage. Pay special attention if you're doing any camping, and make sure you pack food
away at night.

- **Hunting/Trapping**   Hunting and trapping wildlife is prohibited in Jasper National Park.
- **Motorcycles/Snowmobiles/ATVs (all-terrain vehicles)**   Use
of a motorized off-road vehicle is prohibited in Jasper National
Park.
- **Pets**   Unrestrained pets have been known to harass wildlife,
provoke wildlife attacks, and endanger people. You must keep
your pet on a leash at all times—it's a good idea to keep them
out of the backcountry, too.
- **Smoking**   Smoking is prohibited in many hotels and restaurants in Jasper. If you do smoke, pick up all your cigarette butts
and dispose of them in the brown bearproof garbage bins distributed throughout the park.
- **Swimming**   There are plenty of lakes in Jasper, but only a few
are actually warm enough for a dip. Try Lakes Annette and
Edith, near the Jasper Townsite. Although you won't be fined
or charged for swimming in lakes, rivers, or creeks here, you've
got to be somewhat crazy to even give it a try, given the frigid
temperatures. Jasper's **Aquatic Center** (② **780/852-3663**) has
a large pool with a diving board and a children's area.
- **Vandalism/Defacement**   Whatever you find—be it a rock, a
wildflower, or a set of antlers—it belongs where it is.
- **Wildlife**   It is illegal to feed, touch, entice, disturb, or otherwise harass any wild animal—big or small.

FAST FACTS: Jasper National Park

ATMs & Banks **Canadian Imperial Bank of Commerce (CIBC)**
(416 Connaught Dr.; ② **780/852-3391**), **TD Canada Trust** (606
Patricia St.; ② **780/852-6270**). There is a currency exchange
house in **Whistlers Inn** (105 Miette Ave.; ② **780/852-3361**). All
of these locations have ATMs.

Car Trouble & Towing Services **Jasper Towing** has 24-hour
service and trucks capable of towing your RV (② **780/852-
3849**).

Drugstore **Cavell Drugs** has a pharmacist on duty (602 Patricia St.; ℰ 780/852-4441).

Emergencies For fire, ambulance, or police, dial ℰ **911.** There are emergency call boxes located sporadically along major park highways. For park-related emergencies, contact the **Warden Service** ℰ **780/852-6155.**

Gas Stations There are a handful of gas stations in the town of Jasper, including **Avalanche Esso** (702 Connaught Dr.; ℰ 780/852-4721) and **Jasper Shell** (638 Connaught Dr.; ℰ 780/852-3022). There is another gas station at **Saskatchewan Crossing,** just south of the border between Banff and Jasper national parks on Highway 93 (the Icefields Pkwy.) (ℰ **403/761-7000**). It is usually closed from mid-November to mid-March.

Groceries Stock up at **Robinson's IGA Foodliner** (218 Connaught Dr.; ℰ **780/852-3195**), **Super A Foods** (601 Patricia St.; ℰ **780/852-3200**), **Tags Jasper** (401 Patricia St.; ℰ **780/852-5460**), or **Nutter's Bulk Foods** (622 Patricia St.; ℰ **780/852-5844**).

Internet Access Log on to check your e-mail at **More Than Mail** (620 Connaught Dr., Square Mall; ℰ 780/852-3151), or the **Soft Rock Café** (622 Connaught Dr.; ℰ 780/852-5850).

Laundry Get your camping clothes clean at **Coin Clean** (607 Patricia St.; ℰ 780/852-3852).

Medical Services **Seton Hospital,** in the Town of Jasper (518 Robson St.; ℰ **780/852-3344**).

Permits You can purchase all park permits at the **Jasper National Park Information Centre** (500 Connaught Dr.; ℰ **780/852-6716**).

Photo Supplies Get your digital photos printed at the **Tekarra Color Lab** (600 Patricia St., below Earl's Restaurant; ℰ 780/852-5525), or head to **Jasper Camera & Gift Ltd.** (412 Connaught Dr.; ℰ 780/852-3165).

Post Offices You can mail letters and packages from **Canada Post** (502 Patricia St.; ℰ **780/852-3041**).

Taxis Try **Heritage Cabs** (ℰ 780/852-5558), or **Jasper Taxi** (ℰ 780/852-3600).

Weather Updates For weather updates in Jasper National Park, call ℰ **780/852-3185.** The service is available 24 hours.

2 Tips from Park Staff

The key to getting the most out of your visit to Jasper is to do what the locals do—slow down and follow nature's lead. "It's a big, grand place," says Gloria Keyes-Brady, tourism specialist for Jasper National Park. The scale of nature here can be overwhelming, so don't try to do or see everything.

"Jasper is about kicking back and getting into the rhythms of nature," she says. Even if you don't have lots of time, organizing your visit well will allow you to see the park in-depth. She's got plenty of tips on reaching that goal here.

Before you leave home, take advantage of online tools to help you plan, including the Jasper National Park website (www.pc.gc.ca/jasper) and the Jasper Chamber of Commerce website (www.jasper canadianrockies.com), which list hotels, restaurants, guides, and services. You can book your campsite ahead of time on the Parks Canada site (www.pccamping.ca).

Visitors sometimes feel rushed on their way to Jasper, which can take upward of 3 hours even if you're only coming from Edmonton. Keyes-Brady recommends seeing the trip to Jasper as part of the journey. "Take time to enjoy the drive and the amazing views."

The visitor's wisest first stop is either the **Jasper Information Centre** or the Icefield Information Centre, where local staff offer fabulous advice and have the latest information. From what to do when it rains to where you can ride your mountain bike, take any doubts or questions to these knowledgeable and friendly folks.

Jasper has its list of must-sees, including the **Icefields Parkway,** which Keyes-Brady calls "a wonderful place to experience glaciers," mountain rivers, and the thundering Sunwapta and Athabasca falls. **Maligne Valley Road** is an excellent place to spot wildlife (which makes it important to drive slowly here), and has lots of great short hikes and interpretive trails. And Keyes-Brady also recommends taking the **Jasper Tramway** to the top of Whistlers Mountain to get "a really good sense of the landscape of Jasper."

Wildlife encounters along Jasper roads are quite common and are always thrilling. But visitors need to remember their responsibility to ensure a healthy and enduring ecosystem. "Remember that we share this space with wildlife," she says. They may appear harmless and seem to ignore you, but don't be fooled. Wildlife is unpredictable by nature. "I can't emphasize enough how important it is to give wild animals their distance."

Children growing up here, like Keyes-Brady's two sons, are blessed to be able to "watch the patterns of nature all around them all the time." But they also learn early to respect the wildlife. And their parents are lucky to have so many great places to help them discover the natural world.

Kids—and their parents—will love exploring the **Miette Hot Springs** area, where there are short hikes in the Fiddle Valley, picnic spots, and, of course, the newly renovated hot springs pool. Keyes-Brady recommends camping at the **Wabasso campground,** which is a bit farther from town than the two "biggies," Wapiti and Whistlers, but offers excellent sites and is situated along the river. Other kid-friendly spots are the beaches at lakes Annette and Edith, which also have playgrounds. Finally, she suggests parents look into the Junior Naturalist programs run by the Friends of Jasper.

In the Town of Jasper, perhaps the most exciting new opportunity is the newly expanded **Jasper Discovery Trail.** With a total distance of 8km, the trail loops all around the townsite. It's also quite wide, giving lots of room for kids to run and parents to push strollers. It's a great way for parents to take their kids out for a hike without risking child meltdown or burnout, since they're never far from town.

Fun Fact   **Ranger Rick versus Warden Wayne**

If you're looking for Ranger Rick or Rhonda, you've come to the wrong country. In the United States, all employees of the National Park Service are called "park rangers." The work a park ranger does is incredibly varied, ranging from cleaning picnic sites and maintaining trails to being on safety duty, conducting wildlife studies, and leading guided tours.

In Canada, you'll meet Warden Wayne or Wendy, and you'll find that the work they do is much more specialized than that of a park ranger in the US. Canada's park wardens are in charge of public safety and natural and cultural heritage conservation. They work alongside a slew of other Parks Canada staff, who may be administrators, information center staff, or trail crew. But these people are not wardens. While a US park ranger can (and often does) do anything and everything, a Canadian park warden's work has less variety, but requires more specialization.

"The Buildings Should Reflect the Landscape"

The building that currently houses the **Jasper National Park Information Centre** was built in 1914 and is now a National Historic Site. It's one of the finest and most influential examples of rustic architecture in Canada's national parks, says Jasper tourism officer Gloria Keyes-Brady.

The ground floor of the building used to contain various administrative offices and, until 1931, the park superintendent's living quarters. Jasper's first superintendent, **Maynard S. Rogers**, who served from 1913 to 1914 and again from 1917 to 1929, felt that the buildings should reflect the landscape, so builders used materials such as cobblestone, river rock, and timber. "Since the mountains aren't symmetrical, they thought the buildings shouldn't be either," Keyes-Brady says. Architects strived for a harmonious and balanced style.

For the more adventurous, several kilometers of trail on the "bench" behind town pass through Aspen forests, old Douglas fir stands, spruce wetlands, and ponds. The larger trail system around Jasper is under review to ensure better wildlife travel corridors, reduce trail erosion, and improve recreational experiences. For more information about the review process, and to add your opinion, visit the Parks Canada website.

At the end of the day, Keyes-Brady suggests you reward yourself with a meal at one of the town's **great restaurants.** "The number of quality chefs here per capita is extremely high. Jasper competes with the best in terms of food."

Those keen on venturing into the backcountry need to have a good grasp of their abilities and be organized. First-timers should definitely consider hiring a local guide for hiking or backpacking. Trail conditions in Jasper are variable, so always check in with the staff at the Jasper Information Centre before hitting the trail. "This town has fabulous guides. I can't recommend them highly enough."

If you're weary of crowds (a relative phenomenon in Jasper), consider coming in September or October. "The weather is beautiful, it's usually warm, and with the golden and yellow in the forests and the smell of the fall in the air it's my favorite time of year here," says Keyes-Brady.

Even though it has a major ski resort at **Marmot Basin,** people will be surprised to know that winter is a quiet season in Jasper. And thanks to its setting beneath tall peaks, the town itself is quite sheltered from the cold winter winds.

History is always alive in Jasper. Over the next few years, the park is celebrating the bicentennial of explorer, fur trader, naturalist, and mapmaker David Thompson's epic trip across Canada. Check out www.davidthompson200.ca for event listings.

3 The Highlights

You can spend a fun day exploring **Jasper Townsite.** Take the guided history tour of the town "Jasper: A Walk in the Past Tour" (reviewed in the section "What to See & Do in Jasper Townsite" below) and visit the **Heritage Railway Station,** the **Post Office,** the **CIBC Bank building,** and the **Parks Canada–run Jasper Information Centre,** as well as a number of outlying heritage buildings. Another must-see is the **Athabasca River,** which flows near the town and is excellent for river paddling and rafting. Just to the southwest of town, ride the **Jasper Tramway** to the top of **The Whistlers.**

There is much to see and do along the stunning **Icefields Parkway** (Hwy. 93), which connects Banff and Jasper national parks. You can hop in a giant **"snocoach"** and go for a ride on a glacier, or hire a guide and actually go for a *walk* on a glacier. Drive up to **Mount Edith Cavell,** south of the Town of Jasper, watching for mountain goats and bighorn sheep along the way. The parkway also takes you to two spectacular waterfalls: **Sunwapta** and **Athabasca falls,** both located just off the highway.

A short drive east of Jasper Townsite, turn south on the Maligne Lake Road. As you drive along, you'll see the turnoff for **Maligne Canyon** and pass right beside **Medicine Lake.** Maligne Lake Road culminates in **Maligne Lake** itself—the largest and arguably most beautiful lake in the park.

No visit to Jasper National Park is complete without a soak in the 104°F (40°C) **Miette Hot Springs,** the hottest mineral springs in the Canadian Rockies. To get there, take another very scenic drive south from Highway 16 east of Jasper Townsite, along the **Miette Road.**

4 Suggested Itineraries

Most visitors will come to Jasper National Park via Banff, driving north along the Icefields Parkway (Hwy. 93). Make a stop at the **Icefield Information Centre** (© 780/852-6288), just north of the Banff–Jasper park boundary, for maps, any special directions or information you need, and maybe a warm drink, before heading on your way. If you're planning to start out from Jasper Townsite itself, farther inside the park, you can get information from the **Jasper National Park Information Centre** (500 Connaught Dr., Jasper, AB T0E 1E0; © 780/852-6176; www.parkscanada.gc.ca/jasper).

IF YOU HAVE ONLY 1 OR 2 DAYS

If you have 1 day and time for one major outing in Jasper National Park, make it a drive along the **Icefields Parkway.** The road is lined by massive glaciers squeezed between towering peaks in a lunar-like landscape unlike any other area of the Rocky Mountains. This is nature on its grandest scale. The most mind-boggling yet visitor-friendly destination in the park, the **Columbia Icefield** (the **Athabasca Glacier,** specifically) is unforgettable. There are a handful of good outings that you can take in the Icefield area and many excellent hikes (ranging 1 hr.–3 days). (See "Day Hikes" and "Exploring the Backcountry" in chapter 7.)

If you're planning on spending the night in Jasper, make a hotel reservation well ahead of time (at least 2 months ahead, if you're coming between June and Sept). If you're car camping, reserve your site ahead of time at © 877/737-3783 or www.pccamping.ca so you can spend more time exploring. (The range of accommodations Jasper has to offer is detailed in chapter 8.) On your second day, visit **Maligne Lake** first thing in the morning, when there are greater chances for wildlife viewing, and take the **cruise to Spirit Island.** Have lunch in Jasper Townsite, and then head up the **Jasper Tramway.**

For more close-ups of big mountains, another potential scenario for Day 2 starts with a drive down the parkway to **Mount Edith Cavell** with a hike to the toe (lowest end) of the glacier. Then visit the pounding cascades at the broad **Athabasca Falls** and the steep **Sunwapta Falls.** (More information about these attractions is included in the later sections "What to See & Do in Jasper Townsite," "Driving Tours," and "Organized Tours.")

Both of these Day-2 trips have good wildlife-viewing opportunities. Watch for elk east of Jasper Townsite, bear on the Maligne Lake

Tips   Jasper in the Rain

Weather in the mountains can change at the drop of a dime. Being flexible and seeing the opportunities inclement weather presents will help make sure you enjoy every minute of your trip.

Here are a few Jasper activities that are fun no matter what the weather is doing:

- **Go on a rafting trip.** Hey, you'll be getting wet anyway! Head to the Sunwapta, Athabasca, Whirlpool, or Fraser rivers.
- **Soak in the Miette Hot Springs,** the hottest natural springs in the Canadian Rockies.
- **Go fishing.** Some say rain makes for the best fishing conditions.
- **See a movie** at the **Chaba Theatre** (604 Connaught Dr.; *C* 780/852-4749).
- **Visit** the **Jasper–Yellowhead Museum,** which has a video viewing room featuring videos on Jasper and the Canadian Rockies (400 Pyramid Lake Rd.; *C* 780/852-3013).
- **Surf the Internet and check your e-mail** at the **Soft Rock Café** (622 Connaught Dr.; *C* 780/852-5850).
- **Take in teatime at the "JPL,"** a good way to experience the stunning Fairmont Jasper Park Lodge if you aren't staying overnight. Lunch and afternoon tea are served in the lobby at the Emerald Lounge. Call *C* 780/852-6052 for reservations.
- **Go for a misty-day photo shoot,** a nice change of focus from the bright blue skies.

Road, and mountain goats and bighorn sheep along the Icefields Parkway. However, since this route includes most of the popular attractions in the park, it also includes crowds. If you want peace and solitude, leave the parking lot behind for even an hour and hike into the **Brazeau, Fiddle River,** or **Tonquin valleys** (see "Day Hikes" and "Exploring the Backcountry" in chapter 7).

IF YOU HAVE 3 OR MORE DAYS

You can accomplish a lot in 3 or more days in Jasper National Park. Some visitors come here for a couple of weeks, or even a month, reserving a bungalow with a kitchen (see "Lodging in Jasper National Park" in chapter 8). They spend some days touring the park and others sitting by the river wrapped up in a good book. Or, they may enjoy a leisurely picnic lunch followed by a trip into town for dinner and a movie.

In fact, packing a **picnic** is what I suggest you do, if you've got a bit more time to spend. Take it to one of the outstanding **viewpoints along the Icefields Parkway,** or to a lakeside or riverside picnic spot (try **Lake Annette, Pyramid Lake,** or **Athabasca Falls**). Several restaurants/eateries in Jasper will pack a picnic lunch for you. Another way to enhance your park visit is to do some hiking, and ideally some overnight backpacking. Jasper's best hiking trails are reviewed in chapter 7.

5 What to See & Do in Jasper Townsite

The town of Jasper is located in an expansive valley on the west bank of the Athabasca River. Its off-season population hovers around 5,000, but it blossoms to more than 20,000 in the summer, when university students from across Canada head here for summer jobs and mingle with the thousands of travelers passing through, turning the somewhat sleepy mountain town into a vibrant destination. The town itself is quite large, but most visitors will stick to the two main drags, **Connaught Drive** and **Patricia Street.** That's where the good restaurants, shops, and outfitters are. It's also where you'll find the **Jasper National Park Information Centre** (500 Connaught Dr.; ⓒ **780/852-6176;** www.parkscanada.gc.ca/jasper), housed in the former park superintendent's office. Though it's recently been renovated, don't be fooled by the modern signage. The architects kept the building's old-fashioned style intact on the inside. It feels as expansive as the mountain vistas outside. Here, you can pick up permits, maps, brochures, and great tips. The staff are friendly and extremely knowledgeable. Surrounded by a large green lawn with shady gardens, it's also a pleasant place to escape the midday heat and to people-watch.

Across the street is the recently restored **Heritage Railway Station** (which now houses the park administration offices as well as the train station). You can still picture Victorian ladies with their parasols and elaborate dresses mixing with rough 'n' tumble gold diggers at this old frontier outpost.

Jasper Townsite

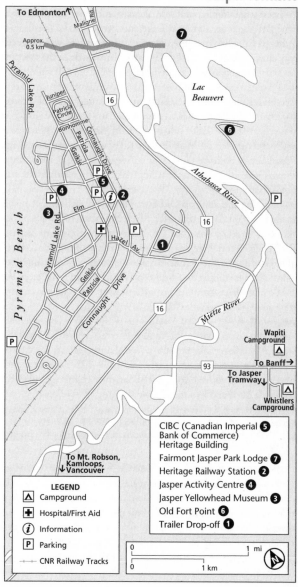

LEGEND

⬛	Campground
➕	Hospital/First Aid
ⓘ	Information
🅿	Parking
┅┅┅	CNR Railway Tracks

CIBC (Canadian Imperial ❺
Bank of Commerce)
Heritage Building

Fairmont Jasper Park Lodge ❼

Heritage Railway Station ❷

Jasper Activity Centre ❹

Jasper Yellowhead Museum ❸

Old Fort Point ❻

Trailer Drop-off ❶

There are a number of lovely lakes around Jasper Townsite. To the north of Jasper are **Pyramid Lake** and **Patricia Lake** (head up the Pyramid Lake Rd. from the townsite), great for bird-watching, fishing, and boating. Patricia Lake is particularly lovely in the fall, when the surrounding aspens turn a lovely shade of gold. It's also a good spot to see beaver and moose. In the winter, you can ice-skate on Pyramid Lake, below the distinctive sandstone peak of Pyramid Mountain. To the southeast of town and at a lower elevation along the valley flats are **Lake Edith** and **Lake Annette** 𝓕 (head east of town and turn left on Maligne Lake Rd. toward the Fairmont Jasper Park Lodge); both are local favorites for swimming in the summertime. There are picnic areas at both lakes, and Lake Annette has a sandy beach as well.

Climbing the stairs up **Old Fort Point** is steep, but worthwhile. Jutting out into the Athabasca River, the point offers great views that take in Jasper Townsite, Lac Beauvert, and the Fairmont Jasper Park Lodge. From here you can also catch sight of mounts Kerkeslin and Hardisty to the southeast, and the snowy triangle of Mount Edith Cavell, shining above all others, to the south. To access Old Fort Point, drive 5 minutes south of Jasper Townsite via Highway 93A and Old Fort Point Road.

Jasper: A Walk in the Past Tour 𝓕 *(Moments)* The Friends of Jasper run this nightly 90-minute leisurely walking tour, which starts at the Jasper National Park Information Centre. It's informative and fun, opening up a part of the area's history you otherwise may not have noticed. Also ask about their full-moon hike! Kids may be a bit bored by the old-time talk.

To sign up, contact the Friends of Jasper at their booth in the Jasper Information Centre (500 Connaught Dr.) or call ✆ **780/852-4767**. C$2 (US$1.85) per person, C$5 (US$4.70) per family. Summer only. Tours leave the Jasper Information Centre nightly at 7:30pm.

Jasper Heritage Folk Music Festival 𝓕 Held every second year on the first weekend of August (the next one will be in 2009), this is one of Western Canada's best outdoor music festivals. Join musicians from all around Alberta, Canada, and the world to celebrate cultural diversity. Just about every kind of music you can think of is showcased, from folk and roots to hip-hop, classical, reggae, and jazz.

Jasper Heritage Folk Music Society. For tickets call ✆ **780/852-3615**. www.jasper folkfestival.com. Admission (weekend passes purchased before July 15) C$49 (US$46) adults, C$27 (US$25) children 11–17, free for children 10 and under. Next festival will be held in Aug 2009.

Jasper Tramway ⟨★★ ⟨Kids⟩   Your quickest and easiest way to the high alpine terrain, this 7-minute gondola ride takes you up 973m (3,191 ft.), just short of the summit of The Whistlers. From the top, the views of the Athabasca and Miette valleys are stunning. Kids love to look out for their car in the parking lot and watch it get smaller and smaller.

The 30-passenger tram takes you out of the cool forest shade to the upper terminal. There's a well-marked, though quite steep, 45-minute self-guided trail to the summit of the mountain. It's tempting to stay at the terminal and soak in the view, but don't miss this chance to travel by foot through tundra and natural rock gardens. The summit is in the alpine region, where the winds are harsh, the sun strong, and the summers short. Vegetation has adapted to this barren environment; most plants are minuscule at best. Flowers can take upward of 25 years to bloom. Watch for squirrels, chipmunks, hoary marmots, and white-tailed ptarmigan. The view is more outstanding with each step upward. Dress warmly and wear comfortable walking shoes. This is the easiest way to a mountain summit in the Rockies, and a great trip for families. At the summit, the panoramic view takes in six mountain ranges, including Mount Robson, the highest point in the Canadian Rockies. Rides leave every 10 minutes or so.

Since more than 150,000 people come up here each summer, expect to stand in line for the tramway upward of 30 minutes, especially in the middle of the day.

ⓒ **780/852-3093.** www.jaspertramway.com. Admission C$24 (US$22) adults, C$12 (US$11) children under 15, free for children 4 and under. Family rate of C$60 (US$56) for 2 adults and 2 children. May 20–June 22 daily 9:30am–6:30pm; June 23–Aug 26 9am–8pm daily; Aug 27–Oct 8 10am–5pm daily. Closed mid-Oct to mid-May. Drive south 4km (2½ miles) from the townsite, on Hwy. 93A, turn west at Whistlers Rd. and continue for 2.5km (1½ miles) to the Tramway terminal, following clearly marked signs.

⟨Moments⟩ **Enjoying the Alpenglow**

Evenings in the Rockies are particularly enchanting, when the mountains take on the rose-colored glow known as "alpenglow." As a special treat, enjoy a casual dinner at **The Treeline Restaurant** (ⓒ **780/852-3093**) in the Upper Terminal of the Jasper Tramway. In the summer, the last tram trip down the mountain departs at 8:30pm.

Titanic Dreams

In 1910, Charles Melville Hays, president of the Grand Trunk Railway, was making big plans for an elaborate resort at Miette Hot Springs, similar to the Banff Springs Hotel. His design called for water from the hot springs to be piped to a luxury hotel situated at the mouth of the Fiddle River. Melville planned to name the hotel Chateau Miette. However, fate had other plans. Melville died on the HMS *Titanic* in 1912. His hot-water dreams went down with him in the chilly waters of the North Atlantic.

Jasper–Yellowhead Museum *Kids*   This museum has exhibits with artifacts from the park's early days, including fur-trade and mountaineering equipment. You'll find Curly Phillips's hand-built cedar-strip canoe, Métis beaded deerskin jackets, and the gear used during the first ascent of Mount Alberta in 1925. There is a video room where you can see videos about area wildlife and the natural history of the Canadian Rockies. Kids enjoy the artificial cave and the telegraph displays. Plan on taking an hour or two to visit the museum. It's great on a rainy day or first thing in the morning to kick off a day of discovering the area.

400 Pyramid Lake Rd. ℭ 780/852-3013. www.jaspermuseum.org. Admission C$4 (US$3.75) adults; C$3 (US$2.80) seniors, students, and children 6–18; free for children 5 and under. Daily 10am–9pm in summer. In winter, closed Mon–Wed.

Maligne Lake Cruise to Sprit Island *Kids*   A 90-minute outing, this guided boat cruise is relaxing for parents and fun for kids. Curly Phillips, a canoe guide and trapper from Ontario, built a floating boathouse on Maligne Lake in 1928 that still stands today. He also began operating commercial cruises on the lake. Guides share historical anecdotes in the glass-enclosed boats (which are heated on chilly days). From the deck, watch for eagles, mountain goats, and even the odd avalanche, if it's the right time of year. The cruise makes a stop halfway up the lake at the mysterious Spirit Island, then returns to the dock.

Reserve and purchase tickets at Maligne Lake Tours office. 627 Patricia St. ℭ 780/852-3370. Admission C$39 (US$36) adults, C$19 (US$18) children 6–12, free for children 5 and under. No seniors' rate. Spring (1st day the ice melts)–June daily 10am–4pm with trips departing every hour; June–Sept daily 10am–5pm with trips departing hourly; after Sept 1, 10am–4pm until the lake freezes.

Miette Hot Springs ✿ Don't miss the chance to soak your tired bones and aching muscles here after a great hike. A series of springs and minor leaks in the narrow and steep-walled valley of Sulphur Creek, there are two hot mineral pools and a deeper, cooler pool with a diving board. The **Ashlar Ridge Café and Gifts** (✆ 780/866-2111) serves cappuccinos, sandwiches, and muffins. Afternoon barbecues feature bison burgers (a must-try).

Miette Rd. ✆ 780/866-3939. Admission C$6.15 (US$5.75) adults, C$5.20 (US$4.85) seniors and children, C$19 (US$18) family pass. Mid-May to June 22 and Sept 4 to mid-Oct daily 10:30am–9pm; June 26–Sept 3 daily 8:30am–10:30pm. Closed mid-Oct to mid-May. 44km (27 miles) east of Jasper Townsite on Hwy. 16; 17km (11 miles) south on Miette Rd.

6 Driving Tours

There are two main driving tours you can do in the park. The first is along the famous Icefields Parkway, which many visitors splitting their trip between Banff and Jasper national parks will drive to get to Jasper. The second is along the Maligne Lake Road, which takes you through the beautiful Maligne Valley.

ICEFIELDS PARKWAY ✿✿

Connecting Banff and Jasper national parks, as well as neighboring national parks Yoho and Kootenay, Highway 93, also known as the Icefields Parkway, is often called one of the most beautiful drives in the world.

The Icefields Parkway deserves an entire, leisurely day to really enjoy. Drive slowly to give yourself time to take in the scenery, which sometimes more closely resembles the moon than the Rocky Mountains. Some visitors stay at one of the campgrounds in the Icefield area and use it as a base for exploring, which gives them more time. (See chapter 8 for information on the campgrounds along the Icefields Pkwy. and in Jasper in general.) Be sure to bring an extra jacket or sweater—it can be much colder here than in Jasper Townsite!

The **Columbia Icefield,** the geographical heart of the Icefields Parkway, is located just north of the Banff National Park border, some 103km (64 miles) south of the Town of Jasper. An area of glacial ice and snow measuring 190 sq. km (74 sq. miles) that is up to 350m (1,150 ft.) deep in places, the Columbia Icefield will give you an idea what the northern part of North America may have looked like during the earth's last ice age.

The Columbia Icefield forms a triple continental divide (one of only two in the world) where water flows in three directions: north

Frequently Asked Icefield Questions

What is a glacier?
A glacier forms in an area where more snow falls in winter than melts in summer. In the Rockies, glaciers are usually found at high elevations, where the average temperature is below freezing. Most of the snow sticks around throughout the year, although some is lost to wind, direct evaporation from ice to water vapor, and summer melting. Glaciers are also formed at lower elevations, in the shaded slopes of steep mountains.

Why is glacial ice so blue?
Unlike the stunning color of many lakes and rivers in the Canadian Rockies, the beautiful color of the Athabasca Glacier has nothing to do with minerals. It's because the ice is so pure. Air and other impurities that reflect white and gray have been squeezed out of the crystals deep within the glacier; thus, wavelengths of light reflect only the blue spectrum.

What is an icefield?
An icefield is a body of ice from which glaciers flow outward in more than one direction. The Columbia Icefield, for example, flows in three separate directions.

How many glaciers flow from the Columbia Icefield?
Six named glacier valleys have outlets from the Columbia Icefield: Athabasca, Dome, Stutfield (these are the ones you can see from the Icefields Pkwy.), Columbia, Castleguard, and Saskatchewan.

What is the highest peak in the Columbia Icefield?
Mount Columbia is the highest peak in the Columbia Icefield, measuring 3,747m (12,290 ft.). It is second only to Mount Robson, the highest peak in the whole of the Canadian Rocky Mountains, at 3,954m (12,969 ft.). It is not visible from either the Icefields Parkway or the ridge behind the Icefield Information Centre.

to the Arctic Ocean, east to the Atlantic Ocean, and west to the Pacific Ocean. There are six main glaciers flowing from the Columbia Icefield: Stutfield and Dome can be seen from the highway as you approach the Icefield area from the north. The Athabasca

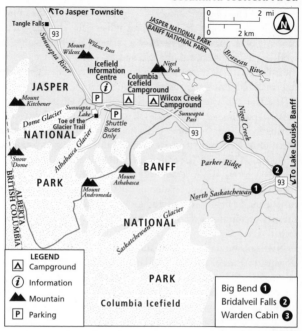

Glacier, by far the easiest to explore, once extended beyond where the Icefield Parkway runs (see the section "Organized Tours" later in this chapter for two great ways to see this glacier up close and personal). If you drive a few kilometers south of the Icefield Centre and into Banff National Park, you can hike Parker Ridge (see "Day Hikes" in chapter 4) and view the spectacular Saskatchewan Glacier. The Columbia and Castleguard glaciers are much less accessible.

The **Icefield Information Centre** (☎ **780/852-6288**) is 103km (64 miles) south of Jasper Townsite; it's 3 miles from the border between Banff and Jasper national parks and is right across the road from the base of the Athabasca Glacier. This is a good spot from which to base your explorations of the Columbia Icefield area. Opened in 1996, this C$7.2-million state-of-the-art center combines an information center, a small hotel, a huge parking lot (with room for 560 cars and 170 RVs), a restaurant, an interpretive gallery . . . even a gift shop. It is somewhat wheelchair-accessible and designed with visitors of all ages in mind. There is a lot to be learned here, but the main reason you need to darken the door is to sign up for a tour. The **Glacier Gallery,** designed for kids, tells the human and natural history of the Icefield area and explains the role glaciers play in global warming. Upstairs is a cafeteria and restaurant. The food isn't anything special, though, and the prices are high, but it's the only restaurant for an hour in either direction. It's a good idea to plan ahead, bring a picnic, and sit outside if the weather is nice.

The Columbia Icefield is a very popular attraction that draws 600,000 people every summer. Book tours early, although if you are driving in on your own (that is, without a guide) you cannot book ahead of time. Be sure to arrive early for a tour—even if you make a reservation in either Jasper or Banff, you still can't get your ticket until you arrive. Tours leave every 15 minutes or so. Visit www.brewster.ca for more information or call ℂ **877/423-7433.** It's best to visit the Icefield in the mornings or late afternoon to avoid the throngs of tourists arriving by bus from the towns of Banff and Jasper.

North of the Icefield Information Centre, the Icefields Parkway slowly drops out of the moonlike landscape into more classic mountain scenery. There are numerous waterfalls along the side of the highway, along with rivers and creeks dropping into the flats of the Sunwapta River. Keep an eye out for mountain goats on the cliffs and bighorn sheep on the road.

One of the most picturesque waterfalls along the way is **Sunwapta Falls.** There are also a hotel and restaurant there, though they are open only in summer. You can explore the falls from the parking lot behind the hotel. The falls tumble through a steep-walled limestone gorge. Follow a 2km (1.2-mile) trail along the north bank of the river for excellent views. From Sunwapta Falls, both the Sunwapta River and the Icefields Parkway enter the broad **Athabasca River Valley.** From this point on, the parkway follows the Athabasca River.

To the west of the Icefields Parkway are the horn-shaped peak of **Mount Fryatt,** the turreted form of **Brussels Peak,** and the jagged **Mount Christie,** with **Mount Edith Cavell** in the distance to the north and **Mount Kerkeslin** to the east. The **Goats and Glaciers Viewpoint,** just off the west side of the highway (you make a wide left turn), has few views of glaciers but offers a decent view of the **Athabasca Valley,** and is one of the best chances in the Canadian Rockies to see mountain goats close up.

The Icefields Parkway soon meets Highway 93A, a scenic road with less traffic. If you take Highway 93A, just past the junction you'll come upon **Athabasca Falls,** pouring through a narrow canyon cut out of quartzite rock. A nearby bridge offers phenomenal views of the thundering falls, and gives you a chance to cool off in the mist and spray. A great spot for a picnic.

Follow Highway 93A north (the former Icefields Pkwy.) along the west bank of the Athabasca River and over the Whirlpool River to **Cavell Road,** which will eventually take you to Mount Edith Cavell—though not without passing some spectacular scenery along the way. Completed in 1924, this narrow, winding road is challenging to drive, and is actually off-limits to most RVs and trailers (anything over 7m/22 ft.). It is also closed from October through June, depending on snow. Follow Cavell Road up to the trail head for multiday hikes into the spectacular **Tonquin Valley.** One of the most popular backpacking areas in Jasper National Park, the Tonquin Valley has beautiful alpine scenery. The main attractions along this trail system are **Amethyst Lake** and its backdrop, the 1,200m (3,936-ft.) cliffs known as **The Ramparts.** At the top of Cavell Road is **Cavell Lake.** Park your vehicle here and head off to explore

David Thompson: Explorer & Mapmaker

David Thompson was one of the first people of European descent to see the Athabasca River, as well as numerous passes, valleys, and peaks throughout what is now known as the northern Canadian Rockies. Born in Wales in 1770, Thompson came to Canada in 1784, at the age of 14, and began working for the Hudson's Bay Company, a fur-trading operation based in Montreal. Ironically, even though he worked for a company located in the eastern part of British North America (today Canada), Thompson spent 28 years exploring and mapping the northwestern part of the area, establishing new trade routes and forging strong relationships with the Native peoples he met. In the winter of 1810 and 1811, Thompson's crew crossed the Athabasca Pass and continued on to the Pacific Ocean, the first group of European descent to do so. From 2007 to 2011 Parks Canada is participating in a celebration of Thompson's feats. For more information, visit www.david thompson200.ca.

⌒ *Fun Fact*　**Maligne: A Wicked Word**

The Maligne River was named in 1846 by a Jesuit missionary, Pierre Jean de Smet, who had some trouble crossing the mouth of the river. It is a French word that means "wicked."

Mount Edith Cavell, the Angel Glacier, or the excellent Path of the Glacier Trail. Come early in the morning or late in the afternoon—the parking lot is often full by midday. At 3,363m (11,030 ft.), **Mount Edith Cavell,** named after a World War I heroine, is the highest and arguably most scenic mountain in the vicinity of Jasper Townsite. **Angel Glacier** saddles the northeastern slope and sends a tongue of ice off the cliff-side. The **Path of the Glacier Trail** takes you over boulders, shrubbery, pebbles, and sand through a landscape which, less than a century ago, was covered by a glacier. New plants, trees, shrubs, and wildflowers have slowly returned to the area, known as a *terminal moraine*. Stay away from the glacier itself since there is a danger of falling rock and ice. If you can spend half a day here, hike the trail to **Cavell Meadows** to see this subalpine meadow brilliant with wildflowers. The best time to do this is mid-July to early August, when the wildflowers are at their most colorful. Recent rehabilitation and restoration projects are helping to heal this trail from overuse.

Head back down the Cavell Road and turn north on to Highway 93A. You'll soon meet the road that leads to **Marmot Basin** ⓕ, one of four commercial downhill ski operations in the Canadian Rocky Mountain national parks. The lifts are obviously closed during the summer, but the drive is scenic nonetheless.

MALIGNE LAKE ROAD ⓕ

This road takes you along through the Maligne Valley and ends at the picturesque Maligne Lake. Head east out of Jasper Townsite on the Yellowhead Highway (Hwy. 16), and turn south on Maligne Lake Road. Wildlife including bighorn sheep, deer, elk, moose, grizzly bear, and black bear can often be spotted along its expanse. The road is open year-round; however, I suggest you steer clear of it in the winter, when driving can be treacherous.

Your first stop along the Maligne Lake Road should be a visit to the **Fairmont Jasper Park Lodge** ⓕⓕ. The largest commercial property in the Canadian Rocky Mountain National Parks, this hotel continues to set the standard for wilderness lodges, attracting tourists and dignitaries from around the world. Non–hotel guests are welcome to tour the grounds, rent a canoe for a paddle on **Lac Beauvert,** enjoy a meal at one of the hotel's six restaurants, or play a round on the award-winning golf course. (For a full review of this and other accommodations options in Jasper, see "Lodging in Jasper National Park" in chapter 8).

Back on the Maligne Lake Road, the route veers east and slides into a parallel run with the **Maligne Canyon,** a spectacular example of the cutting power of moving water. It's a very long, gradual waterfall through a deep limestone canyon.

There are three hiking trails that lead out from the Maligne Canyon parking lot—all of which take you to different parts of the canyon. The shortest trail is paved, and part of it is wheelchair-accessible. If you decide to take either of the two longer trails, both of which lead down into the canyon, remember that the return trip is uphill all the way! Chapter 7 has detailed reviews of these and other Jasper trails.

Mary Schaffer: Hunter of Peace

A Quaker from Philadelphia who first came to the Canadian Rockies in 1889 on a summer vacation, Mary Schaffer made pioneering explorations that would change how the area was perceived. Mary, whose Quaker beliefs promoted the equality of the sexes, decided to shun the city and in 1907 moved permanently to the Rockies, basing herself in the growing mountain town of Banff. From there, Schaffer embarked on a series of adventures, including exploring the remote regions of the Athabasca Valley. In 1908, following a map made by Stoney Chief Samson Beaver, Schaffer became the first woman of European descent to lay eyes on what is today known as Maligne Lake. Schaffer spent her summers exploring the Rockies and roughing it in the bush. Along the way, she painted wildflowers, took photographs, and kept an extensive and humorous journal, which she later published as *Old Indian Trails of the Canadian Rockies*. It is still available under the title *Hunter of Peace*. Schaffer, who married her guide Billy Warren in 1915, died in Banff in 1939.

From Maligne Canyon, the Maligne Lake Road follows the Maligne River (noticing a pattern here?) south through a lodgepole pine valley and continues along the eastern shores of Medicine Lake. Underneath the road and the river, there is a substantial underground river system that begins at the mysterious **Medicine Lake.** This lake seems to evaporate into nothing, with no visible drainage outlet. The Maligne River enters the lake from higher in the valley at the southwest but doesn't appear to drain it. But the river appears another 16km (9.9 miles) down the valley, running at its full course! In fact, most of the water seeps through a series of holes in the bottom of Medicine Lake at a rate of 24,000 liters (6,240 gal.) per second. The spring runoff is particularly large and the underground holes aren't able to handle the capacity, so the lake level rises, sometimes overflowing into the normally dry riverbed beside the road at the northern end of the lake. By late summer, however, the volume of water draining through the holes becomes much less, and the lake's water level drops dramatically. By fall, there's hardly a lake to be seen, only a small stream. The early Natives believed this mysterious lake had healing powers, hence the name.

Farther south along the Maligne Lake Road is the 22km (14-mile) **Maligne Lake,** the largest lake in Jasper National Park and the second-largest glacier-fed lake in the world. Bordered by subalpine forests and mountains, this picturesque lake is a favorite destination for anglers, hikers, and canoeists. There are two parking lots at the end of the Maligne Lake Road (it ends here). Head to the east side parking lot if you're here for a boat tour; drive to the west side lot if you're heading for the **Skyline, Bald Hills,** or **Maligne Pass** hiking trails. There are also a number of shorter hikes around the shores of Maligne Lake. Take the trail to **Lake Mona** and **Lake Lorraine** to get away from the crowds, or the shaded trail to **Moose Lake** to escape the midday heat. See the section "Organized Tours" below for more on boat tours on Maligne Lake. See "Day Hikes" and "Exploring the Backcountry" in chapter 7 for more on these and other hiking trails.

7 Organized Tours

If you think the closest you can get to a glacier is a relatively tame distance at the side of the Icefields Parkway, think again. The guided **Ice Explorer** 𝒦𝒦 will take you via a giant "snocoach" a full 5km (3 miles) onto the surface of the Athabasca Glacier. Snocoaches are massive 56-passenger all-terrain vehicles powered by a 210-horsepower Detroit diesel engine. Tours are 80 minutes and depart from the Icefield Information Centre, where tickets are sold. Call © **877/423-7433,** 780/852-3332, or 403/762-6735. Admission is C$36 (US$34) for adults, C$18 (US$17) for children ages 6 to 15, free for children under 6. Brewster's shuttle from Banff or Jasper townsites is an additional C$98 (US$92) for adults and C$49 (US$46) for children 6 to 15, free for children under 6. The tour operates from April 15 through late September, from 9am to 5pm.

If you want to get even more up close and personal with the Athabasca Glacier, take the **Athabasca Glacier Icewalks** ☞ (reserve at the Columbia Icefields Hotel front desk or call © **800/565-7547** or 780/852-5595), led by naturalist Peter Lemieux. There are two tours: the standard one, which lasts 3 hours, and an extended one, which lasts 5 hours. Both depart from the parking lot at the "Toe of the Glacier" (just below the glacier and off the west side of the Icefields Pkwy., across from the Icefield Information Centre). Tickets for the 3-hour tour cost C$55 (US$51) for adults and C$28 (US$26) for children under 18; for the 5-hour tour tickets are C$65 (US$61) for adults and C$30 (US$28) for children under 18. The 3-hour tour runs Monday to Wednesday, Friday, and Saturday from June 1 to September 30 at 11am, and the 5-hour tour runs Thursdays and Sundays.

For fun and very informative sightseeing tours to the Maligne Valley, the Columbia Icefields, and Mount Edith Cavell/Athabasca Valley, as well as half-day train tours, contact **Sundog Tours** (414 Connaught Dr.; © **888/786-3641** or 780/852-4056). Sundog runs private guided tours as well as shuttles between Jasper and the Edmonton International Airport, and between Calgary, Jasper, and Banff.

7

Hikes & Other Outdoor Pursuits in Jasper National Park

Jasper National Park appeals to outdoor types, with a terrain that is mixed and varied—from broad river valleys and wooded montane slopes to high meadows and alpine tundra. The park is large; in a matter of 15 minutes on foot, you can be far away from the highway enjoying the peace and solitude of the mountains. It's easy to get nowhere fast in Jasper.

Hiking is by far the most popular summer activity. With numerous trails varied enough to suit different fitness levels, you can easily hike here every day for a month and never retrace your steps. The trails are rarely crowded (save for Maligne Canyon trail and the Path of the Glacier trail during the midday hours). If you choose to take a break from hiking, other activities such as mountain biking or whitewater rafting beckon.

Already much more quiet in the summertime than busy Banff to the south, Jasper is even quieter in the winter. Alpine and cross-county skiing are popular winter sports, and ice-skating is a wonderful winter-evening activity. Most outdoor activities are based out of the Town of Jasper, located roughly in the center of the park. From here, you can book a whitewater-rafting adventure or hop on a shuttle to Marmot Basin, Jasper's alpine skiing and snowboarding resort. You can also rent the equipment you'll need to make the most of the outdoors here, from bikes and fly-fishing rods to tents and snowshoes. Perhaps best of all, you can step out of your hotel and within minutes on foot access the trail heads for a dozen hikes.

Jasper locals are enthusiastic, outdoorsy folks who have chosen to live here because they love nature and outdoor recreation. Most of them will be more than happy to give you the lowdown on their favorite trail, viewpoint, or ski hill.

Tips **Trail Conditions**

In the spring, the first hiking trails to clear of snow are usually in the valley bottoms, and this often doesn't happen until late May! Elsewhere in the park, snow may remain on passes well into June and July. Check trail conditions before you head out. Call the **Jasper National Park Information Centre** at *C* 780/ 852-6176.

1 Day Hikes

When selecting a day hike in Jasper National Park, think about the weather, your own fitness level, and the trail conditions. It's generally not a good idea to start out on a hike under threatening skies. Try to go on a sunny day. Many of the trails in Jasper are distinguished by steep ascents and descents—experienced hikers know it's often just as hard to come down as it is to go up. This is mountain terrain; most trails require at least some climbing. Trail conditions are also key. Most trails in the valley are clear of snow before June. Trails at higher elevations are not fully clear of snow until June or July. Come October, most high trails are covered in snow again, although there are still some great hikes to enjoy well into autumn.

The new **Jasper Discover Trail** *R* follows a perimeter around the townsite. It's 8km (5 miles) long and will take you 2½ hours to walk the entire loop; however, it's easy to hop on and off the trail at various points on the edge of town. This makes a good warm-up for more serious hikes, especially the part on the Pyramid Bench just to the north of town. Start at the parking lot between the Jasper Yellowhead Museum and the Catholic Church, then follow the Jasper the Bear trail markings west in a counterclockwise loop to get the best views.

Transportation is another important consideration. A vehicle is not a prerequisite to great hiking in Jasper, since many trails around **Patricia** and **Pyramid lakes** leave right from the streets of the townsite, or can be reached by foot if you walk up the **Pyramid Bench,** above the townsite. If you do have access to a vehicle, however, head to some of the outlying areas for more dramatic scenery. See "Getting There" in chapter 2 for information on renting a car in Jasper.

Jasper National Park Trail Heads

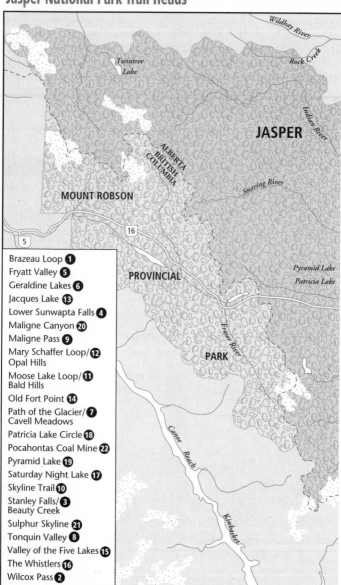

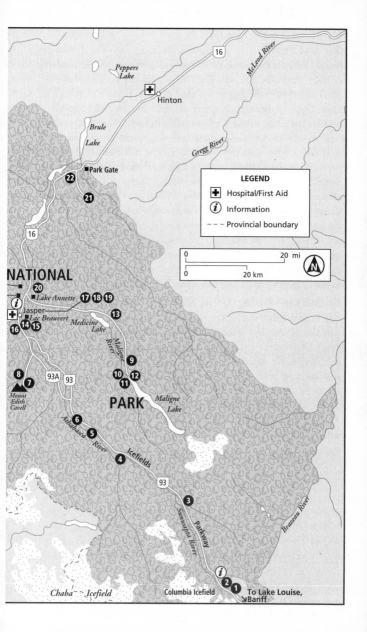

LEGEND

✚ Hospital/First Aid

ⓘ Information

--- Provincial boundary

JASPER TOWNSITE AREA

Old Fort Point   A large hill that protrudes into the Athabasca River, Old Fort Point is a cliffy, classic *roche moutonnée*—a knob of bedrock shaped by a glacier. The trail is steep in places, but has outstanding views of the Jasper Townsite area and beyond. Although it seems unlikely that an actual fort existed here, the first fur-trading post in the area was located just downstream. Also, many early explorers, fur traders, and pioneers passed through the area, climbing atop the hill to scout the rapids along the Athabasca and Miette rivers. If you're in a hurry to get to the top of the hill, you can take a steep climb up the stairs straight to the top. Once there, you'll see a plaque commemorating the Athabasca River as a Canadian Heritage River. If you're not in much of a hurry, take the wide path behind the trail kiosk; it's a longer but gentler climb. The beginning elevation is 1,030m (3,378 ft.) and the elevation gain is 130m (426 ft.). 3.5km (2.2 miles) round-trip. Easy to moderate. Access: From town, follow Hwy. 93A south to Old Fort Point/Lac Beauvert access road. Turn left (west), cross the Athabasca River over the old iron bridge, park in the lot on your right.

Patricia Lake Circle   An easy hike ideal for naturalists, this moderately hilly trail winds through aspen groves and takes you to Patricia Lake, which was named after Princess Patricia of Connaught, the daughter of one of Canada's governors general. The lake is a favorite nesting spot for waterfowl, including songbirds and loons. You may also see deer, bear, moose, and beaver. The beginning elevation is 1,150m (3,772 ft.) and the elevation gain is 70m (230 ft.). 4.8km (3 miles) round-trip. Easy. Access: Take Pyramid Lake Rd. north from the townsite for 3.5km (2¼ miles) to the riding stable parking lot. Or hike from town along the Pyramid Lake trail, which begins across from the Jasper Activity Centre.

Pyramid Lake 𝕮   This is the best of the trails that wind from Jasper Townsite up the Pyramid Bench. Head out from the Jasper Activity Centre and keep to the right when you cross Pyramid Lake Road. Climb up a quick, but steep, trail to end up on a wide bluff. There are lovely views of the Athabasca River from here, and bighorn sheep can often be seen grazing in the area. The trail takes you by Cottonwood Slough, a lovely marshlike area that is a must-see for bird-watchers. In July and August, the meadows and slopes along the benchland are often covered in wildflowers. You'll pass through a montane forest before reaching Pyramid Lake. There are a variety of trails you can take to get back to town. Due to its low elevation, this trail is often hikeable early in spring and well into early winter. The beginning elevation is 1,020m (3,346 ft.) and the elevation gain is 300m (984 ft.). 17.4km (10.8 miles) round-trip. Moderate. Access: Jasper Activity Centre parking lot. You can also start 2km (1¼ miles) farther north up Pyramid Lake Rd., at the Cottonwood Slough parking lot, or at Pyramid Stables, 3.5km (2¼ miles) farther.

Saturday Night Lake ⚐   One of Jasper's best and most challenging longer day hikes, this trail journeys right from the townsite (great if you don't have a car!) through a forested valley west of the townsite, passing several small lakes along the way. Because this is one of the first trails to be snow-free in the spring, you can make this a short day hike if you like, going only as far as Marjorie or Caledonia lakes. Or, you can turn it into an overnight trip, since there are two backcountry campsites (High Lake and Minnow Lake) along the route.

(Moments   The View from the Top of Old Fort Point

Don't forget your camera if you go on this hike. Looking first toward the south and continuing in a clockwise direction, here's what you'll see from the top of the hill on the Old Fort Point trail:

- Mount Edith Cavell (the horizontal lines of snow that you see are there year-round);
- The Whistlers and the Jasper Tramway, to the southwest;
- The Miette River valley, leading west toward the Athabasca Pass and the province of British Columbia;
- The Town of Jasper, across the Athabasca River;
- The Victoria Cross Range, to the northwest behind town, identifiable by its reddish quartzite;
- Pyramid Mountain (the peak with the large satellite station on top of it);
- The Fairmont Jasper Park Lodge, on the shores of Lac Beauvert, to the northeast;
- The Colin Ranges, the rounded top of Signal Mountain, and beside it, Mount Tekarra;
- Mount Hardisty (with sloping layers) and Mount Kerkeslin to the southeast.

The trail leaves the west edge of Jasper Townsite, crosses Cabin Creek, and climbs up a low bluff. Marjorie Lake is to the west, while Hibernia Lake is accessed by a short trail to the east. The trail continues along the shore of Caledonia Lake, and sometimes is very buggy and wet in early summer. Look for wood lilies and wild roses along this part. From here, the route becomes steeper and heads into a forest. It then passes two tiny lakes, Minnow and High lakes (this is where you can camp if you make this an overnight trip). The top of the trail is at the foot of the Cabin Creek waterfall. From here it loops downhill, eventually ending up back at the trail head. On the way back, don't miss the short, steep, side trail to Saturday Night Lake—where one of my favorite campsites is located. The trail also takes you by Cabin Lake, the largest lake on the trail. Perhaps the best viewpoint on the entire hike is on the descent, when the trail opens on an expansive bluff before heading back down through a forest to the trail head. Watch for birds, waterfowl, beaver, and perhaps a black bear or two. This also makes a great winter cross-country-skiing outing since there's no avalanche danger. The beginning elevation is 1,100m (3,608 ft.) and the elevation gain is 540m (1,771 ft.). 24.6km (15.3-mile) loop. Strenuous. Access: Follow Pyramid Lake Rd. west to Cabin Creek Rd. Take the gravel road that branches off to the right to the parking lot and trail head kiosk.

ICEFIELDS PARKWAY AREA

Lower Sunwapta Falls *Moments*   Lower Sunwapta Falls is really three separate waterfalls along the Sunwapta River. And although Sunwapta Falls is on every tour-bus route, and the parking lot, just off the west side of the Icefields Parkway, is often jammed, few visitors venture on to the lower series of falls, just below the main one. Together, they make a powerful natural scene. Start out from the parking lot and follow the main upper-falls viewing trail to where the pavement ends. It's a gradual descent through a lodgepole pine forest, with lovely views of the Sunwapta River, the upper Athabasca Valley, and Mount Quincy's glacier-covered peak. The beginning elevation is 1,320m (4,330 ft.) and the total elevation drop to the falls is 80m (262 ft.). 2km (1.2 miles) one-way. Easy to moderate. Access: Sunwapta Falls junction. From Jasper Townsite, to the north, take Icefields Pkwy. 55km (34 miles) south to the junction. From the Icefield Information Centre, to the south, take the Icefields Pkwy. 49km (31 miles) north to the junction. Take the Sunwapta Falls Rd. .6km (½ mile) west to the parking lot and trail head.

Stanley Falls/Beauty Creek *Finds*   A quiet trail, this route passes no fewer than eight waterfalls as it climbs from the Icefields

Parkway alongside Beauty Creek. The trail goes up a low dam wall across a marsh to reach the old, torn-up Banff–Jasper Highway, which you cross. This isn't the end of the trail, though; the climb ends at the dazzling Stanley Falls. Best done in early summer, when the water level is high and the falls are at their most powerful. The beginning elevation is 1,570m (5,150 ft.) and the elevation gain is 110m (361 ft.). 6.4km (4 miles) round-trip. Moderate. Access: From Jasper Townsite to the north, take the Icefields Parkway 90km (56 miles) south. The trail head is .5km (⅓ mile) past Beauty Creek Hostel. Park in a small pull-off on the east side of the highway, marked with a hiker sign.

Valley of the Five Lakes *Kids*   Families will enjoy this mellow hike, which leads to a series of small woodland lakes ideal for picnicking and fishing. From the trail head, you follow the route through a lodgepole pine forest and cross a boardwalk over Wabasso Creek, where you may spot a beaver or two. Then there's a short climb to an open meadow. From here, the trail splits into a variety of loops—all clearly signed. I suggest you take #9a and return via #9b—there is a panoramic viewpoint that takes in all the surrounding mountain peaks. The trail is well maintained and mostly flat. The beginning elevation is 1,070m (3,510 ft.) and the elevation gain is 30m (98 ft.). 6km (3.7 miles) round-trip. Easy to moderate. Access: From Jasper Townsite to the north, take Icefields Pkwy. 11km (6¾ miles) south to parking lot on east side of the highway. Trail head is well signed.

Wilcox Pass *★★*   This beautiful pass is on the edge of a large alpine valley, just east of the Athabasca Glacier. The view of the Columbia Icefield from the highway pales in comparison to what you can see from up here. The hike begins with a moderate climb through a stunted forest of Engelmann spruce and subalpine fir. Already, you're treated to great views of the Columbia Icefield. On your way up to the ridge, you pass through alpine meadows full of wildflowers. Once you reach the ridge, you can turn around and head back the way you came, or continue on to Wilcox Pass. This is a very good day hike and excellent complement to a tour of the Columbia Icefield. It's also worthwhile to just hike the first part and get the view—you don't have to make it to the top of the pass to enjoy this trail. Avoid the trail until July, though, to give the snow a chance to melt. Watch for bighorn sheep along the way. The beginning elevation is 2,042m (6,698 ft.) and the elevation gain is 335m (1,100 ft.). 8km (5 miles) round-trip to the pass; 11.2km (7 miles) one-way to Tangle Falls. Moderate. Access: From the Icefield Information Centre, follow Icefields Pkwy. 3.1km (2 miles) south to Wilcox Creek Campground entrance road.

HIGHWAY 93A, MOUNT EDITH CAVELL & TONQUIN VALLEY AREA

Cavell Meadows ⋒ This hike is for wildflower lovers. The first part of the trail follows the same route as the Path of the Glacier trail (reviewed below). After a short while, however, it branches off to the east, on its own. The trail climbs steeply up over a moraine (a small hill made up of glacial rock and debris), then levels out. It heads through a well-graded and very colorful upper subalpine forest to a junction where you stay right to choose the more gradual ascent of the two loop sides. The trail then enters sparse tree-line vegetation and the alpine region beyond. There are lovely views of **Angel Glacier** and **Mount Edith Cavell,** and, as you head back down, many, many wildflowers thriving in a cool, damp environment. You return to the trail head via the Path of the Glacier trail. It's best to come in either the early morning or the late afternoon, to avoid the crowds. Early season closures may be in place due to wet conditions and trail erosion. The beginning elevation is 1,738m (5,700 ft.) and the elevation gain is 400m (1,312 ft.). 8km (5 miles) round-trip. Moderate. Access: From Jasper Townsite, follow Icefields Pkwy. 93 south for 7km (5½ miles) to the 93A junction. Follow Hwy. 93A south for 5.4km (3½ miles) to Cavell Rd. Turn right (west). Continue 12km (7½ miles) to end of road and start of trail.

Geraldine Lakes ⋒ Although you can tailor this day hike to the length you want, it's worth your time to hike to the high pass at the head of the **Geraldine Valley,** squeezed between the slopes of **Mount Fryatt** and **Whirlpool Peak.** From the trail head at 1475m (4,839 ft.), the trail climbs a relatively easy 400m (1,312 ft.). The first of the four lakes, Lower Geraldine Lake, which reflects the north face of Mount Fryatt, is an easy 2km (1.2-mile) hike from the trail head. However, I suggest you go as far as the Second Geraldine Lake, which boasts views of a 100m (328-ft.) waterfall. 10km (6.2 miles) one-way. Moderate. Access: From Jasper Townsite, take the Icefields Pkwy. 93 south to the second junction with Hwy. 93A, at Athabasca Falls (31km/19 miles from the townsite). Turn west on 93A and follow it north for 1.1km (.7 mile) to Geraldine Fire Rd. Follow this gravel road west for 5.5km (3.5 miles) to the parking lot.

Path of the Glacier ⋒ (Kids) This interpretive trail takes hikers right up to the north face of the stunning Mount Edith Cavell. In doing so, you cross a rocky landscape that, less than a century ago, was covered in glacial ice. It's amazing to see how animals and plants have moved in since the glacier retreated. The trail climbs steadily up a paved surface, following a lateral moraine (a small hill-shaped mound of glacier rock and debris). Interpretive signs along this part of the trail describe the glaciation process. The route then drops into the exquisite **Cavell Pond,** just below the edge of the Angel Glacier. You may see icebergs floating in the pond's midnight-blue waters. Note that hikers should not hike up to the glacier due to danger of falling rock and ice. The route heads back on a softly pebbled path along Cavell Creek. This is a very popular trail, so try to arrive early in the day or in the late afternoon to avoid the crowds. Early season closures may be in place due to wet conditions and trail erosion. The beginning elevation is 1,378m (4,520 ft.) and the elevation gain is 30m (98 ft.). 1.6km (1 mile) round-trip. Easy. Access: From Jasper Townsite, follow Icefield Pkwy. 93 7km (4½ miles) south to Highway 93A. Take 93A 5.5km (3½ miles) south to Cavell Road. Follow Cavell Road 15km (9 miles) west to parking lot at road's end.

MALIGNE VALLEY AREA

Bald Hills ⚑   The "Bald Hills" extend for 7km (4⅓ miles) in the Maligne Valley area; their highest point is 2,600m (8,528 ft.). This hike is well worth the climb to an old fire lookout for views of Maligne Lake and the hills behind it. Longer and more gradual than the Opal Hills trail (reviewed below), the route first takes you through a forest of lodgepole pine and eventually opens into a subalpine meadow with stunted alpine fir and Engelmann spruce trees. It continues to the foot of a small, rounded mountain (or a "bald hill"). From here, you can follow a variety of trails past the old fire lookout to more impressive viewpoints. Caribou herds often summer in this area. A great choice if you're keen to see wildflowers in high alpine terrain. The beginning elevation is 1,680m (5,510 ft.) and you gain 480m (1,574 ft.). 10.4km (6.4 miles) round-trip. Moderate. Access: From Jasper Townsite, take the Yellowhead Hwy. 16 east 4km (2½ miles) to Maligne Lake Rd. Turn south and follow to the end, past the Maligne Lake Lodge, over the river to the end of the pavement. Turn left into parking lot.

Maligne Canyon ⚑   This hike gives you a good view of the famous Maligne Canyon, the most impressive canyon in the Canadian Rockies. Many people visit the canyon at its upper reaches; few venture down very far. If you are particularly averse to climbing, you can hike the trail from top to bottom. But it's less rewarding, because the views are best when you are looking up from the canyon's depths. An added bonus: You get to hike downhill on your return (when you're tired!). Stay to the right at all crossroads. The beginning elevation is 1,030m (3,378 ft.) and you lose and then later regain 100m (328 ft.). 3.7km (2.3 miles) one-way. Moderate. Access: From Jasper Townsite, follow Hwy. 16 4km (2½ miles) east to Maligne Lake Rd. Turn south and continue 2.3km (1½ miles). Trail head is at the Sixth Bridge parking lot on the east side of Maligne Lake Rd.

Mary Schaffer Loop (also known as Loop Trail) This is a pleasant hike around the north side of Maligne Lake, the largest lake in the Canadian Rockies. The paved trail passes Curly Phillips's historic boathouse and reaches a viewpoint with an interpretive display about explorer Mary Schaffer. (Schaffer was the first woman of European descent to set eyes on the lake, in 1908, and the most prolific writer about the place!) The trail then loops back to the parking lot through a forest. Keep an eye out for "kames," low mounds of glacial debris, on the way back. Stop in at the Maligne Lake Lodge for a cup of tea before heading back to town. The beginning elevation is 1,700m (5,576 ft.) and you gain only a negligible amount. 3.2km (1.9 miles) round-trip. Easy. Access: From Jasper Townsite, follow Hwy. 16 4km (2½ miles) east to Maligne Lake Rd. Follow Maligne Lake Rd. south to the end. Trail head is at the first parking lot at Maligne Lake.

Moose Lake Loop *(Kids* Although this trail follows a route through the woods for its entire length, they are truly amazing woods, filled with mossy, lichen-encrusted boulders. The hike starts out on the same route as the Bald Hills trail (see above), but eventually veers south along the Maligne Pass trail (reviewed below). From Moose Lake, the trail loops back to Maligne Lake and follows the shoreline. The terrain is mostly gentle throughout, making it a good hike for families, especially with younger children, and a nice shady option for a hot summer day. A good escape from the RVs and buses filling up the Maligne Lake parking lot. The beginning elevation is 1,700m (5,576 ft.) and you gain only a negligible amount. 2.8km (1.7 miles) round-trip. Easy. Access: From Jasper Townsite, follow Hwy. 16 4km (2½ miles) east to Maligne Lake Rd. south. Follow Maligne Lake Rd. for 48km (30 miles) to Maligne Lake. Park in the farther west parking lot, Bald Hills trail parking lot. Head up the Bald Hills trail and take a left 200m (656 ft.) on the Maligne Pass Trail toward Moose Lake.

Opal Hills *(* A wonderful, lush area that stands out in the rugged rocky mountains near Maligne Lake, this loop hike is quite steep but displays fascinating geology and a lovely view of the lake. The trail climbs steadily for 1.5km (.9 mile) to a junction where it splits in two directions (the trail that leads to the south is shorter and steeper). The trail to the north offers quite a stunning and varied view from the meadow below Opal Hills. You'll see the Maligne Valley from top to bottom, and the smoothly rounded Bald Hills. To the south, you'll see Mount Unwin (3,268m/10,719 ft.) and Mount

Charlton (3,217m/10,552 ft.). If you take this trail nice and slow, allowing for many rests, and if your own rapid heartbeat doesn't scare you (it *will* beat rapidly!), it's a lovely place to be on a hot and sunny summer day. The beginning elevation is 1,680m (5,510 ft.) and you gain 460m (1,509 ft.). 8.2km (5.1 miles) one-way. Strenuous. Access: From Jasper Townsite, follow Hwy. 16 4km (2½ miles) east to Maligne Lake Rd. Follow Maligne Lake Rd. 44km (27 miles) east to parking lot.

MIETTE HOT SPRINGS AREA

To access the Miette Hot Springs area, take the Yellowhead Highway 16 east from Jasper Townsite 42km (26 miles) and turn south on Miette Road. Though the 17km (11-mile) road is winding and narrow, it's also very scenic. There are often black bears along the roadside.

Pocahontas Coal Mine 🐾   More a short walk than an actual hike, the upper section of this trail, in the shadow of the Roche Miette peak, has wonderful views of the **Athabasca Valley.** The trail is lined with interpretive signs and artifacts that relate the story of the coal mine that operated in the area in the early 1900s, and the town that grew up around it. It is particularly lovely in the fall, when the leaves on the trees along the Athabasca River turn golden. The lower loop is wheelchair-accessible. The beginning elevation is 990m (3,247 ft.); you gain 90m (295 ft.) on the upper loop and next to nothing on the lower loop. Upper loop 1.8km (1.1 miles) round-trip; lower loop .8km (.5 mile) round-trip. Easy. Access: From Jasper Townsite, follow the Yellowhead Hwy. 16 42km (26 miles) east to Miette Rd. Trail head is in the parking lot just after the turnoff.

Sulphur Skyline 🐾   This is the best hike in the eastern reaches of Jasper National Park. The trail starts out on an old road and climbs gradually through a mixed forest. About 2.4km (1.5 miles) into the hike, you'll come to a junction. Take the trail to the right. The route then climbs steadily over **Shuey Pass,** switchbacking across a series of avalanche slopes. A cairn marks the top of the ridge. It's just a few steps from here to the true summit, which is bare and rocky. From the summit, you'll see views of the front ranges of the Canadian Rockies, including the **Fiddle River Valley** to the southeast. If you look farther toward the east, you'll be able to spot the foothills of the Rockies. The beginning elevation is 1,370m (4,494 ft.) and you gain 700m (2,296 ft.). 9.6km (6 miles) round-trip. Strenuous. Access: From Jasper Townsite, follow the Yellowhead Hwy. 16 42km (26 miles) east to Miette Rd. Follow Miette Rd. 17km (11 miles) south to the end of the road. Park in the lot in front of the Miette Hot Springs.

2 Exploring the Backcountry

Allowing yourself time to spend at least 1 night in the backcountry will definitely enhance your trip. For detailed information on backcountry trip planning, see "Planning a Backcountry Trip" in chapter 2 and "Exploring the Backcountry" in chapter 4.

In Jasper National Park, you can rent camping equipment from **Jasper Source for Sports** (406 Patricia St.; ✆ **780/852-3654**). For information on the steepness of trails and trail conditions, ask the staff at the **Jasper Information Centre** (500 Connaught Dr.; ✆ **780/852-6176**).

BACKCOUNTRY TRAILS

Brazeau Loop   You can complete this hike in anywhere from 5 to 7 days. This popular backpacking route actually begins in Banff National Park and crosses into Jasper. As such, it provides an opportunity to tour the mountains in the border area between the two parks. It starts out following the same route as the **Nigel Pass trail** ⋆ (see chapter 4, p. 99), and in about 2 hours reaches the first of three passes along the entire route. From this first pass, the trail follows the Brazeau River, dropping into a lush meadow. After passing Boulder Creek Campground, it drops into another meadow, arriving at Four Point Campground, where I suggest you spend your first night. The following morning, head along the Four Point Valley and over Jonas Pass, making camp at the Jonas Cutoff Campground. On Day 3, hike over Poboktan Pass, then down alongside John-John Creek to Brazeau Lake—a wonderful reward after 2 days of hiking, Brazeau Lake happens to be one of the largest backcountry lakes in Jasper National Park. On your third night, camp at Brazeau River Bridge Campground. On your fourth day, hike up the Brazeau River Valley, past Marble Mountain and Mount Athabasca. Camp at the **Four Point Campground** ⋆. On your fifth day, you'll weave through a series of meadows and forests before hooking back up with the Nigel Pass trail. Watch for grizzly bears, elk, moose, wolves, cougars, and wolverines throughout the area. The beginning elevation is 1,860m (6,101 ft.) and the elevation gain is 750m (2,460 ft.). 78.6km (48.7-mile) loop. Moderate. Access: From the Icefield Information Centre, follow Icefields Pkwy. 93 13km (8 miles) south to Nigel Creek.

Fryatt Valley ⋆   This hike will take you 3 or 4 days. Tucked between mounts Fryatt and Christie, Fryatt Valley may not be large, but it's chock-full of classic Rockies scenery, including mountain lakes, colorful wildflower meadows, and towering peaks. You approach the valley gradually on the first day, taking in views of the Athabasca Valley. On your first night, camp at Lower Fryatt campground, which is tucked beside Fryatt Creek. The next day is challenging, as you cross Fryatt Creek and climb deeper into the hanging valley, which joins the main (and lower) Athabasca Valley from a higher level, dropping down to the side. Stop at picturesque Brussels campground on your second night. On your third day, use the campground as a base for a day hike toward the headwall separating the gentle lower and rugged upper valley. Leave your heaving backpack behind. You'll appreciate it. The beginning elevation is 1,220m (4,002 ft.) and you gain 820m (2,690 ft.). 23.2km (14.4 miles) one-way. Moderate. Access: From Jasper Townsite, follow Icefields Pkwy. 93 32km (19 miles) south to the 93A junction. Follow 93A 1.1km (¾ mile) northwest to Fryatt Valley–Geraldine Lakes road. Follow road 2.1km (1⅓ miles) west to trail head.

Maligne Pass   This 3-day trip takes you along a trail through the alpine zone, passing a handful of pretty little lakes and traversing a beautiful meadow. Starting at the north end of Maligne Lake, the trail climbs up the Maligne Ridge, past the junction for the Bald Hills trail (reviewed above). There's a short descent into Trapper Creek. After crossing a suspension bridge over the Maligne River, the climb is long and gradual until it reaches the Mary Schaffer Campground, where I suggest you spend your first night. On Day 2, the trail climbs through diverse forests to the tree line, eventually heading above it to Maligne Pass. As you approach the pass, be sure to turn around to take in the views of the Maligne Valley below. From Maligne Pass, the trail climbs a short distance farther before beginning a gradual descent to Avalanche Campground. Camp here on your second night. On Day 3, the route is almost all downhill, zigzagging across the Poligne Valley. The trail hooks up with the Poboktan Creek trail before concluding at the Poboktan Creek parking lot, on the Icefields Parkway. The beginning elevation is 1,540m (5,051 ft.). You lose 610m (2,000 ft.), then gain 760m (2,493 ft.). 48km (30 miles) one-way. Moderate. Access: From Jasper Townsite, either follow the Maligne Lake Rd. 4km (2½ miles) east to its end or, if you decide to start the trail from the west trail head, follow the Icefields Pkwy. 93 from Jasper Townsite 72km (45 miles) south to a small parking lot on the east side of the road.

Skyline Trail ⍟   You can complete this hike in 2 to 4 days. This is the most popular backpacking route in Jasper National Park, running along a ridge from high above Maligne Lake to Maligne Canyon. The trail reaches the highest elevations of any trail in the park, with more than half the distance above the tree line.

The hike begins as a gentle climb, but gets steeper once you cross Evelyn Creek and start heading up Little Shovel Pass. Don't forget to look back over your shoulder every once in a while for views of Maligne Lake. After you reach Little Shovel Pass, the trail drops into the Snowbowl, a lush meadow with small creeks and streams crisscrossing through it. Camp at the Snowbowl campground on your first night. The following morning, continue on to the top of Big Shovel Pass and, if you feel like it, take the short side trip to Watchtower Basin, the site of the old Watchtower Cabin, which was a base for alpine skiing in the 1930s (it burned to the ground in the early 1970s). After reaching the Wabasso trail junction, you'll make it to Curator Lake, a remarkable little lake that is tucked peacefully into a barren alpine tarn set amid harsh terrain. From here, the trail heads up to the summit ridge of Amber Mountain. Take some time to admire the views. Reserve at **Tekarra Campsite** *⚿* for your second night, for the best sunset views in Jasper National Park. The beginning elevation is 1,540m (5,051 ft.). You lose 1,350m (4,428 ft.), then gain 820m (2,690 ft.). 44.1km (27.3 miles) one-way. Moderate. Access: From Jasper Townsite, follow Hwy. 16 3.7km (2⅓ miles) east to Maligne Lake Rd. Follow Maligne Lake Rd. 45km (28 miles) east to parking lot.

Tonquin Valley *⚿*   You can complete this route in 3 to 5 days. The star of this backpacking trail is the Ramparts, a massive 1,000m (3,280-ft.) cliff face of Precambrian quartzite, which towers above beautiful Amethyst Lake and the 5km (3.1-mile) pass that is the Tonquin Valley. With horseback trips and exploring hikers (not to mention mosquitoes as late as mid-Aug), this is a busy area. On your first day, hike straight up the bank of the Astoria River into the scenic Surprise Point campground. Stay here your first night. The trail along the river isn't too steep; it follows Mount Edith Cavell's north face and crisscrosses the river over a series of bridges. On Day 2, take a day hike to Chrome and Arrowhead lakes and the Eremite Valley, just as spectacular as the more famous Ramparts nearby. Take the time to explore the upper end of Eremite Valley, where glaciers top almost every summit. For your second or third night, reserve a night at the **Amethyst Lake campground** *⚿*, where you'll first begin to admire the Ramparts. My advice: Hold off on this hike until early September. This trail often has grizzly bear warnings. The beginning elevation is 1,480m (4,854 ft.); you lose 235m (771 ft.), then gain 730m (2,394 ft.). 48.1km (29.8-mile) loop (includes side trip to Emerite Valley). Moderate. Access: From Jasper Townsite, follow Icefields Pkwy. 93 6.7km (4¼ miles) south to Hwy. 93A junction. Follow 93A 5.2km (3¼ miles) south to Mount Edith Cavell Rd. Follow Mount Edith Cavell Rd. 13km (7¾ miles) west to trail head parking lot.

3 Other Activities

The **Jasper Adventure Centre** (604 Connaught Dr.; © **800/565-7547** or 780/852-5595; www.jasperadventurecentre.com) will help you plan a variety of outdoor activities during your stay in the park, from rafting and canoeing to horseback riding and sightseeing. The staff here can help you choose the right trip for you, then will make the reservations for you. They operate year-round, daily from 9am to 9pm.

ROAD BIKING & MOUNTAIN BIKING

Biking is a great way to get around the Town of Jasper, and to visit the nearby attractions. But, while you can bike through the town's streets and paved paths to your heart's content, road and mountain bikes are permitted on only a select number of hiking trails in Jasper National Park. Many of the trails where mountain biking is permitted remain snow-covered into June and are quite muddy for many weeks after the initial melt-off. In the spring, trails along fire roads are the driest. It's very important to follow trail etiquette and to stick to designated trails—for more information, pick up the **Mountain Biking in Jasper National Park** handout from the **Jasper Information Centre** (500 Connaught Dr.; © **780/852-6176**).

If you're on a regular road bike, head to Old Fort Point and follow the road to Lac Beauvert, and lakes Annette and Edith, via the Fairmont Jasper Park Lodge. You might also want to bike to Pyramid Lake or Maligne Canyon.

The best mountain-bike trail in the area is the 14km (9-mile) **Overlander Trail,** which follows a route along the Athabasca River between Maligne Canyon's Sixth Bridge and the Yellowhead Highway (Hwy. 16). While there are some challenging sandy sections and tricky sidehill riding, there are also some great views!

Novices will like the trail ride along Trail 7 from Old Fort Point to Maligne Canyon and the rides along the Valley of the Five Lakes. Families should try the relatively flat and very pleasant 5km (3-mile)

Tips Bike Rentals

The bike shops will likely try to rent you their most expensive bikes. If you're a beginner mountain biker, however, and will just be heading out on a few trails around town, you do not need a full-suspension bike. If you want to just cruise the main streets of the townsite, opt for the cheapest bike.

Biking Do's & Don'ts

- Bike only on designated trails.
- Stay on the trail. Riding around mud puddles and veering off the trail damage vegetation.
- Select a trail that matches your ability.
- Treat other trail users with courtesy, especially on downhill stretches. Make sure your bike has a bell, horn, or whistle, and use it to let other trail users and wildlife know you are there.
- Know that horses have the right of way. If you meet a party of horses, get off your bike and step aside to let them pass.
- Realize that you can get much farther into the backcountry on two wheels than on two feet. Bring enough water and snacks to tide you over if you wind up spending more time on the trail than you planned.

trail along the lush, vegetated valley to the **Summit Lakes.** There are more bike trails along the benchlands above the townsite.

The folks at **Freewheel Cycle** (681 Patricia St.; © **780/852-3898;** www.freewheeljasper.com) are the local experts on two-wheeling. They rent front-suspension mountain bikes that can also be used on roads, from C$30 (US$28) a day. You can rent both road and mountain bikes from **Jasper Source for Sports** (406 Patricia St.; © **780/ 852-3654**). Rates are C$26 (US$24) to C$42 (US$39) per day.

CANOEING & RAFTING

There are dozens of tranquil lakes in Jasper National Park that are perfect for canoe outings. Some of the more accessible areas are **Pyramid Lake, Lac Beauvert** in front of the Fairmont Jasper Park Lodge, **Maligne Lake,** and the Fifth Lake in the Valley of the Five Lakes.

The **Athabasca River** is the best bet for canoeing in fast-moving water. The best canoe route in Jasper National Park—perhaps the best one in the Canadian Rockies—is from the **Athabasca River at Old Fort Point to Jasper Lake** ✖✖. The river moves fast, but there are few obstacles or rapids. It passes through the favorite route of fur trader and mapmaker David Thompson, who paddled the river in 1800, and practically anyone else who has paddled it since. The river slows down when it hits Jasper Lake (which is spotted with shallow sand bars that make navigating a challenge). Don't be afraid to step onto the sandy bottom to help you make it through. Stay to the right side of the lake to hit the take-out point, alongside Highway 16.

Pick up a copy of the **Athabasca River Touring Guide** at the **Jasper Information Centre** (500 Connaught Dr.; © 780/852-6176).

Rent a canoe, kayak, or pedal boat at the **Fairmont Jasper Park Lodge's Boathouse** (4km/2½ miles east of Jasper Townsite on Hwy. 16, south at Maligne Lake Rd. and a quick right/west after the bridge, continue 3.2km/2 miles to the Lodge; © 780/852-5708). Rental rates are C$25 (US$23) for 30 minutes, or C$35 (US$33) for 1 hour. Canoes, kayaks, and rowboats can be rented at the **Maligne Lake** boathouse (4km/2½ miles east of Jasper Townsite to Maligne Lake Rd., follow 48km/30 miles to end of the road; © 780/852-3370). Rates are C$25 (US$23) per hour, or C$75 (US$70) per day. There are a number of whitewater-rafting trips that head out from the Town of Jasper, including a scenic family float trip on the Athabasca River and a bit bumpier introduction to whitewater on the Athabasca—with Class II rapids that will make a lifelong river-lover out of any kid. There are also challenging and technical Class III rapids on the Sunwapta River (*Sunwapta* is a Stoney Indian word meaning "turbulent river"). The big rapid is known as "the Whopper."

None of the whitewater trips mentioned above should be attempted on your own. Children age 12 and up are usually allowed on the Sunwapta River trip. Two guiding companies run Athabasca and Sunwapta River trips. **Jasper Raft Tours** (604 Connaught Dr.; © 780/852-2665) rates for the Athabasca family trip are C$49 (US$46) for adults and C$15 (US$14) for children age 11 and under.

FISHING
You need a Parks Canada permit to fish in Jasper National Park. Permits cost C$10 (US$9.30) for a day or C$35 (US$33) for a year. You can purchase a permit at the **Jasper Information Centre** (500 Connaught Dr.; © 780/852-6176) or at the boathouse at Maligne Lake.

Of the lakes that are warm enough to support fish, I recommend **Talbot Lake,** northeast of the townsite along the Yellowhead Highway 16 (a good destination for families, since it's easy to get to), or **Beaver Lake,** which has a healthy supply of brook trout, especially on summer evenings. The large and scenic **Maligne Lake** has a public boat launch, a boathouse with rentals, and record-setting rainbow and Eastern brook trout. A provincial record 9-kilogram (20-lb.) rainbow trout was caught here! The best way to ensure you catch fish is to hire a local guide. Get in touch with the fly-fishing specialists at **Currie's Guiding** (620 Connaught Dr.; ℂ **780/852-5650**). Their trips last 4 to 7 hours, and cost between C$179 (US$167) and C$219 (US$205). Rates include transportation to the water, tackle, rain gear, and lunch.

If you've got your own ideas about where to go trolling but didn't bring your rod, you can rent fly and spin rods from **Jasper Source for Sports** (406 Patricia St.; ℂ **780/852-3653**).

GOLFING

One of only nine golf courses in the world to receive a Gold Medal in *Golf Magazine*'s 1999 international rankings, a round or two at the **Fairmont Jasper Park Lodge's course** (4km/2½ miles east of Jasper Townsite on Hwy. 16, then south on Maligne Lake Rd. and a quick left/west after the bridge, follow 3.2km/2 miles to end; ℂ **780/852-6090**) is a must for any golfer visiting Jasper. It's a scenic 18-hole course, with 73 sand traps and three water hazards. Oh yes, and the odd wild animal might wander through your drive. Pretty as it is, though, it's not inexpensive to play here. Green fees range from C$95 (US$89) to C$200 (US$187) per person, including cart. A good deal during the June to mid-August summer months is the **twilight golf** option, for C$74 (US$69) per person for tee times after 5pm. If you're a guest at the lodge and are playing with children under 19 years of age, wait until after 3pm, when junior fees drop considerably.

HORSEBACK RIDING

A wide variety of guided horseback trips are available in Jasper National Park, from 1-hour tours of the trails above Jasper Townsite to 5-day backcountry pack trips. **Pyramid Lake Stables** (Pyramid Lake Rd., Jasper, AB T0E 1E0; 4km/2½ miles north from the Town of Jasper on Pyramid Lake Rd.; ℂ **780/852-3562**) takes short trips up to the benchlands above the townsite. Ponies are available for children to ride. Rates are C$35 (US$33) per person for 1 hour, C$57 (US$53) per person for 2 hours, C$175 (US$163) per person for an all-day ride including lunch.

4 Winter Sports & Activities

Uncrowded and friendly, Jasper National Park is a wonderful place to be in the winter. You can take part in just as many activities as are on offer in Banff, but you benefit from fewer crowds and an inti-mate, small-town feel. You can rent downhill skis, snowboards, and cross-country gear at a number of shops in town. A basic ski pack-age goes for under C$25 (US$23) a day. If you want the most modern equipment available, you're looking at a price near C$50 (US$47) a day, including boots, skis, and poles. Try **Totem Ski Shop** (408 Connaught Dr.; ✆ 780/852-3078), **Freewheel Cycle and Snowboards** (618 Patricia St.; ✆ 780/852-3898), **Edge Control Outdoors** (626 Connaught Dr.; ✆ 780/852-4945), or **Jasper Source for Sports** (406 Patricia St.; ✆ 780/852-3654). Shop around for the best price. You can both rent and purchase ski and snowboard equipment at these stores.

CANYON CRAWLING

As the winter freeze hardens the spectacular Maligne Canyon just east of Jasper Townsite, a whole new outdoor adventure is reborn. The Maligne River freezes solid through the limestone gorge, while small waterfalls cascading off the canyon cliffs grow into giant cur-tains of ice. Canyon crawling involves walking through portions of the canyon bottoms and inside caves in the ice. Do this activity with a guide who can show you the safest ways to explore the ice. For trip information, contact the **Jasper Adventure Centre** (604 Con-naught Dr.; ✆ **780/852-5595;** www.jasperadventurecentre.com).

CROSS-COUNTRY SKIING

Popular with locals, **Maligne Lake** ✶ is the best area for cross-coun-try skiing. There are a number of trails to suit different levels of abil-ity. Novices will enjoy the gentle **Maligne Lakeside Loop** and the trails to **Moose Lake.** Intermediates can try the **Lorraine Lake Trail,** while those with good stamina and experience will like the **Evelyn Creek Trail.** There is an impressive network of trails at the **Fairmont Jasper Park Lodge.**

⎛Tips⎞ Be Weather Wary

A sunny winter day in the Canadian Rockies with temperatures hovering around the freezing mark can plummet into bitterly cold winter whiteout conditions in a matter of hours. Winds often come up out of nowhere, bringing clouds and snow with them. Dress warmly and in layers. And don't leave a hat or pair of gloves behind. Call ✆ **780/852-3185** for weather updates.

DOWNHILL SKIING & SNOWBOARDING

You won't find the same celebrity ski resorts in Jasper that you do in Banff. Jasper has only one ski and snowboard resort, and that's **Marmot Basin** 𝕽𝕽 (P.O. Box 1300, Jasper, AB T0E 1E0; ℂ **780/852-3816;** www.skimarmot.com; 19km/12 miles southwest of Jasper Townsite on Hwy. 93 and then turn west on 93A). It's a laid-back, rustic ski hill with about 600 hectares (1,500 acres) of terrain. There are 84 marked runs serviced by nine lifts. While many of the runs are groomed, there are also open bowls and tree skiing for expert skiers and snowboarders. A huge expansion project (under the watchful eye of Parks Canada) opened up a glorious new wilderness area for expert skiers and snowboarders in 2001, and new runs open up each season. The Eagle Ridge includes some of the best glade skiing in Canada, fantastic terrain where you'll feel like you are outabounds. There's also a new rental shop at the base and an improved snow-making system that should help extend the season past Easter. The scenery at Marmot is phenomenal, especially if you catch one of those bright and blue Alberta winter days. A great family package includes lessons for kids. There are also packages for beginner skiers and snowboarders, and great package deals with local hotels, especially during the "Jasper in January" promotion. Full-day lift tickets cost C$59 (US$55) for adults, C$48 (US$45) for youth ages 11 to 17, and C$21 (US$20) for children ages 6 to 11. Children under age 6 ski for free. Prices drop significantly if you purchase multiday passes.

ICE-SKATING

Outdoor rinks are maintained at **Pyramid Lake** and on **Lac Beauvert** 𝕽, in front of the Fairmont Jasper Park Lodge. East of town, try Talbot Lake or Snaring Pond. You can rent skates at **Jasper Source for Sports** (406 Patricia St.; ℂ **780/852-3654**).

SNOWSHOEING

Once an activity reserved for rugged fur traders trudging through snowy passes, snowshoeing has hopped on the adventure-sports bandwagon. The best spots for snowshoeing are marshy or gladed areas like the **Pyramid Lake Bench,** just above Jasper Townsite, or on the frozen surface of **Maligne Lake,** where the snow is most soft, flat, and consistent. You could also try the golf course at the **Fairmont Jasper Park Lodge.** Rent modern snowshoes at **Jasper Source for Sports** (406 Patricia St.; ℂ **780/852-3654**). You can pick up maps, trail information, and the brochure **Winter Trails** at the **Jasper Information Centre** (500 Connaught Dr., Jasper, AB T0E 1E0; ℂ **780/852-6176**).

8

Where to Stay, Camp & Eat in Jasper National Park

Jasper doesn't have the variety of hotels and restaurants that Banff has, but what is here is generally reliable and well managed. Another trade-off between Jasper and Banff: The lodging in Jasper is more secluded than that in Banff, giving visitors a usually much-sought-after sense of privacy. There are some very scenic frontcountry campgrounds, and there are more backcountry campsites here than in Banff, meaning more opportunities to spend peaceful nights in the wilderness.

1 Lodging in Jasper National Park

Almost all the lodging possibilities in Jasper National Park are within a 10-minute drive of Jasper Townsite. There's a wide range of options, from the legendary Fairmont Jasper Park Lodge, to midrange motels, to bed-and-breakfasts.

There was a boom in hotel building in Jasper during the 1970s and early 1980s. The majority of the hotels that went up are located around the outskirts of town. They're of the cookie-cutter variety, though, and I think they charge too much for a service that is generally ordinary. The lodging options in this chapter have more character and are mostly (with a few exceptions) a better value. You can opt for a room in one of these newer hotels or motels; however, think instead about renting a small, private cabin or bungalow. This is what Jasper excels at, and it's something you won't find a lot of in Banff. There are a dozen or so such lodgings, open only in summertime.

Jasper has an impressive network of B&Bs and home accommodations, where local families rent out rooms or suites in private homes. From fancy to frugal, and for a wide range of budgets, there are up to 125 to choose from. They are all inspected and licensed by Parks Canada, and are a great way to meet locals. For more information, contact the **Jasper Home Accommodation Association** ⚑ (P.O. Box 758, Jasper, AB T0E 1E0; stayinjasper.com). The most interesting ones are self-contained, with private entrances and kitch-enettes, allowing you to cook in and spread out.

Another good source of accommodations information is **Jasper Tourism & Commerce** (P.O. Box 98, Jasper, AB T0E 1E0; ℂ **780/ 852-3858;** www.jaspercanadianrockies.com). They have a booth at the **Jasper National Park Information Centre** (500 Connaught Dr., Jasper, AB T0E 1E0; ℂ **780/852-6176**) with updates on availability.

VERY EXPENSIVE

Fairmont Jasper Park Lodge ☆☆   Built in 1923, this historic lodge epitomizes the pampered wilderness experience. The queen of the Jasper area, it's like an upscale summer camp for adults spread over the largest commercial property in the Canadian Rockies. But it's not cheap; in the summer, expect to pay upward of C$400 (US$374) for a single night in the smallest room. However, several different kinds of packages are available, geared toward golf, ski, or romance holidays, and they are usually a much better deal.

The hotel has undergone many waves of renovations, the most recent being upgrades in heating systems and redecoration to 180 rooms in 2005. The guest rooms are mostly in single-story cabins and cottages spread throughout the property. The main lodge and reception area are quite stunning. This is where you'll find gracious sitting areas and porches overlooking Lac Beauvert, as well as the restaurants and pool. Guest rooms are quite large and open, with very comfortable beds. Bathrooms all have vanities and large tubs. Of the regular-size rooms, the Jasper Premier rooms are the only ones with a lakefront view, and they're considerably more expensive. If you have a larger budget or are traveling in a bigger group, there's no shortage of suites and specialty cabins to tempt you. Before you call to book a room, decide how important a lakefront view is to you because they'll immediately try to sell you one of the most expensive ones, always quoting you a lakefront Jasper Premium or deluxe room rate first. Ask about the skiing, romance, bed-and-breakfast, and golf packages, which can be a good way to save some cash. In winter, ask for a room close to the main lodge.

P.O. Box 40, Jasper, AB T0E 1E0. 4km (2¼ miles) east of Jasper on Hwy. 16, 3.2km (2 miles) southeast off Maligne Lake Rd. ℂ **800/441-1414** or 780/852-3301. Fax 780/852-5107. www.fairmont.com/jasper. 446 units. Rates vary based on views, dates, and availabilities. Jan 1–May 15 and Oct 10–Dec 18 starting from C$229 (US$214); May 16–Oct 9 starting from C$429 (US$401); Dec 19–31 starting from C$329 (US$307). Suites and large-cabin rates vary dramatically. Extra person C$25 (US$23). Children 17 and under stay free in parent's room, except with some package deals. AE, DC, DISC, MC, V. **Amenities:** 6 restaurants; 3 lounges; large heated outdoor pool; golf course on property; 4 outdoor tennis courts; exercise room; Jacuzzi; sauna; riding stables; bike and canoe rentals; business center; salon; 24-hr. room service; massage; spa; shopping; babysitting; laundry service. *In room:* TV, video games, coffeemaker, hair dryer, iron, Internet.

EXPENSIVE

Alpine Village 👁👁👁 This is my favorite hotel in Jasper. Located on the banks of the rushing Athabasca River, its rustic log cottages are the ideal romantic getaway for visitors who don't feel the need to socialize or to go out for dinner each night, but instead want to enjoy the natural beauty of the park. It's owned by a couple who were married one day and started running the business the next. It has been renovated many times, most recently in 2004 when six cabins were expanded to two stories. These now sleep up to five, and have a modern kitchen, fireplace, and heaps of rustic ambience.

Sunshine pours into the cabin kitchenettes. Deluxe bedroom suites are newer and more modern than the one-room cabins, although quite small. They do have lovely balconies, cozy kitchenettes smaller than those in the cabins, wood-burning fireplaces, and private barbecues. The cabins farthest from the road are quieter, but those along the river (next to the road) have the best views. The quaint older cabins (some dating back to 1941) are larger than the deluxe suites; each has two bedrooms, living room, and kitchen. All have a balcony, fireplace, and private barbecue. Bathrooms are very small.

P.O. Box 610, Jasper, AB T0E 1E0. 2.5km (1½ miles) south of Jasper Townsite on the Icefields Pkwy. Hwy. 93; at the junction with Hwy. 93A. © **780/852-3285.** Fax 780/852-1955. www.alpinevillagejasper.com. 41 units, 28 with kitchenettes. Mid-June to mid-Sept and all holidays C$190–C$350 (US$178–US$327); mid-May to mid-June and mid-Sept to Sept 30 C$160–C$290 (US$150–US$271); May 1 to mid-May and Oct 1 to mid-Oct C$130–C$220 (US$122–US$206). Extra person C$10 (US$9.30). Children 6 and under stay free in parent's room. MC, V. Closed mid-Oct to end of April. **Amenities:** Jacuzzi; laundry service. *In room:* Kitchenette in some, fridge, coffeemaker, hair dryer.

Coast Pyramid Lake Resort (Kids Nestled on a hillside overlooking picturesque Pyramid Lake, this small resort offers plenty of activities, solitude, and lovely new rooms with an open atmosphere. It's now open summer-only, from May through October. The main lodge—including a restaurant with a stunning view of the lake—sits atop the boat rentals and lounge. The old Founders Cabins, built in 1952, have thin walls and tiny bathrooms, but offer the best views of the lake. The top-floor Cavell Rooms, built in the late 1990s, are the largest and most modern guest rooms, perfect for families planning on staying a few days. Guest rooms are decorated in earth tones with plenty of plaid as an accent. Bathrooms are bright and have large bathtubs. All have pullout sofas. There's a new fitness room and outdoor hot tub. It's slow-paced up here, although there are plenty of outdoor activities. You'll need a car of your own to get around. This is a lovely, peaceful lodge, ideal for active visitors who don't want to be distracted by anything but the outdoors. Kids under 18 stay free with parents.

P.O. Box 388, Jasper, AB T0L 1E0. 6km (3¾ miles) north from Jasper Townsite on Pyramid Lake Rd. © **800/663-1144** or 780/852-4900. Fax 780/852-7007. www. coasthotels.com. 62 units. May C$109–C$169 (US$102–US$158); June–Sept C$194–C$234 (US$181–US$219); Oct C$114–C$194 (US$107–US$181). Extra person C$15 (US$14). Children 18 and under stay free in parent's room. AE, DC, MC, V. **Amenities:** Restaurant; fitness room; outdoor Jacuzzi; canoe rentals. *In room:* Color TV, minibar, coffeemaker, hair dryer.

Mount Robson Inn   This motel has a wide variety of uniquely decorated and well-appointed guest rooms. The options range from basic guest rooms with queen-size beds to fancy suites with private Jacuzzis, not to mention a plush honeymoon suite. I like this two-story motel because it's locally owned and the managers put a lot of care into making it a welcoming place. It has character compared to the other motel-esque inns in Jasper (and there are a lot of them), marked by long, ordinary hallways with identical rooms. All the bathrooms got an upgrade in the fall of 2007. There are also new down comforters and larger televisions. The restaurant next door is nothing special, but provides room service.

902 Connaught Dr., Jasper, AB T0L 1E0. © **800/587-3327** or 780/852-3327. Fax 780/852-5004. www.mountrobsoninn.com. 80 units. June 10–Sept 25 C$214–C$325 (US$200–US$304); Sept 26–Oct 15 C$149–C$268 (US$139–US$251); Oct 16–Dec 27 and Jan 2–Feb 28 C$104–C$220 (US$97–US$206); New Year's C$119–C$269 (US$111–US$252); Mar 1–Apr 30 C$109–C$239 (US$102–US$224); May 1–June 9 C$142–C$261 (US$133–US$244). Extra person C$10 (US$9.30). Children 11 and under stay free in parent's room. AE, DC, DISC, MC, V. **Amenities:** Outdoor Jacuzzi; wireless Internet; ski lockers; laundry. *In room:* A/C, TV, fridge, coffeemaker, hair dryer, iron.

MODERATE

Lobstick Lodge   Located in the northeast corner of town, this hotel has reasonable prices and an unpretentious atmosphere. Built in the late 1960s, the hotel was completely renovated in 1995 and all rooms received new bathrooms in 2007. The lobby now has a coffee shop and a slightly more upscale look. The guest rooms with kitchens are ideal if you're visiting for a few days, although the kitchens themselves are quite dark. Standard guest rooms have queen-size or double beds. Request a guest room on an upper level that overlooks the street and the mountains beyond. Otherwise, you may end up with a disappointing view of the courtyard or pool patio. Although it's nothing particularly special and feels a bit like a Howard Johnson, it's a serviceable hotel.

94 Geikie St., Jasper, AB T0L 1E0. © 888/852-7737 or 780/852-4431. Fax 780/852-4142. www.lobsticklodge.com. 139 units, 45 with kitchenettes. June–Sept C$225 (US$210) standard room; C$247 (US$231) with kitchenette. May and Oct C$149 (US$139) standard room; C$177 (US$166) with kitchenette. Nov 1–Dec 24 C$90 (US$84) standard room; C$109 (US$102) with kitchenette. Dec 25–31 and Feb–Apr C$112 (US$105) standard room; C$149 (US$139) with kitchenette. Jan C$99 (US$93) room; C$119 (US$111) with kitchenette. Extra person C$10 (US$9.30). Children 15 and under stay free in parent's room. AE, DC, DISC, MC, V. **Amenities:** Restaurant; lounge; large heated indoor pool; Jacuzzi; sauna; laundry service. *In room:* TV, coffeemaker, iron, hair dryer.

Park Place Inn ★ *(Finds* Jasper's newest hotel is in a category all its own—urban and friendly, it's a classy boutique inn with reasonable rates. The 12 unique and spacious rooms are attractively decorated, with an upscale cowboy heritage theme. The ambience is created by beautiful linens, goose-down duvets, hardwood floors, huge tubs (many are claw-foot style), and plenty of space. Located upstairs on the bustling Patricia Street, it feels downtown (if that's possible in Jasper). Downstairs are two new luxurious, albeit somewhat dark, suites with all the trimmings. You're literally steps away from the cafes and restaurants.

P.O. Box 2122, 623 Patricia St., Jasper, AB T0E 1E0. © 866/852-9770 or 780/852-9770. Fax 780/852-1180. www.parkplaceinn.com. 14 rooms. June–Sept C$219–C$239 (US$205–US$223), suite C$265 (US$248); Oct 1–15 and mid-Dec to early Jan C$155–C$175 (US$145–US$164), suite C$195 (US$182); Oct 1 to mid-Dec and early Jan to May 30 C$129–C$159 (US$121–US$149), suite C$195 (US$182). Extra person C$15 (US$14). Children under 15 stay free in parent's room. AE, MC, V. *In room:* Color TV, A/C, minibar, coffeemaker.

Pine Bungalows ★ *(Value* Like Alpine Village, reviewed above, these cabins are also ensconced along the Athabasca River. Staying at Pine Bungalows will take some guests on a nostalgia kick, back to road trips with the family to cabins up north. That's because most of the cabins were built in the 1940s and still have that look and feel. Depending on their experience, some visitors will relish this trip back in time, while others will want to stay far away!

Cabins are clean and simple, with comfortable beds. Most of them have fireplaces, and nearly all of them have kitchenettes.

Bathrooms are tidy and simple, all with tubs and showers. There's a brand-new 25-room motel building and convention center that is of interest only to large groups. The best cabins are nos. 1 through 12, right on the river. I think this is a romantic place, a good choice if you don't need to be pampered and want your privacy. In the evenings, enjoy the trails along the river and gather to mingle with neighbors over a campfire. And no, the bugs aren't bad.

P.O. Box 7, Jasper, AB T0E 1E0. Just off Hwy. 16 and the Jasper Townsite turnoff. ℗ 780/852-3491. Fax 780/852-3432. www.pinebungalows.com. 72 cabins, 57 with kitchens and 25 motel rooms. May–Oct C$150 (US$140) motel room; C$150 (US$140) double with kitchen; C$200 (US$187) 2-bedroom cabin with kitchen; C$145 (US$136) king without kitchen. Extra person C$10 (US$9.30). 3-day minimum stay in some cabins. AE, MC, V. Closed Nov–Apr. **Amenities:** Coin-op washers and dryers. *In room:* No phone, no TV.

Whistlers Inn   This reasonably priced hotel has a plum location in downtown Jasper, right across the street from both the heritage railway station and the Jasper Information Centre. The guest rooms are large and have all been renovated in the past few years, though the furnishing is rather uninspiring. There's a nice new top-floor outdoor hot tub. It's a good bet if you are on a moderate budget and want to be close to the action, since all the restaurants, bars, shops, and outfitters are around the corner. Don't choose Whistlers if you plan on being in your room a lot or you are looking for a suite. Choose a standard room here for the location and the price.

105 Miette Ave., P.O. Box 250, Jasper, AB T0E 1E0. ℗ 800/282-9919 or 780/852-3361. Fax 780/852-4993. www.whistlersinn.com. 64 units. June–Sept C$177–C$311 (US$166–US$291); Oct–May C$97–C$209 (US$91–US$195). Extra person C$15 (US$14). Children 17 and under stay free in parent's room. AE, MC, V. Limited free parking. **Amenities:** Lounge; Jacuzzi; ski storage. *In room:* A/C, TV, coffeemaker, hair dryer.

INEXPENSIVE

Jasper International Hostel   This hostel is located in what was the first ski lodge serving the Jasper area, 7km (4⅓ miles) southwest of the townsite, on Whistlers Mountain Road. This is the best choice for budget travelers in Jasper. It's a good location if you have a car or are a big group, although there is a shuttle service available. There are two dorms that are very big, where you'll sleep in bunk beds. Bathrooms are all shared. Family rooms are also available. The shared kitchen is very handy. There is a fun full-time activity program that will get you out exploring Jasper.

P.O. Box 387, Jasper, AB T0E 1E0. 4km (2½ miles) south of Jasper Townsite on Hwy. 93, turn west on Tramway Rd. and follow for 3km (2 miles). ℗ 877/852-0781 or

780/852-3215. Fax 780/852-5560. www.hihostels.ca/alberta. 5 units (2 dormitory-style rooms and 3 private family rooms), 84 beds total. May 31–Sept C$23 (US$22) dorm room for Hostelling International members, C$28 (US$26) dorm room for nonmembers, C$56 (US$52) private room per person for Hostelling International members, C$66 (US$62) private room per person for nonmembers; Oct–May 30 C$21 (US$20) for Hostelling International members, C$26 (US$24) for nonmembers, C$52 (US$49) private room per person for Hostelling International members, C$62 (US$58) private room per person for nonmembers. MC, V. **Amenities:** Lounge; Jacuzzi; bike rentals; coin-op washers and dryers, kitchen; barbecue. *In room:* No phone.

2 Frontcountry Camping in Jasper National Park

Select frontcountry campsites in Jasper National Park (at the Pocahontas, Whistlers, Wapiti, and Wabasso campgrounds) can now be reserved ahead of time at www.pccamping.ca or © **877/737-3783.** A number of sites are set aside for drive-up campers; these are available on a first-come, first-served basis. Visitors traveling in RVs should head to **Whistlers** or **Wapiti** campgrounds. Whistlers has full hookups (electrical and sewage), while Wapiti has only electrical hookups. Tenters looking for a central location can bunk in beside the RVs at these campgrounds or head to one of the more outlying, rustic campgrounds. Refer to the table later in this section for an at-a-glance comparison of frontcountry campgrounds in Jasper.

A note on campground rates: Rates quoted are per site, and are applicable for occupancy up to six people. Therefore, a family of four will pay the same rate as a couple or a person traveling alone. If you're in an RV, I suggest you stick to the campgrounds that have hookup facilities, although RVs are welcome to park for the night at many of the outlying campgrounds that do not have hookups. In Jasper, however, Jonas Creek, Snaring River, and Columbia Icefield campgrounds are for tenters only. Also please note that opening and closing dates change annually depending on Canadian holidays and on weather conditions.

FRONTCOUNTRY CAMPGROUNDS

Columbia Icefield Campground This small and rustic camping area (tent-only) is close to the main hub of activities at the Columbia Icefield Centre. I prefer Wilcox Creek because it's more removed from the bustle. But Columbia Icefield campground opens earlier and closes later, making it a real gem during the quiet shoulder-season months.

106km (66 miles) south of Jasper Townsite on the Icefields Pkwy. 93. 33 sites. No RV hookups. C$15 (US$14). Open mid-May to mid-Oct.

Honeymoon Lake Campground *(Moments)*   This small, secluded campground is located beside a lake that's perfect for early-evening canoeing.

52km (32 miles) south of Jasper Townsite on the Icefields Pkwy. 93. 35 sites. No RV hookups. C$15 (US$14). Open mid-June to early Sept.

Jonas Creek Campground   This is a lovely, quiet campground. Amenities are basic—it's almost like being in the backcountry.

78km (48 miles) south of Jasper Townsite on the Icefields Pkwy. Hwy. 93. 25 sites. No RV hookups. C$15 (US$14). Open mid-May to early Sept.

Mount Kerkeslin Campground *ᖴ*   There are striking mountain views from this campground south of Jasper Townsite.

36km (22 miles) south of Jasper Townsite on the Icefields Pkwy. Hwy. 93. 42 sites. No RV hookups. C$15 (US$14). Open mid-June to early Sept.

Pocahontas Campground   This is the first campground you pass if you arrive in Jasper National Park from Edmonton, on the Yellowhead Highway (Hwy. 16). The campground is large, with a field for games and activities. It you've had a long day, stop here for the night and save the drive into the heart of Jasper for the morning. It's close to the Miette Hot Springs.

44km (27 miles) east of Jasper Townsite on Yellowhead Hwy. 16. 140 sites. No RV hookups. C$21 (US$20). Open mid-May to mid-Oct.

Snaring River Campground *ᖴ (Finds)*   Located east of the townsite, this peaceful campground does not have hookups for RVs and tent-trailers, nor any amenities save dry toilets, firewood, and kitchen shelters. Still, it's an ideal spot for those looking for a more secluded and rustic place to camp that isn't too far from the townsite or the Maligne Canyon area for hiking. This is my first choice if I'm tenting.

13km (8 miles) east of Jasper Townsite on Yellowhead Hwy. 16. 66 sites. No RV hookups. C$15 (US$14). Open mid-May to mid-Sept.

Wabasso Campground *ᖴ*   This pretty campground is located between the Athabasca and Whirlpool rivers—a beautiful, scenic spot. There are 228 sites, a sanitary station with flush toilets, and interpretive programs in the summer. This campground is popular—book ahead of time online at www.pccamping.ca.

16km (10 miles) from Jasper Townsite on Athabasca Hwy. 93A. 228 sites. No RV hookups. C$21 (US$20). Open late June to early Sept.

Wapiti Campground   This is the only campground in the park that's open year-round. There are 362 sites, 322 of which are for tents only. All 362 sites remain accessible in winter, with full RV hookups available on 40 sites. There are often elk roaming about here—remember to keep your distance.

4km (2½ miles) south of Jasper Townsite on the Icefields Pkwy. Hwy. 93, on the east side. Summer: 362 sites; 40 with electrical hookup. C$26 (US$24) tents; C$30 (US$28) RVs. Open Victoria Day long weekend (late May) and mid-June to early Sept. Winter: 93 sites; 40 with electrical hookup. C$17 (US$16) tents; C$20 (US$19) RVs. Open early Oct to early May.

Whistlers   This is the biggest campground in Jasper, with 781 sites. It's also just south of town, on the Icefields Parkway (Hwy. 93). Although it's not a particularly private place, Whistlers does have all the standard campground amenities, which is why it's usually the first campground in the area to fill up. It can also accommodate large groups. The months of June through September see fun interpretive programs put on in the summer evenings. Of the 177 RV sites, 100 have electrical hookups only; the other 77 sites have full hookups. I've twice seen a bear here—keep your food stored properly.

3km (2 miles) south of Jasper Townsite on the Icefields Pkwy. Hwy. 93, on the west side. 781 sites; 100 with electrical hookup only, 77 with full hookup. C$22–C$26 (US$21–US$24) tents; C$30 (US$28) electrical hookup; C$36 (US$34) full hookup. Open early May to early Oct.

Wilcox Creek Campground   It's cold at this small, tents-only campground at the **Icefield Information Centre,** but it's a good choice if you want to beat the crowds on a snocoach or walking tour of the Athabasca Glacier, or if you're planning on waking up early to go hiking in the Brazeau Valley. Did I mention that it's cold up here? Be prepared for chilly nights.

108km (67 miles) south of Jasper Townsite on the Icefields Pkwy. 93. 46 sites. No RV hookups. C$16 (US$15). Open early June to early Sept.

Reservations can be made at www.pccamping.ca or ℂ **877/ 737-3783** for sites at Pocahontas, Whistlers, Wapiti, and Wabasso. A small number of campsites are also available on a first-come, first-served basis.

Please note that these dates are roughly matched to coincide with major Canadian long-weekend holidays, including Victoria Day (third Mon in May), Labor Day (first Mon in Sept), and Thanksgiving (second Mon in Oct). Exact dates will fluctuate from year to year and are also weather-dependent.

Jasper National Park Frontcountry Campgrounds

Campground	Total Sites	RV Hookups	Dump Station	Flush Toilets	Drinking Water	Showers	Firepits/ Grills	Laundry	Public Phones	Self-register	Fees	Open
Columbia Icefield	33	No	No	No	Yes	No	Yes	No	No	Yes	C$15 (US$14)	May 18–Oct 8
Honeymoon Lake Campground	35	No	No	No	Yes	No	Yes	No	No	Yes	C$15 (US$14)	June 21–Sept 3
Jonas Creek Campground	25	No	No	No	Yes	No	Yes	No	No	Yes	C$15(US$14)	May 18–Sept 3
Mount Kerkeslin Campground	42	No	No	No	Yes	No	Yes	No	No	Yes	C$15 (US$14)	June 21–Sept 3
Pocahontas Campground	140	No	No	Yes	Yes	No	Yes	No	No	Yes	C$21 (US$20)	May 18–Oct 8
Snaring River Campground	66	No	No	No	Yes	No	Yes	No	No	Yes	C$15 (US$14)	May 18–Sept 17
Wabasso Campground	228	No	Yes	Yes	Yes	No	Yes	No	No	No	C$21 (US$20)	June 21–Sept 4
Wapiti Campground (summer season)	362	40 Yes (electrical only)	Yes	Yes	Yes	Yes	No	Yes	No	No	C$26–C$30 (US$24–US$28)	May 18–21; June 15–Sept 3
Wapiti Campground (winter season)	93	40 (electrical only)	No	Yes	Yes	No	Yes	No	Yes	No	C$17–C$20 (US$16–US$19)	Oct 8–May 9
Whistlers Campground	781	77 full hookups; 100 electrical only	Yes	Yes	Yes	Yes	Yes	Yes	Yes	No	C$22–C$36 (US$21–US$34)	May 4–Oct 8
Wilcox Creek Campground	46	No	Yes	No	Yes	No	Yes	No	No	Yes	C$16 (US$15)	June 8–Sept 10

3 Backcountry Camping & Lodging in Jasper National Park

Take advantage of the outstanding backcountry camping available in Jasper National Park—some of the best in Canada. There's more than enough space to find some real solitude and privacy. See "Exploring the Backcountry" in chapter 7 for more information on backpacking trails in Jasper.

BACKCOUNTRY CAMPING

You need to reserve a backcountry campsite before you head out on a backpacking trip. Reserve by calling the **Jasper National Park office,** at © **780/852-6177,** or visit the **Jasper National Park Information Centre** (500 Connaught Dr.; same telephone number). I recommend that you reserve 3 months before your trip if you have a particular campsite in mind. Rates are C$10 (US$9.30) per person per night. There is a nonrefundable reservation charge of C$12 (US$11).

There are more than 100 backcountry campsites in Jasper National Park. The most popular ones, including those on the **Skyline Trail,** the **Brazeau Loop,** around Maligne Lake, and those in the **Tonquin Valley,** book up in early spring. When you reserve a spot to camp at a marked campsite, you can't select a specific site within the camping area. You choose the site once you get there, on a first-come, first-served basis.

BACKCOUNTRY HOSTELS

Hostelling International (© **877/852-0781** or 780/852-3215; www.hostellingintl.ca/Alberta) runs a number of rustic backcountry hostels in Jasper National Park, as well as in Banff. They do not have direct phone lines.

The **Beauty Creek Hostel** on the Icefields Parkway (Hwy. 93), 17km (11 miles) north of the Icefield Information Centre (87km/54 miles south of Jasper Townsite), is in a fabulous location for hiking. It sleeps 24 people in 2 cabins, and has wood-stove heating, propane cooking, and lamplights. There is an outdoor toilet. There is no electricity or showers. Rates are C$18 (US$17) per person per night for Hostelling International members and C$23 (US$22) per person per night for nonmembers.

The **Mount Edith Cavell Hostel** (take Hwy. 93A south from the townsite to Cavell Road; turn west and continue for 13km/8 miles to the hostel, on the east side of the road) offers shelter and a base for exploring the Tonquin Valley. In winter, you must ski in. It sleeps 32 people in two cabins. It also has no electricity or flush toilets. Rates are C$18 (US$17) per person per night for Hostelling International members, C$23 (US$22) per person per night for nonmembers.

BACKCOUNTRY HUTS

The **Alpine Club of Canada** (© **403/678-3200;** www.alpineclubof canada.ca/facility/index.html) runs a handful of backcountry huts in Jasper National Park. They are ideal places to stay if you're going on a long backpacking or ski touring trip. But they are rustic—many do not have even the barest of amenities, such as electricity and running water. The largest and best-equipped ACC hut in Jasper National Park is the **Wates-Gibson Hut,** in the **Tonquin Valley.** (Access is via the Astoria River hiking trail: Take the Icefields Pkwy. south from Jasper Townsite 7km/4⅓ miles to Hwy. 93A. Continue for 5.5km/3½ miles to Cavell Road, turn west and follow for 13km/7¾ miles to the parking lot above Cavell Lake, on the west side of the road.) Rates are C$22 (US$21) for Alpine Club of Canada members, C$32 (US$30) for nonmembers.

4 Where to Eat in Jasper National Park

Jasper doesn't have an extensive selection of restaurants, but the ones that are here serve good food at reasonable prices. Most restaurant managers and chefs have been in town for at least a decade, and have developed unique takes on some of the more common dishes. Prices are lower than in Banff and there are fewer lineups. My favorite dining experience here involves dropping in to see Glen at the stellar **Patricia Street Deli** (606 Patricia St.; © **780/852-4814**), then taking a deluxe picnic to the shores of Lake Annette—dinner alfresco amid the mountains is divine in and around Jasper Townsite.

Andy's Bistro ★ *(finds* FUSION   Andy Allenbach has been a chef in Jasper for more than 30 years. Now his own boss, he's created a fun and creative menu featuring local ingredients, plenty of fresh herbs and fruit, and the traditional recipes of his Swiss homeland blended with tastes from around the world. The atmosphere is casual, but the service is first-rate—it's a classy but comfortable place to come and meet fellow travelers or to chat with Andy after dinner. Tables are candlelit and intimate, but there aren't many of them; the restaurant seats only 45 people. The friendly *stammtisch* table—a great place to mingle—seats 10.

606 Patricia St. ⒸⒸ **780/852-4559.** Reservations recommended June–Aug daily and on weekends during the rest of the year. Main courses C$19–C$34 (US$18–US$32). AE, MC, V. Mon–Sat 5–11pm.

Coco's Café VEGETARIAN Head to this popular spot on Patricia Street to mingle with the young locals and enjoy some fresh, healthy food. Lunches and dinners come from the same menu and offer sandwiches, wraps, and vegetarian burgers. Daily specials include curries, veggie lasagna, and soups. There's also great cappuccino, latte, and espresso. The cafe is small and can be cramped; expect to literally rub elbows with your neighbors.

608 Patricia St. Ⓒ **780/852-4550.** Breakfast C$4–C$10 (US$3.75–US$9.30); lunch and dinner main courses C$7–C$17 (US$6.50–US$16). AE, MC, V. June–Sept daily 7am–11pm; Oct–May daily 8am–10pm.

Denjiro Japanese Restaurant JAPANESE Formerly known as Tokyo Tom's, this sushi house has a loyal local following. Sushi and sashimi-grade fish is brought in on ice from Vancouver. For the more squeamish types, there is chicken, beef, and salmon teriyaki or Japanese pork curry. A highlight is the Jasper Roll, which consists of shrimp, cucumber, tobiko (flying-fish roe), and spicy sauce in a nori wrap. For a fun, festive night, reserve one of the *Tatami ozashiki* booths and order hot pots that you cook on your own table. Specials offered Sundays and Wednesdays during ski season (Dec–Apr).

410 Connaught Dr. Ⓒ **780/852-3780.** Reservations recommended for Tatami booths. Lunch items C$7–C$12 (US$6.50–US$11); main dinner courses C$8–C$22 (US$7.50–US$21). AE, MC, V. Daily noon–2:30pm and 5–10:30pm.

Earl's CANADIAN A real crowd-pleaser, Earl's is a good choice for just about anybody—families, couples, or friends. Part of a popular Western Canada chain, there's a bit of Mexican, Asian, and European served here. The menu is extensive, ranging from burgers to Thai curries to forno-oven pizzas. The open kitchen and domed ceiling provide a lively atmosphere. They also have the nicest outdoor patio in the townsite, including heaters on a chilly evening.

600 Patricia St., upstairs. Ⓒ **780/852-2393.** Reservations recommended in summer. Entrees C$10–C$28. AE, MC, V. Daily 11:30am–midnight.

Edith Cavell Dining Room *(Overrated* CANADIAN Hailed as the premier dining establishment in Jasper, this restaurant, located in the Fairmont Jasper Park Lodge, appears to be first-class all the way, but look a little deeper and the veneer starts to wear thin. The menu reads impressively enough, with main-course features such as seared ahi tuna, guinea fowl, boar bacon, AAA beef tenderloin, and arctic char. There's a fancy six-course sampler if you don't know what to choose. And yes, the wine list is extensive and varied. But the food's not worth the prices charged, and the tuxedoed waiters always seem to be rushing away to another "more important" cloth-draped table. The setting, however, is undeniably special: floor-to-ceiling windows overlooking Lac Beauvert line the restaurant. To catch a glimpse without committing yourself to a full meal, come for a drink and then head somewhere else.

In the Fairmont Jasper Park Lodge. Take Hwy. 16 4km (2½ miles) east of Jasper to Maligne Lake Rd., turn south and then west as soon as you get over the bridge. Follow to the end. ② 780/852-6052. Reservations recommended June–Aug daily. Jacket advised for men Nov–Apr. Main courses C$34–C$42 (US$32–US$39). AE, DC, MC, V. Daily 6–10pm.

Fiddle River CANADIAN   The new owners at Fiddle River have shifted the emphasis off fresh fish and put it squarely on popular Canadiana dishes. Now, there's Alberta-raised beef, caribou meat-loaf, and a steaming bison stew, as well as pumpkin-seed trout and a seafood kettle. In the winter, they have a three-course *table d'hote* for C$23, a great value. The service is casual and friendly, and the views are divine.

620 Connaught Dr., upstairs ② 780/852-3032. Reservations recommended June–Aug daily. Main courses C$15–C$35 (US$14–US$33). AE, MC, V. Daily 5pm–midnight.

North Face Pizza ⊛ PIZZA   With free delivery anywhere in the Jasper Townsite area, this is the place to call when you just feel like staying in. The pesto sauce is particularly good and makes a healthy base. Ask the counter servers for their favorite combination. There are also burgers, salads, pastas, sandwiches, and wings on offer, plus locally brewed beer from Big Rock Brewery on tap. Eat in (order at the counter) if you want to mingle with the local under-30 crowd.

618 Connaught Dr. ② 780/852-5830. Pizzas C$6–C$20 (US$5.60–US$19). AE, MC, V. Daily 11am–2am.

Palisades ⊛ *Value* *Kids* GREEK/CANADIAN   This is my choice for best affordable restaurant in Jasper. With high-quality food at moderate prices, this family-run joint highlights the owners' Greek heritage with generations-old moussaka and souvlaki recipes. There's also lasagna, veal Parmesan, and grilled prime rib burgers. The decor is far from fancy, with outdated wooden tables and green carpets. But the views and the friendly service will distract you from any design flaws. There's also a kids' menu.

401 Patricia St., at the corner of Cedar. ② 780/852-5222. Entrees C$8–C$21 (US$7.50–US$20). MC, V. Daily 3–11pm.

Jasper Treats

For a quick snack, drop by the **Bear's Paw Bakery** (at a new location at 610 Connaught Dr; the original is still at 4 Cedar Ave.; ℂ **780/852-3233**). The bakery offers fresh sandwiches, granola to go, superb fruit tarts, and a huge variety of cookies, bars, and yummy delights—including dog treats! Their freshly baked bread is served at nearly every restaurant in town. If you need a late-afternoon pick-me-up, visit **Café-Mondo** (inside Jasper Marketplace at 616 Patricia St; ℂ **780/852-9676**) for a cup of coffee, a sandwich, and/or a sweet treat.

Tekarra Restaurant ⓕ *(Finds)* CANADIAN/FUSION   Putting a new twist on comfort food, chef Dave Husserau's little-known restaurant is a gem in the Jasper area. The setting is a rustic cabin on the property of the Tekarra Lodge, and the menu inspires equal feelings of warmth and coziness. The rack of lamb comes with a macadamia-nut crust, and there's a banana-crusted chicken dish that is sensational. For breakfast, try the spinach salsa omelet or the French toast with fresh strawberries. The service is equally warm and friendly. Vegetarian items available. A local favorite.

In the Tekarra Lodge. On Hwy. 93A, 1km (½ mile) south of Hwy. 16, at Jasper Townsite. ℂ **780/852-4624**. Reservations recommended June–Aug daily. Breakfast C$6–C$13 (US$5.60–US$12); dinner main courses C$18–C$42 (US$17–US$39). AE, DISC, MC, V. Daily 8–11am and 5:30–10pm.

5 Jasper After Dark

Jasper's nightlife doesn't even try to rival that of Banff's, but things do stay lively here well into the evenings. All bars are now smoke-free. Locals hang out at the **Atha-B Pub,** in the Athabasca Hotel (510 Patricia St.; ℂ **780/852-3386**), grooving to hits from the '60s, '70s, and '80s. The **De'd Dog Bar and Grill,** in the Astoria Hotel (604 Connaught Dr.; ℂ **780/852-3351**) is a casual favorite, with pool table, darts, big-screen TV, and a long list of ales and Scotches. **Pete's on Patricia** (614 Patricia St.; ℂ **780/852-6262**) is the place to go for live music and dancing. The **Downstream Bar** (620 Connaught Dr.; ℂ **780/852-9449**) often has live music and has a more mature, upscale crowd than the Atha-B. There's a new brewpub in town, the **Jasper Brewing Co.** (624 Connaught Dr.; ℂ **780/852-4111**), with homemade lagers and ales.

9

Gateways to Banff & Jasper National Parks

Banff and Jasper national parks don't exist as islands. More beautiful mountain wilderness and facilities for visitors surround them both. To the east of Banff National Park is the booming town of Canmore, Alberta, home to some of Canada's hottest real estate and an increasingly popular place to base your exploration of the Canadian Rockies. The sprawling protected area known as Kananaskis Country lies to the southeast. To the west of Banff are Kootenay and Yoho national parks, both in the province of British Columbia, and both full of backcountry hiking trails—not to mention beautiful mountain lodges. To the west of Jasper National Park is Mount Robson Provincial Park, also in British Columbia. This provincial park protects the highest peak in the Canadian Rockies: Mount Robson, at 3,954m (12,969 ft.). As you make your way to Banff or Jasper, it's worth setting aside some time to visit these gateways to the parks. You can make it a daylong excursion, or base your trip from one of them.

1 Canmore & Kananaskis Country

106km (66 miles) west of Calgary, 22km (14 miles) east of the Town of Banff, 6km (3⅔ miles) east of the Banff park gates

The secret is out. Savvy travelers (not to mention wealthy investors) are discovering that Canmore is less touristy, more active, and more authentically Canadian than its popular neighbor, Banff. Once a small coal-mining town that was hardly noticed by the throngs that motored past from the city of Calgary into Banff National Park, these days Canmore is hip and happening. Increasingly well-known to adventurers and weekend warriors, this town of 13,000 nestled below the picturesque Three Sisters Mountain has fabulous restaurants and shops, not to mention great skiing, biking, hiking, and climbing opportunities.

Known as "Alberta's Aspen," Canmore is home to a community of outdoors-lovers and artists, many of whom moved here because of its appeal as a healthy and active place to live. Many of the people who work in Banff live in Canmore, and the tourists are taking note: On their first visit to the Canadian Rockies, most visitors stay in Banff. On their second, they stay in Canmore. Because hotel rates are lower than they are in Banff, it's a good place to set up a base and take day trips into the park. It's a relaxed and friendly place.

To the south of Canmore lies **Kananaskis Country**—a vast area that contains four provincial parks (Peter Lougheed, Bow Valley, Bragg Creek, and Elbow/Sheep Wildland) and beautiful valleys of undisturbed mountain wilderness. It's quiet compared to Banff, and offers a good variety of outdoor activities including whitewater rafting, hiking, fishing, mountain biking, and skiing. At its center is **Kananaskis Village,** home to a golf course, hotels, and the nearby **Nakiska** ski resort (where the Alpine skiing events were held during the 1988 Calgary Winter Olympics).

ESSENTIALS

GETTING THERE   Although the **Trans-Canada Highway 1** runs right through Canmore on its way from Calgary to Banff, you'll need to exit the highway to access downtown Canmore. There are four exits; take the third one and follow the wooden signs to **Main Street.** Most of the shuttles that run between the Calgary International Airport and Banff make a stop in Canmore. Try the **Banff Airporter** (② **888/449-2901** or 403/762-3330; www.banff airporter.com; C$50/US$47 one-way or C$92/US$86 return trip). Although there've been efforts to get it going for many years, no shuttles currently run between Banff Townsite and Canmore.

Once you find it, Canmore's downtown area is easy to navigate. It's organized in a grid pattern, with streets numbered from 1 through 15 running north–south, and avenues numbered 1 through 17 running east–west. **Main St.,** for example, is **7th St.** It'll be your main destination for strolling, shopping, and dining. Parallel to that is **9th St.,** also known as Olympians Way, with great restaurants and shops. The Bow Valley Trail 1A is just to the south of the Trans-Canada Highway 1, and runs parallel to it. That's where many hotels are located.

To get to Kananaskis Country from Banff, Canmore, or Calgary, exit the Trans-Canada Highway 1 at the **Kananaskis Trail Highway 40 South.** It's 30km (19 miles) east of Canmore.

VISITOR CENTERS & INFORMATION   The **Travel Alberta Visitor Information Centre** (2801 Bow Valley Trail, Canmore, AB T1W 3A2; ℭ **800/252-3782** or 403/678-5277; www.discover alberta.com) has information about Canmore, as well as the entire province of Alberta. It's just off the Trans-Canada Highway 1 at the western Bow Valley Trail exit at Canmore.

WHAT TO SEE & DO

Canmore Centennial Museum and Geoscience Centre

This museum displays the history of the town, from its coal-mining years to the 1988 Calgary Winter Olympics and beyond. There is also an interesting First Nations exhibit and an extensive interpretive display on geological history covering the past 350 million years, great for budding young scientists and those of us who may have forgotten what we learned in high school science class. The museum is housed in Canmore's new Civic Centre, which has won awards for its eco-friendly design.

902b 7th Ave. Half a block north of Main St. ℭ **403/678-2462.** Admission C$3 (US$2.80) adults, C$2 (US$1.90) students and seniors. Summer Mon–Tues noon–5pm, Wed–Sat 10am–6pm; Sept 5–May 17 Mon–Fri noon–5pm, Sat–Sun 11am–5pm.

North-West Mounted Police Barrack

Take a moment to drop in to this unprepossessing white shack at the end of Main Street that once housed Canmore's early lawkeepers. The post was built in 1893 to establish—and maintain—order in the then-rambunctious frontier town. A Provincial Historic Site, it stands in its original spot beside Policeman's Creek. There's a lovely garden out back.

609 Main St. south of Railway Ave. ℭ **403/678-1955.** Free admission, but donations welcome. June–Aug Mon–Tues noon–4pm, Wed–Sun 10am–6pm; Sept–May Sat–Sun noon–4pm.

Summer Festivals

Canmore is home to some wonderful summertime festivals, starting with the **Canmore Children's Festival** (ℭ **403/678-1878**) on Victoria Day weekend in May. The **Canmore Folk Music Festival** (ℭ **403/678-2524**), held the first weekend in August, showcases an eclectic and inspiring array of musicians from across Canada and around the world at an outdoor stage in **Centennial Park.** Join Celts in their kilts for music, dancing, and unique athletic competitions at **Canmore's Highland Games** (ℭ **403/678-9454**), held on Labor Day weekend (the weekend of the first Mon in Sept). Bring your lawn chair and sun hat!

Oh Canada Eh?! Dinner Show ☆ Proving the stereotype that Canucks have a great sense of humor, this lively dinner theater includes all the classic Canadian characters, from the Mountie and the lumberjack to Anne of Green Gables and the requisite hockey star. Dinner is a five-course, family-style Canadian meal. The combination makes for a high-energy, fun-filled evening.

125 Kananaskis Way. ⓒ 800/773-0004 or 403/609-0004. Tickets C$59 (US$55), children 6–16 C$29 (US$27). May–Oct nightly at 6:30pm.

OUTDOOR PURSUITS

CLIMBING There are countless areas for sport climbing (rock-climbing on fixed routes) throughout the Canmore area, including Cougar Creek, Grassi Lakes, Heart Creek, and Grotto Canyon. **Yamnuska Mountain School** ☆ (Suite 200, 50 Lincoln Park, Canmore, AB T1W 1N8; ⓒ 403/678-4164; www.yamnuska.com) offers guided outings. The weekend-long Intro to Rock Climbing course is C$255 (US$238) per person. (There are no children's rates.) In the cooler months or on a rainy day, you can climb indoors at the **Vsion Climbing Gym** (109–109 Boulder Cres., Canmore, AB T1W 1L4; ⓒ 403/678-8803; www.vsion.com) in Canmore's Elk Run Industrial Park. A drop-in pass is C$16 (US$15) for adults, C$13 (US$12) for youth 13 to 18, and C$11 (US$10) for children under 13. It's a good place to go on a rainy day.

DOG SLED TOURS In winter, mush with "dogs that have jobs" in traditional style with **Snowy Owl Sled Dog Tours** (104–602 Bow Valley Trail; ⓒ 888/311-6874 or 403/678-4369; www.snowy owltours.com). A 2-hour trip is C$127 (US$119) for adults, C$85 (US$80) for children age 8 and under.

FISHING Head to the **Bow River** (near the old train bridge at the end of 10th St.) for bull trout, brown trout, and whitefish. There is good lake trout fishing at **Spray Lakes** (take the Spray Lakes Rd. 15km/9⅓ miles south from town, past the Canmore Nordic Centre) and the **Barrier Lake ponds,** in Kananaskis Country (take Hwy. 40 south from the Trans-Canada Hwy. 1 7km/4⅓ miles to the Barrier Lake Visitor Centre). Get lessons and equipment at **Wapiti Sports and Outfitters** (1506 Railway Ave.; ⓒ 403/678-5550).

GOLFING **Kananaskis Country Golf Course** (Hwy. 40 south from the Trans-Canada Hwy. 1 for 26km/16 miles; ⓒ 877/591-2525 or 403/591-7272; www.kananaskisgolf.com) has two 18-hole, par-72 courses. It's one of the top-rated and most scenic courses in

Canada, and, amazingly, it's easy to get a tee time. Green fees are C$85 (US$80) per person (C$65 per person for Alberta residents).

There are three outstanding golf courses closer to Canmore, including the 18-hole **Canmore Golf and Curling Club** (2000 8th Ave.; ☎ **403/678-4785;** www.canmoregolf.net) on the edge of town, along the Bow River. Green fees are C$75 (US$70) per person. The clubhouse has a decent restaurant and one of the best patios in town. On the north side of Canmore is **SilverTip** (1000 SilverTip Trail, exit at the main Canmore exit and turn left just before the Sheraton Four Points Hotel; ☎ **877/877-5444** or 403/678-1600; www.silver tipresort.com). Calling what it offers "extreme mountain golf," this Les Furber–designed 18-hole, par-72 course is one of a kind. Green fees range from C$125 to C$175 (US$117–US$164). **Stewart Creek Golf Course** (1 Stewart Creek Rd., via the Three Sisters Pkwy. exit just east of Canmore; ☎ **877/993-4653** or 403/609-6099; www.stewartcreekgolf.com) winds along the picturesque lower slopes of the Three Sisters Mountain. A second 18-hole course is slotted to open in 2008. Green fees are C$155 (US$145) Monday through Thursday, C$175 (US$139) Friday through Sunday.

HIKING   Kananaskis Country has a number of guided hikes led by staff from the **Peter Lougheed Provincial Park Visitor Centre.** Some of the more popular trails you can hike on your own outside the park and closer to Canmore include Heart Creek and Grotto Canyon, just north of Canmore. A short but strenuous trail up **Ptarmigan Cirque,** in Kananaskis Country, takes you to spectacular alpine highs in only 5km (3.1 miles). At the base of Kananaskis Lake, you can head 8.6km (5.3 miles) up Mount Indefatigable for superb valley views (hiking boots a must!). Closer to Canmore, try the **Grassi Lakes Trail,** Cougar Canyon, or head to the top of one of the local mountains—**Ha Ling Peak** or **Mount Lady Macdonald**— for a bird's-eye view.

HORSEBACK RIDING   In Kananaskis Country, saddle up at **Boundary Ranch** (on Hwy. 40 just south of Kananaskis Village Junction; ☎ **877/591-7177** or 403/591-7171; www.boundary ranch.com). The "Adventure Ride" costs C$80 (US$75) per person and includes a trail ride and a steak lunch. They also offer back-country pack trips from overnight to 6 days in length. Rates start at C$395 (US$370).

KAYAKING   If you're looking for something a bit more interactive than just bobbing along in a raft, **Blast Adventures** (119–120 B Rundle Dr., Canmore, AB T1W 1G8; ☎ **888/802-5278** or

403/609-2009; www.blastadventures.com) will show you the joys of negotiating whitewater in the relative safety of an inflatable kayak. Both the half-day trip on the bumpy Kananaskis River and a trip on the calmer Bow River cost C$79 (US$74). It's a lot of fun for the whole family.

MOUNTAIN BIKING   Mountain biking is almost a mandatory community event in Canmore, where the wealth of dirt trails and fire roads means there is an off-road route at the end of virtually everyone's driveway. Locals have constructed obstacles like log jumps and wood ramps along the Bow River and beneath Lawrence Grassi Ridge. Those looking for a challenge will want to take their thick, off-road tires and front suspension directly to the **Canmore Nordic Centre Provincial Park** (1.8km/1 mile southwest of Canmore on Spray Lake Rd.; ✆ **403/678-2400**), site of many World Cup Mountain Bike races and home to more than 100km (62 miles) of paved and dirt trails. The trail system was updated and trails refurbished in 2005. **Trail Sports** at the Canmore Nordic Centre, in the park (✆ **403/678-6764;** www.trailsports.ab.ca), will lead you on a 1½ hour tour of the center for C$60 (US$56) per person (adults and children) plus rental, which costs C$16 (US$15) hourly for front-suspension and C$20 (US$19) hourly for full suspension. You must book the tour in advance.

You can rent bikes at **Gear Up** (1302 Bow Valley Trail; ✆ **403/678-1636;** www.gearupsport.com). Full-suspension bikes (with shock absorbers on the front and back tires) cost either C$15 (US$14) per hour or C$45 (US$42) per day. Or try **Rebound Cycle** (902 Main St.; ✆ **403/678-3668;** www.reboundcycle.com). They've got full-suspension bikes for C$35 to C$59 (US$33–US$55) per day. Their staff are very knowledgeable.

RAFTING   **Canadian Rockies Rafting** (1727 Mountain Ave.; ✆ **877/226-7625** or 403/678-6535; www.rafting.ca) has trips for every member of the family, from 2-hour paddle raft trips through big rapids on the Kananaskis River (C$72/US$67 for adults, C$67/US$63 for children ages 5–15) to a whitewater adventure with some very big rapids on the Kicking Horse River (C$118/US$110) for adults, C$110/US$103 for kids 14–18, including a buffet lunch in Lake Louise). There is also a lovely evening float trip on the Bow River, with good chances of seeing birds and wildlife (C$50/US$47 for adults, C$36/US$34 for seniors, C$45/US$42 for children ages 6–15, and C$40/US$37 for children age 5 and under).

Moments **The View from Up High**

If you want the best in sightseeing, try a helicopter tour from **Alpine Helicopters** (91 Bow Valley Trail, Canmore, AB T1W 1N7; © **403/678-4802**; www.alpinehelicopters.com). Leaving from the Canmore Helipad, this bird's-eye view takes you to remote and spectacular mountain scenery quickly. From 12-minute scenic helicopter rides that don't touch down (C$95/US$89) to guided alpine walks with flight, lunch, and guided hike (C$319/US$299).

SKIING & SNOWBOARDING **Nakiska** was the site of the Alpine skiing events for the 1988 Calgary Winter Olympics and is a great family ski hill (Trans-Canada Hwy. 1 to Hwy. 40 south to Kananaskis Village, follow road straight for 5 min.; © **403/591-7777;** www.skinakiska.com). Full-day lift tickets cost C$52 (US$49) for adults, C$42 (US$39) for seniors, C$37 (US$35) for students and youth ages 11 to 17, C$17 (US$16) for children ages 6 to 10, and free for children age 5 and under. It's steps from Kananaskis Village on the lower slopes of **Mount Allan.**

Cross-country skiers will want to hit the trails at the **Canmore Nordic Centre Provincial Park** (1.8km/1 mile south of Canmore, take Rundle Dr. across the Bow River bridge, left at Three Sisters Dr. and right at Spray Lakes Rd., follow signs; © **403/678-2400**), host of the Nordic skiing and biathlon events for the 1988 Calgary Winter Olympics, site of the Canadian cross-country skiing team's training center, and the only Canadian stop on the Nordic World Cup tour. This is the big time, folks! There are more than 27km (17 miles) of trails for all abilities as well as a lovely day lodge. Novice skiers should head out on the **Banff Trail,** which hits the east boundary of Banff National Park, 6km (3¾ miles) from the trail head. Full-day tickets are C$7.50 (US$7) for adults; C$6 (US$5.60) for seniors, students, and youth ages 11 to 17; and C$4.50 (US$4.20) for children ages 6 to 10. Children 5 and under ski for free.

WHERE TO STAY

There's a slew of chain motels strung along the Bow Valley Trail on the outskirts of Canmore, and B&Bs (see www.bbcanmore.com for full listings) dotted throughout town. Like in nearby Banff, hotel rates are generally much lower in wintertime, from October to May, although they do peak during the holiday season.

HOTELS

Chateau Canmore (Kids)

Although it's right beside the train tracks, the Chateau Canmore may be the best hotel in town for families. It's located on the Bow Valley Trail, just off the Trans-Canada Highway 1. The rooms are all very large; each is essentially a suite with a separate living room equipped with a kitchenette. On the top floor are the spacious lofts, great for groups of four or more. All rooms have a gas fireplace. Unless you're a big group (and should select the largest rooms in the hotel, which are track-side), choose a room away from the railway tracks—trains go by up to four times a night. There's a special check-in for kids, an indoor pool and fitness facility, and a tennis court that converts to a skating rink in winter. The log-cabin-styled lobby, with a waterfall and fireplace, reminds you that you're in the Rockies.

1720 Bow Valley Trail, Canmore, AB T1W 2X3. (C) **800/261-8551** or 403/678-6699. Fax 403/678-6954. www.chateaucanmore.com. 93 units; 77 suites, 16 lofts. June–Sept C$196 (US$183) suite, C$215 (US$201) loft; Oct–Dec 22 C$120 (US$112) suite, C$140 (US$131) loft; Dec 23–Jan 3 C$175 (US$164) suite, C$195 (US$182) loft; Jan–May C$125 (US$117) suite, C$150 (US$140) loft. Extra person C$15 (US$14). Children 17 and under stay free in parent's room. AE, DISC, MC, V. **Amenities:** Restaurant; lounge; large indoor heated pool; Jacuzzi; sauna; concierge; business center; massage; laundry service. *In room:* A/C, TV/VCR, dataport, kitchenette, hair dryer.

Fire Mountain Lodge (★) (Value)

Get it while it's still shiny, swanky, and new. A brand-new row of upscale condos, the Fire Mountain Lodge offers privacy, luxury, and a fully equipped home for a few nights. Offering much more than a hotel at the same price, these units include high-end kitchens with stainless steel appliances, barbecues, oak doors, and a full concierge service. There are two- and three-bedroom units; all have 2½ bathrooms, patios, flatscreen TVs, and puffy duvets. The downside? It's overlooking a parking lot and a few blocks from downtown. Top floors have the best views.

121 Kananaskis Way, Canmore, AB T1W 2X2. (C) **866/740-3473** or 403/609-9949. Fax 403/609-8204. www.firemountain.ca. 24 units. Jan 2–Feb 14 and Oct 9–Dec 20 C$199 (US$186) 2-bedroom suite, C$249 (US$233) 3-bedroom suite; Feb 15–Jan 21 and Sept 4–Oct 8 C$229 (US$214) 2-bedroom suite, C$279 (US$261) 3-bedroom suite; June 22–Sept 3 and Dec 21–Jan 1 C$349 (US$326) 2-bedroom suite, C$399 (US$373) 3-bedroom suite. Children 15 and under stay free in parent's unit. AE, MC, V. **Amenities:** Hot tub; fitness center; meeting room. *In room:* Barbecue, laundry.

Mystic Springs Chalets (Kids)

Families can settle in here for a few days and feel like they have their own little home in the mountains. In the booming area between the Bow Valley Trail and the Trans-Canada Highway 1, this facility is essentially a series of two-bedroom town houses. Suites have two stories, with kitchens and fireplaces. Units have been quite abused over time and are in need of some refreshing. Nestled in the middle is a hot pool that makes for lovely late-night dipping after a day's ski or hike. There's also a helpful concierge service.

140 Kananaskis Way, Canmore, AB T1W 2X2. © 866/446-9784 or 403/609-0333. Fax 403/609-0264. www.mysticsprings.ca. 44 units. June–Sept C$349 (US$326); Feb–June and Sept–Oct C$259 (US$242); Jan and Oct–Dec C$209 (US$195). Extra person C$15 (US$14). Children 15 and under stay free in parent's room. AE, MC, V. **Amenities:** Outdoor hot pool and Jacuzzi; exercise room; tour desk; laundry. *In room:* A/C, TV, kitchen.

Paintbox Lodge   A winner for its cozy vibe, friendly service, and location (just steps from Main St.), this is Canmore's best boutique-style inn and a particularly good choice for couples looking for some mountain romance. Holding Rocky Mountain heritage as its style compass, there's a blend of antiques, fireplaces, and ultra-cozy beds. The eight guest rooms are all different and all comfortable; upstairs ones have high ceilings with a cozy sitting area. The two-bedroom suite is good for families. Service is pretty hands-off and low-key, so be prepared to fend for yourself. Breakfasts are currently held at a nearby cafe.

629 10th St., Canmore, AB T1W 2A2. © 888/678-6100 or 403/609-0482. No fax. www.paintboxlodge.com. 8 units. Doubles C$159 (US$149) in autumn, winter, and spring, C$199 (US$186) in summer and over Christmas. Suites C$199 (US$186) in autumn, winter, and spring, C$279 (US$261) in summer and over Christmas. Extra person C$30 (US$28). AE, MC, V. **Amenities:** Library; meeting room. *In room:* Fireplace, coffeemaker, iron, minibar, Internet, CD player.

WHERE TO EAT

Chef's Studio Japan *(Finds* SUSHI   Canmore's downtown sushi restaurant is one of the best deals in town. The food is presented with award-winning artistic flair. Sushi, sashimi, tempura, and teriyaki are fresh and healthy. It's a casual, very friendly atmosphere worth searching out (behind the Avens Art Gallery).

709 Main St. (at the rear). © 403/609-8383. Dinner only. Main courses C$15–C$30 (US$14–US$28). MC, V. Tues–Sun 4:30–10pm.

Communitea Café *Ⓡ* CAFE   Choose from more than 80 blends of looseleaf tea at this funky and thoughtful new spot downtown. It makes a great hangout, with cool music, board games, and beanbag chairs, and also serves healthy, affordable, and tasty meals. The breakfast options include organic granola; for lunch or dinner, build your own rice bowl with organic brown rice, steamed veggies, and flavorful Asian sauces. There are also great snacks like sushi, shrimp rolls, organic edamame—and quite possibly the best lattes in town, brewed in a one-of-a-kind espresso machine. This is a place with heart, where efforts are made to be sustainable and community-focused.

117–1001 6th Ave., corner of 10th St. (✆ 403/678-6818. Lunch C$5–C$12 (US$4.70– US$11); dinner entrees C$8–C$14 (US$7.50–US$13). MC, V. Daily 8am–9pm.

Quarry Bistro and Wine Bar EUROPEAN/CANADIAN   Step out of the laid-back life and into this Main Street swanky and chic bistro, which manages to blend rustic with refined. The menu, rooted in classical French and Italian bistro cuisine, is varied and excellent, with a clear focus on fresh local ingredients and simple flavors. That means the menu changes frequently. For dinner, try the delicious Sooke Hills rainbow trout or braised pork shoulder; for lunch, the tuna confit panzanella is a creative twist on a salade nicoise. There's also a lovely weekend brunch and a bustling Main Street patio. With an upscale, Scandinavian decor, this is an enjoyable place to dine or to enjoy a glass of wine—10 whites and 10 reds are served by the glass from the ever-changing, Old World–friendly wine list.

718 Main St. (✆ 403/678-6088. Reservations recommended. Lunch C$12–C$17 (US$11–US$16); dinner C$14–C$32 (US$13–US$30). AE, MC, V. Mid-May to mid-Sept Mon–Fri 11:30am–2:30pm and 5–10pm, Sat–Sun brunch 9am–2:30pm; Mid-Sept to mid-May Thurs–Mon dinner 5–10pm, Sat–Sun brunch 9am–2:30pm.

Rocky Mountain Flatbread Company (Kids) MEDITER-RANEAN   A sunny and colorful place, the Flatbread Co. offers heaps of atmosphere for folks who like to watch their food being made. The wood-fired clay oven is allegedly the largest in Canada. Handcrafted flatbread pizzas are made with organic flour, regional cheeses, and fresh, creative toppings. The Nemo has prawns, arti-chokes, and Asiago cheese. The restaurant also offers hearty salads and fresh pastas and a weekly curry night during the winter. Pint-size portions for kids and a kid-friendly play area, where they can bake their own pretend pizzas, are available.

838 10th St. (✆ 403/609-5508. Reservations recommended. Entrees C$14–C$18 (US$13–US$17). AE, MC, V. July–Aug daily 11:30am–2pm and 5–10pm, Sept–June daily 5–10pm.

Santa Lucia ITALIAN   A casual and budget-friendly alternative, Santa Lucia just happens to have the best Italian food in town. Run by the Barbaro family for decades now, its manicotti, cannelloni, and lasagna are all homemade and the real deal. There's a kids' menu with four yummy choices for $6. This is a great option for families on the much-yuppified Canmore dining scene. They'll also deliver their excellent flatbread pizza to your hotel room.

714 Main St. ✆ **403/678-3414.** Entrees C$10–C$20 (US$9.30–US$19). MC, V. Mon–Sat 4:30–10pm.

The Trough ✷✷ BISTRO/INTERNATIONAL   With a cheeky attitude, a relaxed and intimate vibe, and a stunning menu, this is the new hot spot in Canmore's competitive bistro scene. Not for the faint of heart, flavors here are powerful and intense. Appetizers like oriental duck confit, an unpredictable Caesar salad (with speck, Meyer lemons, and fresh basil), and the Trough bruschetta dough balls are staples. Labor-intensive entrees from the often-changing menu include duck breast with nectarine and orange chutney, wild salmon with fennel and citrus rub, and jerk-spiced pork ribs, all chock with fresh ingredients and surprising tastes. The highly professional waitstaff are also very knowledgeable about the extensive wine list. If you're on a budget, come for a glass of wine and dessert.

725 9th St., behind Main St. between 6th and 7th Aves. ✆ **403/678-2820.** Reservations highly recommended. Main entrees C$20–C$34 (US$19–US$32). AE, MC, V. Winter Wed–Mon 6–10pm; summer daily 5–11pm.

CANMORE AFTER DARK

Locals head to **The Drake Inn** (909 Railway Ave., corner of Main St.; ✆ **403/678-5131**) for dinner on the patio, live music, and billiards. The **Canmore Hotel** (738 Main St., corner of 7th Ave.; ✆ **403/678-5181**) hosts some of the funkiest live bands in Canada. The building itself is more than 100 years old. **The Grizzly Paw**

Fun Fact   **What's with All the Coffee Shops?**

Coffee has become an honored local specialty in Canmore—there are more coffee shops here than in some of Alberta's largest cities. There's a Starbucks in town, but locals generally prefer to enjoy the abundance of unique little cafes. Downtown is **Beamer's Coffee** (120–737 7th St.; **403/609-0111**), with huge muffins and plenty of magazines. The **Rocky Mountain Bagel Company** (830 Main St.; ✆ **403/678-9968**) has a great variety of bagels and cream cheeses (try the spinach and roasted garlic on a parmozza bagel, or the strawberry and honey on a cinnamon-raisin bagel). Yummy soups and herb bread can be found at **The Coffee Mine** (103–802 8th St.; ✆ **403/678-2241**). Finally, there's **Mountain Mercato** (102–817 Main St.; ✆ **403/609-6631**), a Euro-inspired espresso bar with fabulous panini sandwiches.

(622 Main St., between Railway and 6th Aves.; ⓒ **403/678-9983**) houses the only microbrewery in the Canadian Rockies and a heated outdoor patio. If you want to dance, head just out of town to **Hooligan's Nightclub** (103 Bow Valley Trail, 1km/½ mile west of Railway Ave.; ⓒ **403/609-2662**).

2 Radium Hot Springs, British Columbia & Kootenay National Park

Radium Hot Springs is 105km (65 miles) southeast of Golden, British Columbia, 134km (83 miles) west of the Town of Banff, 449km (278 miles) north of Spokane, WA. Kootenay National Park's eastern entrance is 38km (24 miles) southwest of the Town of Banff. The western entrance is .5km (⅓ mile) east of the village of Radium Hot Springs

A small town (the population is around 675 people) at the southern end of Kootenay National Park in the province of British Columbia, Radium Hot Springs—often simply called Radium—is named for (you guessed it) its famous hot springs, mineral pools that have been drawing visitors to soak in their supposedly healing waters for more than a century. The town is essentially a strip of motels and restaurants, but if you explore some of the back roads you'll discover a pretty spectacular setting and bump into more than a few Calgary residents who make this their second home. It's also a good area for golfing and hiking.

You can cross from one end of Kootenay National Park to the other in around an hour. If you're coming from Banff, you'll feel the temperature rise and see the cactus appear, as the Kootenay Parkway (Hwy. 93) drops slowly and steadily from the high peaks of the Continental Divide into the semi-dry forests and grasslands of the Columbia Valley.

ESSENTIALS

GETTING THERE FROM BANFF NATIONAL PARK   Highway 93 South, the Kootenay Parkway, runs from the little settlement at Castle Junction, in Banff National Park, through Kootenay National Park and into the town of Radium Hot Springs. The distance is around 100km (62 miles) and takes about an hour. Highway 93 between Banff and Radium goes over the Vermillion Pass. The road is open year-round, although it is sometimes closed in winter due to poor driving conditions and avalanches.

Most hotels and restaurants in Radium are on or very near Highway 93.

GETTING THERE FROM THE UNITED STATES   Radium is 224km (140 miles) north of the Canada–US border. Take US Highway 2 northwest from Spokane, Washington, into northern Idaho and cross the border. Continue north on Highway 93 through Cranbrook, British Columbia, into Radium.

VISITOR CENTERS & INFORMATION   The **Radium Chamber of Tourism** (© 250/347-9331) shares an information center with **Kootenay National Park,** in Radium (7556 Main St. E., Radium Hot Springs, BC V0A 1M0; © 250/347-9505; www.pc.gc.ca/kootenay). If you want information on the town of Radium Hot Springs, call © 250/347-9331 or log on to www.radiumhotsprings.com. There's another park information center at **Kootenay Crossing,** where's there's also a shop, snack bar, and hotel in the middle of the park, 31km (19 miles) south of the Banff–Kootenay park border.

WHAT TO SEE & DO

A drive through **Kootenay National Park** (© 250/347-9505; www.parkscanada.gc.ca/kootenay) makes a great day trip, whether you're coming north from the United States or south from Banff National Park. Established in 1920, the park is long and narrow (94km/58 miles long; 8km/5 miles across) and has a remarkably diverse landscape. The main road through the park traverses the scars of the massive 2003 forest fire; two large lighting-caused fires eventually merged and burned 12.6% of the park. Parks Canada sees the fire as a natural—and therefore healthy—episode in the forest's makeup.

You can make a number of short stops along Highway 93, one of them being the trail head for **the Rockwall Trail**—which is, in my opinion, one of the best backcountry hiking trails in all of the Canadian Rockies. Just past the Continental Divide and over the Alberta–British Columbia border, make a stop at the Vermillion Pass to hike the **Fireweed Trail,** a short 20-minute loop with interpretive signs that explain why natural forest fires are healthy and good for the environment and are no longer suppressed by Parks Canada.

If it's a hot day, you'll particularly enjoy a short hike at **Marble Canyon** (on the north side of Hwy. 93, 7km/4⅓ miles past the provincial border), a narrow trail of limestone carved by two retreated glaciers. The farther up the trail you walk, the more impressive the canyon. It's cool and shady here. And don't be fooled by the name: There is no marble, only white and gray dolomite rock. Kids will find the hike intriguing, but keep an eye on them because the trail can get slippery.

The **Paint Pots** (on the north side of Hwy. 93, 10km/6¼ miles past the provincial border) is a fascinating area where Natives gathered ocher, an iron-based mineral that was baked, crushed, mixed with grease, and used as a paint for tepees, pictographs, and personal adornment. There is an excellent, wheelchair-friendly, 30-minute **interpretive trail** at the Paint Pots.

Kootenay closes with a bang at the spectacular red cliffs of Sinclair Canyon, which welcome you to the Columbia Valley just after the Radium Hot Springs pools.

Radium Hot Springs Pools ✪   The "sacred mountain waters" of the Radium Hot Springs have been drawing visitors to the Columbia Valley since 1914. There is one hot pool (104°F/40°C) and a cooler pool (81°F/27°C). The pools are settled in a canyon rich with oxide, giving the walls a permanent orange-sunset look. They are open daily throughout the year, but I prefer the pools in winter, when their warmth is more appreciated and there are fewer crowds. There's also a massage clinic at the pools.

3km (2 miles) northeast of the town of Radium on Hwy. 93. ✆ **250/347-9485.** Admission C$6.50 (US$6.10) adults, C$5.50 (US$5.15) seniors and children. Mid-May to mid-Oct daily 9am–11pm; mid-Oct to mid-May Mon–Fri noon–9pm, Sat–Sun noon–10pm.

OUTDOOR PURSUITS

BIRD-WATCHING   The **Columbia River Wetlands,** 10km (6¼ miles) north of the town of Radium on Highway 95, is the largest continuous wetland remaining in North America. More than 250 species migrate through here annually. In June, the annual "Wings over the Rockies" is an excellent birding festival celebrating the annual migrations through the Columbia Valley.

GOLFING   The Radium Resort owns and operates two golf courses. The **Springs Course** (at the end of Stanley St., which runs west off Main St.; ✆ **800/667-6444** or 250/347-6200; www.radium resort.com) is an 18-hole championship course ranked sixth in British Columbia. Located along the cliffs that border the Columbia River below, this course has four tee boxes at every hole to please golfers of all levels. Green fees range from C$91 (US$85) per person on weekdays to C$140 (US$131) per person on weekends.

Radium Resort's other course, called the **Radium Course** (8100 Golf Course Rd., 4km/2½ miles south of Radium on the east side of Hwy. 93/95; © **800/667-6444** or 250/347-9311; www.radium resort.com) is another scenic 18-hole course, tucked along the edge of Kootenay National Park. Green fees are C$81 (US$76) per person during the week and C$100 (US$93) per person on weekends. Featuring tree-lined fairways, undulating greens, and plenty of elevation changes, this course is more challenging than the Springs Course. Both courses are open daily from late March until October.

HIKING IN KOOTENAY NATIONAL PARK The premier multiday hiking route is the **Rockwall Trail** 🐾🐾, considered by many to be the best backpacking trip in the Canadian Rockies. It heads up-valley to a dramatic limestone cliff that runs 40km (25 miles) along Kootenay's northwest border. If you have time for only a single-day outing, you can do the first section of the Rockwall Trail, 21km (13 miles) round-trip, which takes you up to stunning **Floe Lake.** It's the most popular day hike for strong hikers and leads past gorgeous glaciers, through an alpine meadow scattered with larch trees, along an avalanche run to the lake named for the ice floes often floating in the water. This turquoise jewel is in an incredible setting below the 1,000m (3,280-ft.) limestone cliffs of the Rockwall. **Stanley Glacier** 🐾 is an excellent half-day hike that takes you through a series of switchbacks into a high valley and pulls you forward to the glacier. Watch for moose and marmots and have your camera ready for waterfalls cascading from the steep walls of Stanley Peak. The 3.2km (1.9-mile) **Juniper Trail** winds up from the hot springs through a lovely forest of ponderosa pine and juniper trees to a cool canyon with waterfalls. Great spot on a hot summer day!

RAFTING **Kootenay River Runners** (in Radium, on Hwy. 93, 2km/1¼ miles west of the Kootenay National Park entrance on the north side of the highway; © **800/599-4399** or 250/347-9210; www.raftingtherockies.com) has pioneered whitewater trips in the area and offers a variety of trips in and around Radium, including one on the **Kootenay River** that's great for families. Rates for the full-day Kootenay River trip are C$90 (US$84) for adults, C$74 (US$69) for children 13 and under. Their **Kicking Horse River Adventure** is for experienced paddlers only and costs C$90 (US$84) per adult (no children under 14 allowed and no seniors' discounts). A more placid trip is the **Voyageur Canoe Trip** on the Columbia River, a wonderful spot for bird lovers and a chance to experience Canada's canoeing heritage. Rates are C$49 (US$46) for adults, C$35 (US$33) for children age 13 and under. Trips run from late May to September.

WHERE TO STAY
IN RADIUM HOT SPRING

The Lido Motel   A comfortable motel located in the heart of the village of Radium, this is a classic road-trip favorite. All rooms here have kitchenettes, which make it a good choice for families and those who'll be spending lots of time outdoors. The rooms themselves are quite dark, but there's a large garden and barbecue area outside to spread out in. Run by a friendly German couple, this is a relaxed and unpretentious option.

4876 McKay St., Radium Hot Springs, BC V0A 1M0. 1 block west of Highway 93/95.
(℃*)* **877/347-9533.** Fax 250/347-9533. www.thelidomotel.com. 10 units. June–Sept C$75 (US$70) double with kitchenette, C$85 (US$80) 2-room unit with kitchenette; Oct–May C$60 (US$56) double with kitchenette, C$70 (US$65) 2-room unit with kitchenette. Extra person C$10 (US$9.30). MC, V. **Amenities:** Picnic area; barbecues; mini-golf. *In room:* A/C, TV, Internet.

Radium Resort   This four-season resort located 5 minutes south of the village of Radium is primarily for golfers (rooms are located right on an 18-hole course that is part of the resort), but it has managed to bridge the season by supplying a variety of other amenities. Accommodations are moderately priced and the staff are friendly. The rooms are all large, and most have excellent views and large balconies. The two-level lofts are great for families and groups; they feel more like apartments than hotel rooms. All rooms have balconies. Bathrooms have large tubs; some are jetted.

P.O. Box 310, Radium Hot Springs, BC V0A 1M0. 4km (2½ miles) south of Radium on Hwy. 93/95, east side. *(*℃*)* **800/667-6444** or 250/347-9311. Fax 250/347-6299. www.radiumresort.com. 90 units. May–Sept C$129 (US$121) double; C$179 (US$167) quad-occupancy loft. Apr and Oct C$109 (US$102) double; C$159 (US$149) quad-occupancy loft. Nov–Mar C$99 (US$93) double; C$139 (US$130) quad-occupancy loft. Golf packages available. Children 15 and under stay free in parent's room. AE, MC, V. **Amenities:** 2 restaurants; large indoor heated pool; golf course on property; outdoor tennis court, 2 racquetball and squash courts; health club; Jacuzzi; sauna; limited bike rentals; video arcade; babysitting. *In room:* A/C, TV, coffeemaker, hair dryer.

IN KOOTENAY NATIONAL PARK
Kootenay Park Lodge ⭐   Built by the Canadian Pacific Railway in 1923 to offer a stop on the drive from Banff to Radium, these cabins still look the way they did when the first car travelers made their way through the Rockies. Cabins are surrounded by huge spruce trees and have wood verandas on two sides. They narrowly escaped the huge forest fire that swept through Kootenay in 2003. Facilities are very well cared for, and renovations in the 1990s have

retained the old style of the cabins. The bedrooms and bathrooms are quite small and very rustic in design; there are no marble vanities or poster beds, although the beds do have gorgeous goose-down duvets. All 10 cabins have private bathrooms. The kitchens in some of the cabins are on the small side. There's a library, a general store next door, and trail access in every direction. The main lodge has a gorgeous stone fireplace. This is a rustic and relaxing place to stay—guests are the quiet type who like to read a book by the fireplace, go for a stroll along the river, and get away from it all.

P.O. Box 1390, Banff, AB T1L 1B3. Located on Hwy. 93 at Vermillion Crossing, 42km (26 miles) west of Castle Junction and 61km (38 miles) east of Radium Hot Springs. © 403/762-9196. Fax 403/283-7482. www.kootenayparklodge.com. 10 cabins. May 18–June 14 C$75–C$95 (US$70–US$89); June 15–Sept 29 C$99–C$145 (US$93–US$136). Extra person C$10 (US$9.30). Children 4 and under stay free in parent's room. MC, V. Closed Oct 1–May 17. Pets accepted, C$7 (US$6.50) per night. **Amenities:** Restaurant; extensive library; laundry service. *In room:* Minibar, coffeemaker, no phone.

Redstreak Campground There's lots to do here in Parks Canada's largest campground in Kootenay National Park, including nightly entertainment in the summer and a network of trails leaving the campground and heading into the park. It's located behind the Visitors Centre. You can reserve a campsite online at www.pccamping.ca or © 877/737-3783, which is a smart plan since this is a very popular spot.

2.5km (1½ miles) southwest of Radium Hot Springs, turn east off Hwy. 93 at the sign. © 250/347-9505. 242 sites; 38 with electrical hookup only, 50 with full hookup. C$26–C$36 (US$24–US$34). Open May 11–Oct 8.

WHERE TO EAT
IN RADIUM HOT SPRINGS

Helna's Stube ★★ *(Finds) (Kids)* AUSTRIAN Owned by Helmut and Natascha Kendler (hence the name "Helna") this quiet gem of a restaurant has carved itself a niche in the Radium food scene and stands out for quality meals and reasonable prices. The menu is straight from Austria, with a hint of Rocky Mountain cuisine. Starters include baked tomato soup and escargots. The house specialty entrees are homemade ravioli, spaetzle, and sauteed veal liver Tyrol. The Wiener schnitzel is a classic. There are also seafood and vegetarian entrees and a kids' menu.

7547 Main St. © 250/347-0047. Reservations required for dinner. Entrees C$14–C$28 (US$13–US$26). MC, V. May–Sept daily 5pm–midnight.

Horsethief Creek Pub PUB The menu here is almost as expansive as the views across the Columbia Valley. The famous half-pound burger comes with mushrooms, bacon, and melted cheese. Pasta lovers will be tempted by Kootenai curry fettuccini or Louisiana prawn penne. There are also great salads, classic oven roasts, and fish and chips—something for everyone! It's also a nice spot for an afternoon beer and nibbles—pub favorites like bacon-wrapped prawns, chicken wings, potato skins, and nachos. They've also got microbrews on tap and a good list of fun summer cocktails.

7538 Main St. ✆ 250/347-6400. Entrees C$9–C$22 (US$8.40–US$21) MC, V. Sun–Thurs 11am–10pm; Fri–Sat 11am–11pm. Pub open weekends until midnight.

IN KOOTENAY NATIONAL PARK

Kootenay Park Lodge ✦ CANADIAN   If you're driving from Banff to Radium in a half- or full-day outing, plan to stop for either breakfast or lunch at this lodge in the heart of Kootenay National Park. Otherwise, make a night of it and get away from the busy streets of Banff (see "Where to Stay," above). Owned and operated by mother-and-son team Frances and Paul Holscher, the restaurant serves home-style food from a diverse and comfortable menu. Try their breakfast crepes filled with fruit and yogurt. For dinner, select the rainbow trout in hollandaise sauce.

Hwy. 93 at Vermillion Crossing, 42km (26 miles) west of Castle Junction, 61km (38 miles) east of Radium Hot Springs. ✆ 403/762-9196. Reservations required for dinner. Breakfast C$4–C$12 (US$3.75–US$11); lunch items C$7–C$16 (US$6.50–US$15); main dinner courses C$15–C$32 (US$14–US$30). MC, V. Mid-May to mid-June and Sept 8–10am and 6–8pm; mid-June to end of Aug 8–10am, noon–2pm, and 6–8pm. Closed Oct–Apr.

3 Golden, British Columbia & Yoho National Park

Golden is 361km (224 miles) east of Kamloops, British Columbia, 135km (84 miles) west of the Town of Banff. Yoho National Park's east gate is 60km (37 miles) west of the Town of Banff; the west gate is 20km (12 miles) east of Golden, British Columbia

Golden, British Columbia, is located just off the Trans-Canada Highway (Hwy. 1) at the confluence of the Kicking Horse and Columbia rivers. The small town (pop. 4,200) has been on the verge of a boom for a few years now as it shifts gears from a resource-based economy to one based more on outdoor recreation. This is largely due to the recently redeveloped **Kicking Horse Mountain Resort** (frequently ranked one of the best ski resorts in North America). Although it is not located within Yoho National Park (it's 20km/12 miles outside the park's west gate), Golden is the park's major gateway and service center.

Yoho National Park makes a great base for exploring the Rockies. You're midway from the Columbia Icefields and the Town of Banff, next door to Lake Louise, and yet in a less-traveled and less-touristy area. Hikers will find a good variety of trails in Yoho, such as those at Twin Falls and Lake O'Hara. There is also the great presence of the railroad for history buffs, and Yoho also has three of my absolute favorite mountain lodges in the Canadian Rockies: **Lake O'Hara Lodge, Cathedral Mountain Lodge,** and **Emerald Lake Lodge.**

ESSENTIALS

GETTING THERE   Yoho National Park lies to the west of Banff and Lake Louise. If you are starting in the Town of Banff, continue west on the Trans-Canada Highway 1 past Lake Louise. The town of Field is 14km (8¾ miles) from the Alberta–British Columbia border and is Yoho's main center. Golden is another 20km (12 miles) west. It will take you about 45 minutes to reach Field from Banff Townsite, another 45 minutes to get to Golden. Highway 1 to Field crosses the Kicking Horse Pass. It's open year-round, although it is occasionally closed in winter due to poor driving conditions and avalanches.

If you're coming east from British Columbia, follow the Trans-Canada Highway (Hwy. 1). Golden is 713km (442 miles) east of Vancouver and 361km (224 miles) east of Kamloops.

VISITOR CENTERS & INFORMATION   In Golden, visit the **Kicking Horse Country Chamber of Commerce Visitor Center** (500 10th Ave. N, P.O. Box 1320, Golden, BC V0A 1H0; ✆ **800/ 622-4653** or 250/344-7125; www.goldenchamber.bc.ca). Drop by the Yoho National Park Visitor Centre (at the intersection of Hwy. 1 and the entrance to the town of Field; ✆ **250/343-6783**) for maps, updated trail reports, and other information. There is an information desk for Yoho National Park (✆ **250/343-6783;** www. pc.gc.ca/yoho) as well as information on **Tourism Alberta & British Columbia** (✆ **250/343-6783;** www.discoveralberta.com or www. travel.bc.ca). You can pick up park permits here and make reservations for backcountry campsites.

WHAT TO SEE AND DO

Yoho National Park, established in 1889, is 1,310 sq. km (507 sq. miles) of visitor-friendly wilderness with a fascinating human history. "Yoho" is an expression of awe and wonder in the Cree language, and that's just what you'll experience in this park, which showcases the western slopes of the Rockies with dozens of spectacular waterfalls and the Kicking Horse River. Give yourself 3 or 4 hours to drive through Yoho National Park. This drive, described below, takes you from Lake Louise southwest on the Trans-Canada Highway 1 through the park toward Golden, BC.

When the Canadian government was trying to figure out how to complete the ambitious transcontinental railway in the 1880s, surveyors spent years determining which was the easiest route over the Rocky Mountains. They finally selected the Kicking Horse Pass. The first trains to make it over the pass had wild rides descending the steep west slope, or really difficult ascents going toward Lake Louise. It was only a matter of time before trains would start crashing into the town of Field, so engineers developed a groundbreaking plan to ease the incline: the **Spiral Tunnels** take trains through two loops inside Cathedral Mountain, easing the steepness substantially. View the Spiral Tunnels from two lookouts: the first (and best) is on the side of Trans-Canada Highway 1 just up the hill from Field and has excellent interpretive signs; the second is on Yoho Valley Road just past the Cathedral Mountain Bungalows.

You can reach **Takakkaw Falls,** the fourth-highest waterfall in Canada, by car along the **Yoho Valley Road** (not recommended for large RVs or trailers); turn north off the Trans-Canada Highway 1. If you love waterfalls, you've come to the right place. Hike in another hour along the Yoho Valley trail past Staircase Falls and Point Lace Falls to see Laughing Falls and beautiful Twin Falls.

The town of **Field** is the service center for Yoho National Park, although it still looks like a tiny railroad stopping post. It makes a good place to stop for lunch but isn't worth a visit in and of itself. Just south of Field is the **Natural Bridge,** where the Kicking Horse River meets with U-shaped sedimentary rock that has so far kept the river from breaking open a deep canyon. The river did manage to erode a small canyon of softer rock just upstream from the tougher section, creating a crooked bridge. Visit it soon—it may be gone in a matter of centuries!

Farther up the road from the Natural Bridge is the spectacular **Emerald Lake,** featuring hiking trails, canoe rentals, horse stables, and the lovely **Emerald Lake Lodge** (reviewed in the section "Where to Stay: In Yoho National Park," below). A visit to Emerald Lake alone is worth an entire roll of film.

The Burgess Shale   The Rockies' greatest contribution to archaeology is the 515-million-year-old Burgess Shale, a fossil bed discovered at the base of Mount Stephen. This discovery transformed our understanding of the evolution of life on earth and gave real examples of the amazing biodiversity of the mass extinction of species—half of the animal groups seen in the shale have since disappeared from earth. You can get there to see them only on a 6-hour, 6km (4-mile) guided hike organized by the Yoho Burgess Shale Foundation. This is a must for archaeology buffs, but only those with the dedication and fitness to trek into the site. You cannot drive to The Burgess Shale or visit it on your own; you must hike in to the site on an official tour with a registered guide. You will not enjoy this trip unless you are quite fit. Kids will enjoy the shorter hike to the Mount Stephen Fossil Beds. Reserve ahead of time at the Shale's website: www.burgess-shale.bc.ca.

Reserve by calling ⓒ **800/343-3006** or 250/343-3006. Hike costs C$70 (US$65) adults, C$38 (US$35) students, C$16 (US$15) children under 12. July 1–Sept 15 daily. The group takes only 15 fit hikers on 1 trip per day.

OUTDOOR PURSUITS

HELI-HIKING   Canadian Mountain Holidays (217 Bear St., Banff, AB T0L 0C0; ⓒ **800/661-0252** or 403/762-7100; www. canadianmountainholidays.com) runs excellent (and expensive) dream-fulfilling multiday hiking trips from their remote lodges—helicopters whisk you deep into the mountains, where a guide will show you the kind of scenery you'd never get to on your own. Although Canadian Mountain Holidays is based in Banff, the majority of their trips head out from Golden into the Purcell, Bugaboo, Monashee, and Selkirk mountains. Four-day trips start at C$2,207 (US$2,061).

HIKING   In Yoho National Park, the best hiking trails are located in two areas. First, spend a day discovering the magic of **Lake O'Hara,** a region that makes some locals misty-eyed just at its mention. There are some easy, shorter hikes around the lake itself, and a handful of excellent 3- to 4-hour trails that take you above Lake O'Hara to some of the equally spectacular surrounding lakes. The best bet is to connect all the short hikes into a challenging day hike known as the **Lake O'Hara Circuit.** The second area to hike is in the Yoho Valley. Park your car at the base of Takakkaw Falls and head up the valley toward Laughing Falls. This trail can be as long as you want it to be—it stretches into a fantastic 3-day hike called the **Iceline Trail** (the shorter version of which can be completed in 1 day). Visit Twin Falls and the Whaleback. Families or novices will particularly like the gentle climb into the valley, where you can pitch a tent and use it as a base for exploring the area. If you've got time to squeeze in one more trip, walk the 5km (3-mile) trail around beautiful **Emerald Lake.**

Tips Getting to Lake O'Hara

Lake O'Hara is a magical section of Yoho National Park, just on the other side of Lake Louise, accessed by a 13km (8-mile) road that can be hiked or cross-country skied in the winter. But daily Parks Canada–run bus rides (from mid-June to mid-Oct) will take you up to the warden station on the shores of Lake O'Hara in a painless 15 minutes. That'll give you the rest of the day for hiking. Reserve a spot on the bus by calling © **250/343-6433**. While you're on the line, you can also reserve a campsite at the **Lake O'Hara Campground** if you plan on staying the night at the lake. It's a good spot for families—it's in the backcountry, but accessible by bus so you don't have to worry about carrying everything in on your back. Bus tickets cost C$15 (US$14) for adults and C$7.50 (US$7.05) for children, return-trip. Buses leave the parking lot daily at 8:30am and 10:30am. The last bus out departs the campground at 6:30pm. The parking lot is located 1km (½ mile) west of the Alberta–British Columbia border, just off the south side of the Trans-Canada Highway 1. Turn south at the sign to Lake O'Hara and west into the parking lot. Campsites go extremely fast; you must reserve well in advance. The reservation line opens mid-March with restricted hours. For more information, visit www.pc.gc.ca/yoho. Lake O'Hara Lodge has its own private bus service for its guests (see below).

MOUNTAIN BIKING   Yoho and Golden are mountain-biking meccas. In Yoho National Park, many former fire roads have been converted to biking trails. Some of the best ones include the 18.8km (11.7-mile) Amiskwi Lake trail and the 8.3km (5.2-mile) Ross Lake trail and 10.5km (6.5-mile) Great Divide trails, which both take you to Lake Louise. Check with the staff at the Information Centre in Field for more information. Downhill biking at Kicking Horse Mountain Resort (from Hwy. 95, turn west at blue sign in downtown Golden, 13km/8 miles uphill; © **866-754-5425** or 250/439-5400; www.kickinghorseresort.com) is for thrill-seekers only. Stick your bike on the gondola and cruise down twisty single-track trails.

RAFTING   The whitewater on the Kicking Horse River is some of the best in British Columbia. You'll dive through narrow canyons and see the valley from a totally different perspective. Plus, it's buckets of fun! **Kootenay River Runners** (1km/½ mile west of the western gates of Kootenay National Park; © **800/599-4399** or 250/347-9210; www.kootenayriverrunners.com) runs a half-day trip along the river. Rates are C$90 with lunch (US$84). Children age 13 and under not permitted. **Wet'n'Wild Adventures** (© **800/668-9119** or 250/344-6549; www.wetnwild.bc.ca) has half- and full-day trips on the river. Rates range from C$65 (US$61) per person for the half-day trip to C$110 (US$103) per person for the full-day trip, including transportation from Banff or Lake Louise; it's C$95 (US$89) if you're already in Golden. Children age 13 and under not permitted.

SKIING & SNOWBOARDING At **Kicking Horse Mountain Resort** (from Hwy. 95, turn west at blue sign in downtown Golden, 13km/8 miles uphill; © **866-754-5425** or 250/439-5400; www.kickinghorseresort.com), the snow is famously so light it's called "Champagne powder." Once known as the Whitetooth Ski Area, this resort has undergone massive investment and development over the past 5 years resulting in what promises to be some of the finest skiing in the Canadian Rockies; the development includes 10 new runs and a slew of new hotels at the base of the resort. Full-day lift tickets are C$60 (US$56) for adults, C$50 (US$47) for seniors and youth ages 13 to 18, and C$28 (US$26) for children ages 6 to 12. Children under age 6 ski for free.

WHERE TO STAY
IN GOLDEN

Kicking Horse Hostel An affordable choice if you want to mingle with some skiers, snowboarders, kayakers, or hikers. The owners are happy to share the latest reports on snow and river conditions. Essentially a place to rent a bed, hang out, and make new friends, this hostel, located just across the train tracks from the main part of town, has a communal kitchen, and the staff are very knowledgeable about the area. There's a sunny deck and barbecue out back, and a fun, laid-back atmosphere.

518 Station Ave., Golden, BC V0A 1H0. © **250/344-5071**. www.kickinghorsehostel.com. 12 units. C$25 (US$23). Not a Hostelling International member hostel. MC, V. Open year-round.

Prestige Mountainside Resort This is Golden's top-end hotel, currently unrivalled by the handful of basic motels in the area but feeling the potential for competition from new developments at the base of Kicking Horse Mountain Resort. It may look run-of-the-mill from the outside, but the rooms have been decorated in a heritage style reminiscent of the old small-town hotels that used to be the only option. The rooms are large and spacious, especially those with king-size beds. There's a restaurant connected to the hotel, where you can get some pretty standard Canadian dishes like grilled cheese or hot turkey sandwiches. It's right on the main thoroughfare—the Trans-Canada Highway. If you want a room with a kitchen, ask for one at the end of the hall for more space.

1049 Trans-Canada Hwy., Golden, BC V0A 1H0. © **877/737-8443** or 250/344-7990. Fax 250/344-7902. www.prestigeinn.com. 82 units. C$100–C$150 (US$93–US$140) standard room; C$130–C$180 (US$121–US$168) standard room with kitchenette; C$120–C$230 (US$112–US$215) king suite. Ski, golf, and romance packages available. Extra person C$10–C$15 (US$9.30–US$14). Children 18 and under stay free in parent's room. AE, MC, V. Small dogs accepted. **Amenities:** Restaurant; lounge; small heated indoor pool; exercise room; Jacuzzi; sauna; laundry service. *In room:* A/C, TV w/pay movies, kitchenette, coffeemaker, hair dryer.

IN YOHO NATIONAL PARK

Cathedral Mountain Lodge ⊛   If it's a cozy yet luxurious log cabin in a peaceful and powerful setting you're after, this is an excellent choice. This lodge offers a lovely blend of privacy and luxury tucked beneath its namesake mountain along the banks of the glacier-fed Kicking Horse River. Quintessential cabins are functional and cute, with fireplaces, modern bathtubs, and fluffy duvets. The earth-tone decor is enhanced with Canadiana antiques and historical photos. There are big porches out front—a great place to relax and ponder nature, since there are no TVs or telephones in the cabins. Cabin nos. 6 to 12 are right on the river. The lovely timber-frame main lodge has a massive fireplace and a superb restaurant. Great views all around. For discounts, consider coming during late May or late September. The lodge is closed October through May.

Mailing address: P.O. Box 40, Field, BC V0A 1G0. Located on Yoho Valley Rd. 15-min. west of Lake Louise. Take the Trans-Canada Hwy. 5km (3 miles) west from the Alberta–British Columbia border or 2km (1¼ miles) east of the town of Field, BC and turn northwest on Yoho Valley Rd., continue 4km (2½ miles) to lodge. © **866/619-6442** or 250/343-6442. Fax 250/343-6424. www.cathedralmountainlodge. com. 31 units. May 23–31 C$160–C$265 (US$149–US$248), premier cabin C$435 (US$406); June C$240–C$415 (US$224–US$388), premier cabin C$510 (US$476); July C$305–C$499 (US$285–US$466), premier cabin C$625 (US$584), Sept C$160–C$415 (US$149–US$388), premier cabin C$555 (US$518). Rates include breakfast. Extra person C$25 (US$23). No children under 8 allowed. AE, MC, V. **Amenities:** Canoeing; guided hiking; library. *In room:* Coffeemaker, iron.

Emerald Lake Lodge ⊛   Whether it's been a warm summer day, a cool rainy day, or a bright but chilly winter day, this is where you want to end it. Relax and enjoy a meal and a glass of wine at this luxurious but cozy historic lodge, made up of 24 buildings on 5 hectares (12 acres) in the heart of Yoho National Park. Each guest room has a fieldstone fireplace and warm, rustic decor, including dark green marble vanities in many bathrooms (although others remain in need of a face-lift). Most rooms have a balcony. The real star, however, is Emerald Lake itself, a glow of turquoise that never escapes the corner of your eye. The guest rooms located in the lakeside buildings, especially nos. 32 and 33, have the best views of the lake. Rates vary depending on availability, so don't hesitate to bargain for a better view at the price you've been quoted. Winter is just as nice as summer here, with cross-country and downhill ski packages and a true retreat atmosphere. The lodge's two restaurants are outstanding, the main one in the lodge serving first-class Canadian cuisine, and Cilantro on the Lake serving Californian-style food and pizzas (open summer only).

Mailing address: P.O. Box 10, Field, BC V0A 1G0. Located on Emerald Lake Rd. Take Trans-Canada Hwy. 2km (1¼ miles) south of Field to Emerald Lake Rd. turnoff; continue 8km (5 miles). ℂ 800/663-6336 or 250/343-6321. Fax 250/343-6724. www. crmr.com. 85 units. June–Sept C$350–C$440 (US$327–US$411) superior room; C$395–C$485 (US$369–US$453) deluxe room; C$480–C$545 (US$448–US$509) suite. Oct–May C$175–C$280 (US$163–US$262) superior room; C$240–C$340 (US$224–US$318) deluxe room; C$290–C$480 (US$271–US$448) suite. Extra person C$25 (US$23). Children 12 and under stay free in parent's room. AE, MC, V. **Amenities:** 2 restaurants; Jacuzzi; sauna; canoe rentals; game room. *In room:* Coffeemaker, iron.

Lake O'Hara Lodge 🏔🏔🏔   Located in a secluded alpine valley on the shore of its namesake lake, this lodge is one of a kind. There are no phones, no television, no roads, and no cars (you either hike 13km/8 miles in or take the lodge's private bus from the Lake O'Hara Campground on the Trans-Canada Highway 1. See the box "Getting to Lake O'Hara," above). When meals are announced with a ringing bell, guests make their way in from the trail or up from lakeside decks to be served modern, international cuisine. The lakefront cabins have large, comfortable beds with down comforters and modern bathrooms, as well as the most privacy and the best views; the guest rooms in the lodge are the least expensive and are still very cozy (they also have a shared bathroom). It's a wonderful getaway for city slickers and a true mecca for mountain lovers of all ages. There is a ton of history on the walls, coupled with personalized service by managers and staff who love this place as much as the guests. It's not hard to understand why it's so hard to get a reservation here in summer. Reservations are usually made 1 year ahead of time. September is a lovely option if July and August are full, although prices are the same. You'll need a National Parks vehicle permit to leave your car in the parking lot (it's unsupervised, so don't

leave any valuables in your car!); see chapter 2 for information on obtaining permits. Though the atmosphere comes very close to making up for it, this isn't an economical place to stay; rates seem very high for the size of the guest rooms. They don't accept credit cards; mail your deposit in as a personal check and pay the rest in cash or check when you arrive at the lodge.

P.O. Box 55, Lake Louise, AB T0L 1E0. Access the lodge via the Parks Canada bus that leaves the Lake O'Hara parking lot just west of the Banff–Yoho border on Trans-Canada Hwy. © 250/343-6418 June–Sept. Oct–May call © 403/678-4110. www.lakeohara.com. 8 lodge rooms, 8 cabins. Rates include all meals, tips, taxes, and bus transportation. June 18–Oct 4 C$485 (US$453) double lodge room; C$675 (US$630) lakeshore cabin; C$710 (US$663) guide's cabin. Each additional adult C$250 (US$224). Children 6–15 C$105 (US$98); children 2–5 C$50 (US$47); children 1 and under stay free. Mid-Jan to mid-Apr only main lodge open C$515 (US$481). Closed Oct–Jan and May. No credit cards. 2-night minimum stay. **Amenities:** Restaurant; canoe rentals; library. *In room:* No phone.

Whiskey Jack Hostel   This hostel was rebuilt after the former building was swept away in an avalanche. Hikers and other outdoor types usually stay here. There are 27 beds, 9 in each of 3 dorms (male, female, and coed), each with a great view of Takakkaw Falls and the Yoho Valley. Guests cook their own meals in the one equipped kitchen (buy your food before you come!), although Olga's happy to share her yummy cornbread with all. Some come and stay here for a week, using it as their base for exploring the area. There's a fun, social campfire every night.

P.O. Box 1358, Banff, AB T0L 0C0. On the Yoho Valley Rd., just below Takakkaw Falls. © 866/762-4122 or 403/670-7580. Fax 403/283-6503. www.hihostels.ca. 3 units, 27 beds total. C$22 (US$21) per person for Hostelling International members; C$26 (US$24) per person for nonmembers. Children 17 and under half-price. MC, V. Closed Oct to mid-June.

WHERE TO EAT
IN GOLDEN
Cedar House Restaurant ✦ CANADIAN   The setting is splendid, and the food is fresh and inspired. Located in a 10-acre forest 5 minutes south of Golden, the Cedar House is a warm and friendly spot that oozes atmosphere. The passionate chefs offer simple and local ingredients, creating entrees like roasted free-range chicken supreme, slow-braised lamb shank, and a spectacular pan-seared peppered duck breast. Meats are all natural, and the fish is wild. For dessert, there are homemade sorbets.

735 Hefti Rd. © 250/344-4679. Reservations recommended. Main courses C$11–C$38 (US$10–US$35). MC, V. Daily at 5pm.

Eagle's Eye Restaurant 𝒻 CANADIAN   With what I'd call easily the best view from a restaurant in the Canadian Rockies, this gondola-accessed restaurant is perched atop Kicking Horse Mountain Resort at 2,350m (7,708 ft.), making it the highest restaurant in Canada. The 360-degree view threatens to distract you, but don't miss out on the superb cuisine. Where else so far above the ocean can you enjoy a wild BC salmon filet? For dinner, try the Rocky Mountain buffalo rib-eye, and don't pass up a mango samosa for dessert. In winter, the view is arguably even better—plus you can ski down! This is a fabulous dining experience—for both the view and the food.

At Kicking Horse Mountain Resort, 1500 Kicking Horse Trail. ✆ **250/439-5400.** Reservations recommended. Lunch with gondola ride C$42 (US$39). Sunset dinner with gondola C$50 (US$47). AE, MC, V. Summer Mon–Thurs 10am–5:30pm, Fri–Sat 10am–8pm. Winter hours daily 11am–3pm; dinners Fri–Sat until 9pm (last reservation).

Eleven22 Grill & Liquids 𝑓𝑖𝑛𝑑𝑠 INTERNATIONAL   This charming little spot inside a heritage home serves up some of the most creative and healthy food in town. The tables are tucked into the three front rooms. Service is very friendly; ask your server for advice on the daily specials. There's a nice patio for cocktails—they have an extensive list of spirits, wines, and mixed drinks. The tajine Moroccan stew is a favorite with the locals; the lamb shanks and daily pasta specials, including a homemade cannelloni with seasonal ingredients, are also delicious.

1122 10th Ave. S. ✆ **250/344-2443.** Lunch items C$8–C$14 (US$7.50–US$13); main dinner courses C$17–C$24 (US$16–US$22). MC, V. Daily 5–10pm.

Jita's Café CAFE   For a healthy meal or a midafternoon coffee break, head to this funky cafe in downtown Golden. Besides baked goods that are served fresh out of the oven, there are soups, sandwiches, and salads. I particularly like the Thai Asian salad.

B–1007 11th St. ✆ **250/344-3660.** Main courses C$4.50–C$12 (US$4.20–US$11). No credit cards. Mon–Sat 8am–6pm; Sun 10am–4pm.

IN YOHO NATIONAL PARK

Emerald Lake Lodge 𝒻𝒻 NEW CANADIAN   Eating at the lodge's main dining room can be a 2-hour experience. It's got a spectacular setting in the old CPR main lodge, built in 1902, and some of the best service I've experienced in the Rockies—not to mention a creatively localized menu and an award-winning wine list. Try the grilled Rocky Mountain ranch elk strip loin on braised elk *osso buco* or northern caribou medallions, or the Rocky Mountain game platter that has buffalo, venison, duck, and jam. If you want something a bit more casual, try the Lodge's other restaurant, **Cilantro on the Lake** (summer only).

On Emerald Lake Rd., 8km (5 miles) off Trans-Canada Hwy., at a turnoff 2km (1¼ miles) south of Field. *©* 250/343-6321. Reservations required if you're not a guest at the lodge. Main courses C$27–C$42 (US$25–US$39). AE, MC, V. Daily 5:30–11pm.

Truffle Pigs Café CAFE   In a funky old home in the heart of the tiny village of Field, Truffle Pigs makes a great stop for lunch or an afternoon snack. There's a bustling general store next to the somewhat cramped, crowded yet cozy restaurant. For lunch, yummy sandwiches include curried egg salad, build-your-own deli sandwiches, and grilled panini. For dinner there are hearty daily pastas, organic buffalo burgers, pizzas, and fondue. They also have delicious home-baked treats, a sunny outdoor patio, and great small-town atmosphere.

318 Stephen Ave., at the corner of Kicking Horse Ave. *©* 250/343-6462. Lunch C$7–C$14 (US$6.50–US$13). Dinner main entrees C$14–C$32 (US$13–US$30). MC, V. Daily 9am–9pm.

4 Mount Robson Provincial Park

25km (16 miles) west of Jasper

Established in 1913, Mount Robson Provincial Park protects the highest peak in the Canadian Rockies, for which it is named. This recreation-focused park, just on the other side of the Alberta–British Columbia border, makes a good side trip from Jasper National Park. You can take a day trip into the park to enjoy some of the area's excellent hiking opportunities. If you're keen to stay longer, camp overnight in one of the park's campgrounds. If you're lucky, you might catch a glimpse of the elusive 3,954m (12,969-ft.) peak of Mount Robson, often shrouded in clouds.

ESSENTIALS

GETTING THERE   Mount Robson Provincial Park is 82km (51 miles) west of Jasper on the Yellowhead Highway (Hwy. 16).

VISITOR CENTERS & INFORMATION   Park headquarters are at the **Mount Robson Visitor Information Centre** (*©* **800/ 689-9025** or 250/566-4325). It's on Highway 16, 60km (37 miles) west of the western gate of Jasper National Park. There are a store and a gas station here, as well as three campgrounds. For camping information, call the **British Columbia Parks office** at © **250/ 422-3212.** The nearby town of Valemount is the main servicing center for the provincial park. Contact **Valemount Tourism and Recreation** at © **250/566-4846** for information.

OUTDOOR PURSUITS

The **Berg Lake Trail,** a 20km (12.4-mile) trail that leads to the foot of Mount Robson, is the most popular hiking trail in the park, widely regarded as the best-maintained trail in the Rockies. With only a few short exceptions, the trail is well graded and broad. The north wall of the towering Mount Robson backs the turquoise glacial lake that is the trail's namesake. The trail passes **Kinney Lake,** heads over the **Valley of a Thousand Falls,** and runs past the gorgeous **Emperor Falls.** There are seven campgrounds spread out along the length of the trail; the best are at the end.

WHERE TO STAY

There are three **campgrounds** adjacent to the **Mount Robson Visitor Information Centre,** including the B.C. Parks–operated **Robson Meadows** (125 sites) and **Robson River** (19 sites) as well as the privately run **Emperor Ridge Campground** (37 sites). **Lucerne Campground** (32 sites) is another 6km (3¾ miles) west of the visitor center. All are open to RVs as well as tenters. To reserve, visit the website for British Columbia Provincial Parks' campgrounds, www. discovercamping.ca or call (tel) **800/689-9025** (Apr 1–Oct 1 only).

Just down the road from Robson Meadows campground is the **Mount Robson Ranch** *(finds* (Box 548, 8924 Hargreaves Rd., Valemount, BC, V0E 2Z0 (© **877/56604654** or 205/566-4658; www. mountrobsonranch.com), where rustic cabins are for rent. This is an incredibly peaceful place, especially when big groups of campers aren't around.

10

A Nature Guide to Banff & Jasper National Parks

The Canadian Rockies are part of a mountain system called the Cordillera that runs along the western edge of North, Central, and South America. It's a cohesive area in the sense that one life zone easily blends into another. However, there are some clear patterns and distinctions at work here that help us understand the complex ecology of Banff and Jasper national parks.

The most important factors that determine what grows where and when in the parks are geology, precipitation, elevation, and exposure to sunlight. On the northern slopes of mountains, for example, snow lingers on the ground much longer (sometimes year-round) and forms glaciers, so very little vegetation grows on these slopes. The southern slopes, by contrast, are sunnier and warmer. It's to these more forgiving areas that you go to appreciate park flora and fauna.

1 The Geology

Geology, the science and language of rocks, has always been a somewhat inaccessible subject. But you can become a lot more enlightened about it by spending some time in the Canadian Rockies, where geology forms the basis of the dominant land formations, the mountains. It's like being in a giant living laboratory.

The Canadian Rockies run from southeast to northwest along the Continental Divide, which also separates the provinces of Alberta and British Columbia. They are only 120km (74 miles) wide at their greatest expanse—you can drive from one side to the other in a day. (You might think that you could in fact make it across in about an hour, not a whole a day, but remember that we're not talking as the crow flies. These are mountains—the road meanders, turns, and twists. You don't drive in a straight line anywhere.) Anyway, in this respect, the Canadian Rockies are much different from the section of the Cordillera range in the United States, which is much wider and takes several days to cross.

Charting the Rockies East to West

The Rockies are a series of mountain ranges, each with unique characteristics. Think of them like successive ripples in a carpet that has been pushed up against a wall.

- **Foothills:** The easternmost "ripples," where the prairies roll in to the Rockies.
- **Front Ranges:** The eastern mountain front, also known as "the big wave."
- **Main Ranges:** The backbone of the Rockies and of North America, including the Continental Divide.
- **Eastern Main Ranges:** Massive limestone cliffs along the west side of the Continental Divide.
- **Western Main Ranges:** No dramatic cliffs, a less rugged profile.
- **Western Ranges:** East of the towns of Golden and Radium, British Columbia. The Western Ranges are outside the Banff and Jasper park boundaries.

The Canadian Rockies are made up of layers of sedimentary rock consisting of limestone, shale, and sandstone. Sedimentary rock is the result of the compression or hardening of sediments—particles that have broken away from pre-existing rock formations and dissolved.

To understand a little more about the geology of the Rockies, it helps to have a bit of a history lesson. About 200 million years ago, sedimentary rock began collecting on the broad, flat seabed underneath the landmass that today is the North American continent. The landmass began to drift westward, slowly moving away from the Euro-Asian continent. Over the next 40 million years or so, the western edge of the North America landmass had drifted as far west as where British Columbia's wine-producing Okanagan Valley sits today. But this western coast was increasingly crammed by volcanic islands moving east from the Pacific, creating a "big squeeze" that compressed the continental plates together. The sedimentary rock on the seabed began being pushed upward toward the east, in the same direction as the advancing volcanic islands. Over the next 60 million years, what are today known as the Main Ranges of the Rockies thrust upward, eventually towering above sea level. Over the next 15 million years, the Front Ranges appeared, followed by the Foothills. During this time, the multi-layered seabed shifted into a series of accordion-like peaks, with A-shaped peaks and V-shaped valleys. Rocks were shorn apart, folding and faulting into new layers.

During the last ice age, about 2 million years ago, a huge sheet of ice covered most of the continent east of the Rockies, leaving the alpine icefields and glaciers to expand and carve even deeper valleys. Glaciers ground up and down the valleys in a repeated process of melting, re-freezing, advancing, and retreating. Retreating glaciers expanded the V-shaped valleys into more scenic, U-shaped ones. One of the most spectacular outcomes of this is what are known as "hanging valleys," where the ground suddenly gives way and plunges into a deep valley or canyon.

You'll see some easily recognizable types of mountains in both Banff and Jasper national parks. Here's a rundown:

Castellated Mountains (Castle Mountain and Mount Temple, in Banff National Park)   Mainly seen along the Eastern Ranges, these mountains, so named because their shape resembles that of a European fortress, have weak layers of shale separated by limestone, dolomite, and quartzite rocks that form unique cliffs, leaving the weak layers to become ledges and the mountain faces looking like layer cakes.

Dogtooth Mountains (Mount Louis, Mount Birdwood, Cinquefoil Mountain)   Common in the Front and Western Main Ranges, these mountains are a result of sedimentary rock being gathered together and thrust vertically toward the summits.

Horn Mountains (Mount Athabasca, above the Icefield Information Centre, in Jasper National Park; Mount Fryatt, also in Jasper National Park; Mount Chephren, in Banff National Park)   These mountains resemble the famed Matterhorn of Europe, created in places where several cirque glaciers eroded different sides of the same mountain at the same time.

Overthrust Mountains (Mount Rundle in Banff National Park)   Typical of the Front Ranges, these mountains tilt southwest and have a steep northeast slope. The "writing desk" shape exemplifies how the sheets slid upward and layered on top of each other from southwest to northeast during the initial collisions of mountain building.

Sawtooth Mountains (Colin Range, east of Maligne Lake in Jasper National Park)   Also common in the Front Ranges, these are the upturned edges of thrust sheets, with ridges that are angled perpendicular to the main wind direction. Hourglass-shaped gullies have been eroded into shale formation. Very photogenic at sunset or with a light sprinkle of snow.

Fun Fact Canadian Rockies vs. American Rockies

No, we're not talking about two competing sports teams. Some 80 million years ago, the mountains in Banff National Park probably looked much like those in Colorado's Rocky Mountain National Park. Not today. Although part of the same chain, there are many differences between the Rocky Mountains in the United States and those here in Canada:

- The Canadian Rockies are made up of layered sedimentary rock, including limestone and shale, while the US Rockies are mostly made of metamorphic and igneous rock, such as granite.
- In the US, the Rockies grew out of a major thrust upward from the underlying continental plate. In Canada, the underlying plate wasn't disturbed much at all. The mountains here are remnants of upper-level layers of rock piled on top of each other.
- The American Rockies are taller than the Canadian Rockies. In the US, many summits top out above 4,000m (13,000 ft.), including the 4,276m-high (14,255-ft.) **Longs Peak,** and **Pikes Peak,** at 4,301m (14,107 ft.) the tallest mountain in the American Rockies. In the Canadian Rockies, only 17 peaks are higher than 3,500m (11,500 ft.), and none are as high as 4,000m (13,000 ft.): **Mount Robson,** the highest peak in the Canadian Rockies, stands 3,954m (12,969 ft.) tall. However, valleys in the Canadian Rockies have been eroded deeper, relative to the peaks, than those in the Rockies south of the border.
- The Canadian Rockies are more heavily glaciated than the American Rockies. Here, glaciers had a hand in shaping the entire region, while in the US glacial activity has tended to be located only in the high-elevation areas.
- Finally, and perhaps most obviously, the fact that the Canadian Rockies are farther north means that the climate is cooler and less snow and ice are able to melt. In Colorado, there is more runoff, evaporation, and snowmelt, making Colorado drier. Many of the same flora grow in both areas, but in general, the flora in the Canadian Rockies are more abundant and colorful, although they have a shorter growing season.

2 The Life Zones

In the Rockies, elevation is what determines which plants and animals can subsist in a given area. The landscape can be divided into three life zones, each supporting a different group of flora and fauna: the montane zone, at lower elevations; the subalpine zone, at midlevel elevations; and the alpine zone, at the highest elevations.

Visitors to Banff and Jasper will probably end up spending most of their time in the montane zone, which in fact represents only 3% of the land area. Subalpine forests make up 55%, 5% is alpine meadows above the tree line, and the remaining 37% is made up of rock and ice.

Montane Zone (low elevation)   This zone includes all the river valleys of Banff and Jasper national parks and the towns of Banff and Jasper. Usually occurring below 1,350m (4,500 ft.) and also on warm and dry southwestern slopes, this is the most temperate part of the mountains. It has the longest growing season, usually running from May to October. Wildflowers and many kinds of plants and shrubs flourish, as do animals that exist on a plant-based diet, like elk and moose. The most common tree is the Douglas fir, but you'll also spot lodgepole pine, white spruce, and aspen. Buffaloberry, juniper, cinquefoil, kinnikinnik (bearberry), and wild rose are the shrubs living here. Montane riverbanks are wintering habitat for elk, deer, and bighorn sheep, and therefore also draw animals that prey on them, like wolves and coyotes. Covering only a minuscule 3% of the Canadian Rockies, this is also where the most human development has taken place, and where most of the area's inhabitants live. The warm Chinook wind blows sporadically through the low-lying montane valleys, especially welcome during the coldest months of the year.

Subalpine Zone (moderate elevation)   Known as taiga in Europe and Asia, the subalpine zone runs above the montane zone up to the limit of tree growth. This zone receives more precipitation than the montane zone, and features mainly coniferous trees (if you see aspen, you're still in the montane zone). This life zone covers the majority of Banff and Jasper national parks—up to 55% of the landmass. It is often cool, wet, and windy here. Heavy forests of tall fir and Engelmann spruce are scattered throughout the subalpine ecosystem, with shrubs including grouseberry and Labrador tea. The climate is cool and damp; during winter, there is considerable snow accumulation. This is ideal habitat for many animals, including black bear and red squirrels. Deer, elk, and moose use the broad branches of subalpine trees for shelter from heat and rain in the summer.

Alpine Zone   This is the land of rock and snow, above the tree line. Also known as the alpine tundra, the ground in the alpine zone stays frozen most of the year. Animals that live here include pika, marmot, and gophers, as well as mountain goats and bighorn sheep. Scattered throughout the mountains, there is no simple line that defines where subalpine becomes alpine. Summer comes late here and is very short, often lasting only a few weeks in July and August. This zone is primarily made up of glacier, ice, and bare rock, although there are some alpine meadows where hummingbirds gather and blooms like alpine arnica and columbine explode in an array of color and fragrance each summer. If you make it there early on a warm July morning, the alpine zone can be unforgettable and live up to the postcard-perfect hype of high places.

Capping the montane, subalpine, and alpine zones is the perpetually frozen land of ice and snow.

3 The Flora

Considering how unforgiving the climate can be at times, Banff and Jasper national parks have a remarkable variety of trees, wildflowers, and shrubs.

The majority of the trees in Banff and Jasper are coniferous (they have cones or needles; no leaves), which are well adapted to cooler climates. Deciduous trees (with leaves instead of cones or needles) don't fare too well, preferring gentler slopes and a more moderate climate.

With a stunning variety of colors, shapes, and scents, wildflowers are perhaps the loveliest surprise in the Canadian Rockies. At times overshadowed by the grandeur of the mountains and lakes, wildflowers stand out nevertheless: a blazing patch of color at the side of the highway, or blanketing an alpine meadow. They exist with a fragile beauty, however, because their growing season is so short.

Moments **Taking Home Wildflowers**

Instead of picking wildflowers (which is in fact illegal in Banff and Jasper national parks), bring a camera or sketchbook along on your hike and either snap a few pictures or take a break and sketch your favorite one.

> ⌒Tips **What the Needles Tell You**
>
> One way to identify a tree is to know what to look for in its needles.
>
> **Spruce needles** are under 3 centimeters (1 in.) in length and are four-sided. They are prickly to the touch, and can be rolled between your fingers.
>
> **Fir needles** grow in singles.
>
> **Pine needles** grow in bunches of two to five, and have long, stiff needles.

Although some flowers start to bloom as early as April, the peak flowering time in Banff and Jasper is mid-July to late August.

At lower elevations, flowers tend to bloom earlier and reach greater heights. And though they often last longer into the fall at higher elevations, they don't grow as tall. Indian paintbrush can reach a height of 60 centimeters (24 in.) in the lower valleys, yet only makes it to 10 centimeters (4 in.) in the alpine zone. Although I adore the mountains throughout the year, when the wildflowers are blooming I'm at my happiest here. Try identifying and photographing them.

TREES
CONIFEROUS TREES

Douglas fir   You'll see the tall Douglas fir growing in damp soil along the eastern slopes of the Bow, North Saskatchewan, and Athabasca Valleys, usually reaching heights between 30 and 40m (98–130 ft.). It is smooth-barked, symmetrical, and delicate looking when young but becomes more gnarled as it ages, the bark becoming furrowed and the limbs heavy and sagging. It has a long life span—sometimes more than 1,300 years. This is largely thanks to its moist trunk and root system, which gives it the ability to survive forest fires.

Engelmann spruce   This is the most common spruce in the Rockies, identified by its thick, dark green (almost blue) needles and shaggy-looking branches. It can grow to 20 to 30m (65–95 ft.) by maturity. When young, this cone-shaped tree starts with pretty, symmetrical branches, becoming more uneven with age. It has a brown, sheddy bark that is often barren when in the shade. Its stiff needles are 2 to 5 centimeters (1–2 in.) long and are twisted in bundles of two. It has dense 2- to 6-centimeter (1–2.4-in.) cones growing at its top.

Douglas fir

Engelmann spruce

Larch Although it is a conifer, the larch (also known as the tamarack) isn't an evergreen. In mid-September, its needles turn yellow, then gold, falling to the ground by late October. Larches appear dead in winter. Subalpine larches, which grow just below the tree line, are branching and scraggly, measuring 5 to 10m (16–33 ft.) in height.

Lodgepole pine The lodgepole pine is the official tree of Alberta, and is also the most common tree in the Rocky Mountains (in both Canada and the United States). It has a slight, gradually tapered trunk that Natives used for making longhouse and tepee poles. The trunk is still used in construction today. Its needles usually grow in bunches of two, between 2 and 5 centimeters (1–2 in.) in length. The lodgepole pine is easily mistaken for a jack pine, more common in eastern North America.

Larch

Lodgepole pine

Fun Fact **The Oldest Trees**

The oldest tree in the Banff and Jasper area is an Engelmann spruce that lives in a subalpine grove just north of the Icefield Information Centre, on Highway 93, in Jasper National Park. It is thought to be between 680 and 720 years old. An estimated 685-year-old Douglas fir was found just east of Banff National Park.

DECIDUOUS TREES

Trembling aspen   Found in moist areas in the montane zone, these are the leafy trees you see along the riverbanks and in the towns of Banff and Jasper. A member of the willow family, aspens have long, slender trunks of quite pale bark that can become riddled with black as the tree ages. Its leaves are pale green and heart-shaped; they turn bright yellow in autumn. When caught by a breeze, they do indeed move in a trembling-like manner, which is likely how it got its name. They also make a lovely whispering sound.

Trembling aspen

FLOWERING PLANTS

Arnica   Arnica blooms every other year, and is often found in montane and subalpine woods. It has a bright yellow flower that curls slightly at the edges and has a small yellow center. There are 15 species of arnica, each with a unique leaf shape, including heart-shaped, broad-shaped, and narrow-shaped. The alpine arnica has show-off all-yellow petals with lance-shaped leaves and a woolly stem.

Arnica

Camas Blooming in different shades for different sub-species, including blue and white, the camas is common in the subalpine and montane zones, below the tree line. It has long, narrow leaves that rise gracefully from the base of the plant. Its stem and leaves are pale green. The white-flowered camas grows 20 to 30 centimeters (8–12 in.) tall. The blue-flowered camas has six petals and long stamens. It grows to a height of 30 to 60 centimeters (12–24 in.). The camas prefers sunny, open areas.

Fireweed Identified by its four-petaled fuchsia flowers, the fireweed is also identified by its unusually tall height: up to 1.5m (5 ft.). Flowers have rod-like seedpods that cover the top two-thirds of the stem. Although it can be found in dense thickets in the montane and subalpine zones, it is at its most forceful in disturbed soil, along the sides of the highways, near construction areas, or in areas where the ground has recently been burned from a forest fire.

Camas

Fireweed

Indian paintbrush   This is perhaps the best-known flower in the Rockies, and the easiest one to identify. Colors range from reddish-orange to purple. If you examine one closely, however, you'll see that the source of the color is not the petals themselves, but the cups on the exterior of the flower, known as bracts. Bracts cradle the actual petals, on the inside. Indian paintbrush is a parasite; it attaches itself to nearby plants so it can survive in harsh areas, like gravel-strewn roadsides.

Lupine   There is a variety of lupine species in the Canadian Rockies, most growing on western slopes in the montane and subalpine regions. Lupine has leaves that resemble teeth spread out along the stem. Small indigo flowers reach upward off the top of the flower.

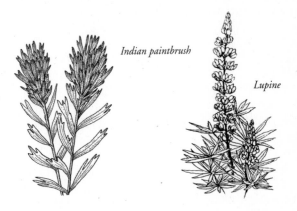

Indian paintbrush

Lupine

⟨Tips⟩ How to Identify Wildflowers

Keep these five factors in mind when you're trying to tell wildflowers apart:

1. **Petal color:** could be white, red, yellow and green, pink and orange, or blue and purple.
2. **Petal shape:** could be daisy- or bell-like.
3. **Petal arrangement:** could be arranged in small or large clusters.
4. **Leaf occurrence and arrangement:** could occur all or partway up the stem, or not at all. Could be arranged in small or large clusters.
5. **Occurrence:** flowers could occur individually or in clusters.

Wild strawberry   You'll know it's a wild strawberry when you spot the berries growing inside the small but showy white flowers. The berry is edible, and for such a tiny thing it's bursting with flavor. The flower has three-part leaflets that resemble teeth in shape, with a red stem that spreads out across the ground. Look for the wild strawberry in dry, open woods during July and August.

Wood lily   The wood lily has a colorful orange flower punctuated by black dots on the inside. The base of its petals is also black. It does have a rather exotic look to it, and for this reason is often mistaken for the Asian tiger lily. As a result of this mistaken identity, the wood lily is picked in large quantities, which is why it has become quite rare. It grows to a height between 5 and 50 centimeters (2–20 in.) on south-facing, open montane slopes and aspen woods. It blooms in early summer.

Wild strawberry   *Wood lily*

Yellow columbine   Growing up to 1m (3.3 ft.) tall, this wild-flower blooms in subalpine meadows and in moist woods. Its flowers are large, with a complex design. It is usually a pale yellow color, although those that grow near the Continental Divide often hybridize with the red columbine to produce pink-tinged petals. Its leaves are dark green and rounded.

Yellow lady's slipper   This member of the orchid family, with its exotic yellow lips and twisted, twirling petals, blooms in late May or early June in shaded woody areas. Its cousin, the mountain lady's slipper, is very similar but has a white flower instead of yellow. The yellow lady's slipper reaches a height of 20 centimeters (8 in.). It's very attractive to bees.

Yellow columbine

Yellow lady's slipper

SHRUBS

Prickly juniper   Very common in Banff and Jasper national parks and easy to recognize, this shrub grows in circular patches to a height of 1m (3.3 ft.). Its branches drop outward from the stem. It has prickly, needle-like leaves and a distinctive odor. Its greenish-blue berry, though edible, tastes bitter.

Sagebrush   The most common shrub on the western slopes of the Canadian Rockies, sagebrush grows at low elevations in dry, open areas. It has gray-green leaves with wide, pointed tips, and doesn't grow much higher than most people's waistlines. It's easy to locate because of the fresh and spicy sage fragrance. In the fall, the sagebrush sprouts tiny white flowers.

Prickly juniper

Sagebrush

Shrubby cinquefoil   This shrub grows just about anywhere in the mountains. With rough brown stems and small leaves that are so stiff they resemble needles, the plant looks prickly, but it isn't. The yellow, five-petaled blossoms make it easy to spot.

Wild rose   There are many different types of wild rose in the Canadian Rockies. If you spot one of the pink-petaled variety, how-ever, you'll be looking at Alberta's provincial flower. Look for small leaves growing in bunches of seven or nine and five-petaled flowers. The wild rose excels in the open, but also grows in lodgepole or aspen forests.

Shrubby cinquefoil

Wild rose

4 The Fauna

Your chances of seeing wild animals in Banff and Jasper national parks are very good. It's a magical experience to spot a mother goat making her way across a steep cliff with a small kid at her side, or a black bear cooling off by an alpine stream. Most wildlife here enjoy a natural and healthy existence. Some are dangerous, though; although you may want to approach them of your own accord, they aren't tame. See "Protecting the Environment" in chapter 2 for more information on what to do if a wild animal approaches you of *its* own accord.

Aside from the common birds listed in this section, keep an eye out in the montane zone for red-winged blackbirds, belted king-fishers, willow flycatchers, yellow throats, and teals. In forested areas, look for warblers, tanagers, and woodpeckers, with warblers and kinglets nesting in higher forests. Finally, in the high alpine zone, you may see fox sparrows, rosy finches, and water pipits.

Tips **For the Birds**

Pick up the brochure *Banff and Vicinity/Lake Louise and Vicinity Drives and Walks* to help plan your birding outing. Top spots include the Cave and Basin marsh, Vermillion Lakes, Johnston Canyon, and Bow Summit. The Friends of Banff and the Friends of Jasper organizations sell "checklists" that let you keep track of the different birds you see.

MAMMALS

Beaver   The beaver is a beloved, though sometimes maligned, member of the Canadian wilderness family. The largest rodent in the Rockies, it has a glossy reddish-brown coat (which is water-repellent), exposed incisor teeth, webbed feet, and a flattened, black tail, which it slaps against the ground when threatened. The beaver eats twigs and bark, especially from aspen, birch, and poplar trees. While you're most likely to see the beaver in lowland ponds, streams, and lakes, it is a largely nocturnal animal. What you're more likely to see is its shelter: beaver "dams" constructed from mud and twigs, which often stretch all the way across narrow streams and creeks. Canoeists, beware! It can be quite a challenge to drag your loaded canoe over one of these beauties, cursing all the way. Hikers need to beware, too, that you don't mistake a beaver dam for a bridge. You could end up waist-deep in a pile of muddy sludge!

Bighorn sheep   Found along rugged slopes and in meadows (and often rummaging along roadsides), the stocky bighorn sheep has a grayish-brown coat and stands approximately 1m (3.3 ft.) tall. When mature, it grows a set of thick, brown horns that spiral forward. A powerful climber, its hooves make it especially adept at walking along rocky slopes. Males and females form separate herds for most of the year, both feeding on grass. They meet in the fall for rutting.

Beaver

Bighorn sheep

Black bear This is the most common bear in the province of Alberta. You can spot the black bear in forested and swampy areas. Its coat, although normally deep black in color, can be cinnamon as well. Its diet consists of vegetation, carrion, fish, and—believe it or not—other bears. An average-size male stands .9m (3 ft.) tall at its shoulders and measures 1.7m (5.5 ft.) from end to end when on all fours. It weighs approximately 170 kilograms (374 lb.). Females are about two-thirds the size of males.

Cougar Also known as the mountain lion or puma, the cougar weighs upward of 70 kilograms (154 lb.). It is the largest representative of the feline family indigenous to the Canadian wild. The cougar lives a rather solitary life in remote forests and swamps, spending most of its time hunting for cloven-hoofed mammals including elk, moose, deer, hares, and small rodents. Rarely seen and extremely strong, cougars hunt by stalking and pouncing.

Black bear

Cougar

Coyote Although the coyote resembles the wolf, this dog-like mammal is smaller, weighing between 13 and 20 kilograms (29–44 lb.). It has a grayish-yellow coat, large ears, a pointed nose, and a black-tipped tail. The coyote feeds on rodents, rabbits, and berries. It is a sly hunter, active mostly at dusk and in the evenings. When it runs, it can reach a quite remarkable speed of 65kmph (40 mph), though a more comfortable running speed sits around 40kmph (25 mph). One of the best identifiers of a coyote is that it runs with its tail down. Coyotes' nightly conversations of chirping, yipping, and barking make for interesting listening.

Deer There are two kinds of deer in Banff and Jasper national parks: the white-tailed deer and the mule deer. The mule deer is more common. Both have a reddish-brown coat during summer that turns gray in winter. Both also have a white tail; however, the mule deer is distinguishable from the white-tailed deer because its tail has a black tip. Both have whitish rump patches.

Coyote

Deer

Elk Also known as wapiti, the elk is commonly seen in open forests and meadows. Distinguished by its large size, shaggy dark neck, and light rump patch, it is most active at dusk and dawn, when you can spot it feeding on grass, lichen, and twigs. The males are the ones with the large antlers, which they shed in the spring. Elk usually travel in herds.

Grizzly bear The grizzly usually lives in higher terrain than the black bear, preferring isolated mountain meadows and tundra areas. It is distinguished by its large shoulder hump and dished face. The male averages 130 centimeters (51 in.) tall and 190 centimeters (75 in.) long, and weighs 250 to 320 kilograms (550–700 lb.). Primarily nocturnal, grizzlies feed on vegetation, fish, and other mammals, both large and small.

Elk

Grizzly bear

Hoary marmot The marmot is not what you would call shy. You can see it in high alpine meadows near rockslides, and hear it scampering across the ground in the high subalpine and low alpine zones. It's a heavy-bodied rodent that resembles a large gopher, with silvery-white fur, black feet, and a black head. It's also a favorite prey of the grizzly bear. Marmots live in small colonies, but are mainly seen individually. Its whistle, an unforgettable shrill alarm call that sounds remarkably like a human whistle, will make you stop and turn around in your tracks.

Moose   Partial to swamps and heavily forested areas near lakes, the moose is quite literally the size of a horse, and is easily identified by its long, thin legs and overhanging snout. The male moose is further distinguished by its enormous set of antlers. Largely solitary, the moose is most active at dawn and dusk. Good spots to see moose include the Vermillion Lakes, Bow Lake, Upper Waterfowl Lake, and in the "Moose Meadow" between Johnston Creek and Silver City, all in Banff National Park.

Hoary marmot

Moose

Sheepish Sheep That Jump

Although wildlife is out and about year-round in Banff and Jasper national parks, you stand a better chance of spotting animals in the springtime. One April day, after the snow had just melted, I decided to go for a hike at Maligne Canyon, in Jasper. My companion and I didn't have much human company—ours was the only vehicle in the parking lot at the trail head. As we neared the tea-house at the top of the canyon, we surprised a small herd of bighorn sheep feeding on the newly exposed grass. One by one upon our arrival, the startled sheep jumped over the teahouse fence and fled down the canyon. The last sheep to do so was obviously the timid one. He took three or four runs up to the meter-high fence—and balked each time. The rest of his herd waited on the other side, seemingly urging him to "Jump!" Finally, the sheepish sheep leaped, made it over the fence, and the herd disappeared down the canyon. But not before we were able to snap the wildlife photograph of a lifetime.

Mountain goat   Found high in the mountains along rocky slopes, the mountain goat has a shaggy white coat and pointed black horns. A fabulous climber, mountain goats are drawn to roadside salt deposits and can scamper up seemingly vertical cliffs with ease. Watch for them at the "Goats and Glaciers" viewpoint, on the Icefields Parkway in Jasper National Park.

Rocky Mountain pika   Often heard but rarely seen, this endearing relative of the rabbit, also known as a rock rabbit, is distinguished by its round body, large ears, and lack of a tail. It looks likes a tennis ball with ears. Active during the day, the pika spends most of its time gathering herbs and grasses, which it dries in the sun before storing. The pika does not hibernate in the winter. Instead, it spends most of the cold, snowy season resting, slowly making its way through its store of food. Look for the pika at the back end of Lake Louise in Banff, and at Moraine Lake in Jasper.

Mountain goat

Rocky mountain pika

Squirrel   The squirrel seems to inhabit every nook and cranny in Banff and Jasper national parks. There are several different species here, including the golden-mantled squirrel, the ground squirrel, the thirteen-lined ground squirrel, Richardson's ground squirrel, and the red squirrel, which cheerfully lives in trees and is far from shy. Don't mistake the squirrel for the common chipmunk, a smaller and friskier cousin with a striped head frequently seen scavenging for nuts.

Wolf   The wolf looks quite a bit like a large German shepherd, but is lankier, with longer legs and bigger feet. And who could forget its wise, piercing yellow eyes? Its coat varies from white to gray to black, but brown is also a common color. This elusive yet aggressive predatory animal lives in groups known as "packs," which have a complex social hierarchy. Its long, quavering howl can be heard on many a mountain evening.

Squirrel

Wolf

BIRDS

Bald eagle   Fairly common along rivers and lakes, usually perching atop a tree or soaring in the sky, the bald eagle is impressive to see and difficult to mistake. The bald eagle is 82 centimeters (32 in.) long from head to toe and has a wingspan of 203 centimeters (80 in.).

Black-billed magpie   A large, photogenic bird with deep-blue iridescent feathers, the key distinguishing feature is that the magpie's tail is as long as its body. The magpie is the rooster of the Canadian Rockies, often waking you up earlier than you wish. The magpie is a loud, aggressive scavenger.

Black-billed magpie

Bald eagle

Tips **The Best Bird-watching Times**

Just past dawn and early evening are the best times of the day for bird-watching, particularly during the busy spring and fall migrating seasons.

Canada goose   From early April until the end of October, the Canada goose is a common sight in the Canadian Rockies. You will spot groups of them along the sides of lakes, calm rivers, and marsh ponds, although the Canada goose does have a special fondness for golf greens—as many golf course staff members who are charged with cleaning up their plentiful droppings will attest to. The Canada goose has a long black neck with a white patch at the top, a brown body, white "underpants," and black tail feathers. Its call is a loud "Honk!"

Clark's nutcracker   Measuring about 30 centimeters (12 in.) in length, the Clark's nutcracker has a white face, pointed black bill, black wings, and a long, light-gray hood. This chirpy bird lives in pine trees, using its long beak to pry limber pines from the cones. It makes guttural, crow-like sounds.

Canada goose

Clark's nutcracker

How Many Mammals?

There are 69 naturally occurring species of mammals living in Banff National Park. The largest is the moose; the smallest, the pygmy shrew. The most recent estimates on mammal populations in Banff are:

- **Bighorn Sheep:** 2,000 to 2,600
- **Elk:** 2,500 in summer, 1,600 in winter
- **Mule deer:** 850 to 950
- **Mountain goats:** 800
- **White-tailed deer:** 300 to 350
- **Coyotes:** 150 to 250
- **Grizzly bears:** 50 to 80
- **Moose:** 50 to 80
- **Black bears:** 50 to 60
- **Wolves:** 30 to 40

Common raven   This black bird resembles a crow, but is larger, with a stouter bill. Its call is a guttural croak. The common raven can be seen throughout the Canadian Rockies, including the Banff and Jasper townsites. The raven is a tame but shrewd bird. It mates with the same partner for life.

Gray jay   Also known as the Canada jay or Whiskey Jack, this bird is gray in color with a black nape and whitish head. It's easy to spot since it's so large, often 30 centimeters (12 in.) long. The gray jay makes a soft "wheer-ooo" sound and whistles pleasantly, although when threatened its call becomes loud and shrill, similar to that of the blue jay.

Common raven

Gray jay

Osprey   Nesting along lakeshores and rivers in a massive treetop nest, the osprey is easily identified by its white head, black eye-stripe, and black bill. It has a brown back and upper wings with black patches at the wing joints, and a black-and-white underside. It flies with its wings dropped and has a plain whistle call.

White-tailed ptarmigan   Pronounced "tar-mi-gun," this bird is common to the alpine zone. Its feathers are whitish-brown in summer, turning all white in winter, when the birds sometimes become indistinguishable from the snowy ground they rest on. Growing no more than 25 centimeters (10 in.) long, the ptarmigan moves through alpine meadows and boulder fields in families of four, "cluck-clucking" or "boo-ow-oo-ing" to each other.

White-tailed ptarmigan

Osprey

5 The Future

The Rockies are undergoing continual change, some of it due to environmental factors, some of it the result of human development. Glacier recession, for example, is a natural process. But the effects of global warming are causing glaciers in Banff and Jasper to recede at an accelerated rate. In the summer of 1994 alone, the surface of the lower Athabasca Glacier in Jasper National Park receded 7m (23 ft.). Icefields and glaciers will continue to melt at these accelerated rates if temperatures keep rising. Travelers are increasingly aware of and interested in climate change, and the Rockies are a great place to witness the effects of global warming before your eyes. Human interaction with the natural environment has also taken its toll. Towns like Canmore, Golden, and Radium Hot Springs, which are outside national park borders and therefore more open to commercial development, have seen swift and broad development of resort homes and golf courses, placed square in the middle of wildlife corridors. Wildlife does not respect the "boundaries," so the animals wander into trouble as they migrate in and out of the parks. The heightened human presence in the parks presents unhealthy ecologies where wildlife struggles to survive.

The new buzzword here in the Canadian Rockies is "ecological integrity," which means allowing nature to maintain its true nature. Native components like water, rocks, flora, and fauna should be allowed to flourish in natural processes. Parks Canada believes nature is ever-evolving, and should be allowed to do so on its own terms.

The usually competing forces of preservation and commercial development are also learning to work together, as preservationists realize the significant economic benefits to be reaped from maintaining the parks as visitor-friendly destinations. Through heritage tourism initiatives, commercial operators are demonstrating greater understanding of and respect for the landscape on which their income depends. Pine Bungalows, in Jasper, is located in prime elk habitat. As the owners renovate and rebuild, they will be reducing their footprint on the landscape. The Fairmont Jasper Park Lodge has a wildlife corridor running through its golf course. To make the area more wildlife-friendly, it has reduced the fenced area. The hotel has also partnered with Jasper National Park to open up the waterway between Lac Beauvert and the Athabasca River. Residents and visitors alike can take an active role in controlling the commercial development in the park. Find out what your hotel is doing to promote ecological integrity, head out hiking with a certified local guide to learn more about the complexities of the wilderness here, and do your part in leaving no trace. As they say here in the Rockies, "Take only photos, leave only footprints."

Index

See also Accommodations and Restaurants Indexes below

RESTAURANTS

The new way to
get AROUND town.

Make the most of your stay. Go Day by Day!

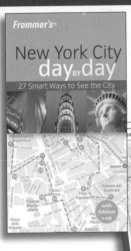

The all-new Day by Day series shows you the best places to visit and the best way to see them.

- Full-color throughout, with hundreds of photos and maps
- Packed with 1-to-3-day itineraries, neighborhood walks, and thematic tours
- Museums, literary haunts, offbeat places, and more
- Star-rated hotel and restaurant listings
- Sturdy foldout map in reclosable plastic wallet
- Foldout front covers with at-a-glance maps and info

The best trips start here. **Frommer's®**

A Branded Imprint of **WILEY**
Now you know.

New series!

Pauline Frommer's

Pauline Frommer's
ITALY
★ SPEND LESS SEE MORE ★
For a New Generation of Smart Travelers

Pauline Frommer's
HAWAII
★ SPEND LESS SEE MORE ★
For a New Generation of Smart Travelers

Pauline Frommer's
NEW YORK CITY
★ SPEND LESS SEE MORE ★
For a New Generation of Smart Travelers

★ SPEND LESS SEE MORE ™ ★

Discover a fresh take on budget travel with these exciting new guides from travel expert Pauline Frommer. From industry secrets on finding the best hotel rooms to great neighborhood restaurants and cool, offbeat finds only locals know about, you'll learn how to truly experience a culture *and* save money along the way.

Coming soon:

Pauline Frommer's Costa Rica
Pauline Frommer's Paris

Pauline Frommer's Las Vegas
Pauline Frommer's London

The best trips start here.
Available wherever books are sold.

Frommer's®
A Branded Imprint of ⊕**WILEY**
Now you know.

Wiley, the Wiley logo, and Spend Less-See More are trademarks or registered trademarks of John Wiley & Sons, Inc. and/or its affiliates.
Frommer's is a registered trademark of Arthur Frommer, used under exclusive license.

Discover North America's National Parks with Frommer's®!

All the up-to-date, practical information and candid insider advice you need for the perfect park vacation

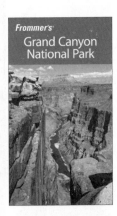

Frommer's
Grand Canyon National Park

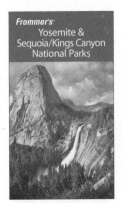

Frommer's
Yosemite & Sequoia/Kings Canyon National Parks

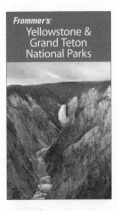

Frommer's
Yellowstone & Grand Teton National Parks

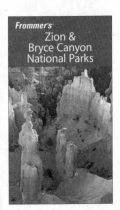

Frommer's
Zion & Bryce Canyon National Parks

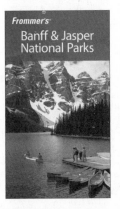

Frommer's
Banff & Jasper National Parks

Frommer's PORTABLE
Algonquin Provincial Park

SECOND EDITION

Available at bookstores everywhere.

Discover Canada with Frommer's®!

All the up-to-date, practical information and candid insider advice you need for the perfect vacation in Canada

Frommer's
Niagara Region

Frommer's
Newfoundland & Labrador

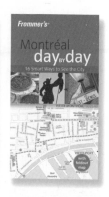

Frommer's
Montréal
day by day
16 Smart Ways to See the City

Frommer's
Ottawa

Frommer's
Toronto 2008

Frommer's
Vancouver Island, the Gulf Islands
& the San Juan Islands

Frommer's
Montréal &
Québec City 2008

Frommer's
Vancouver & Victoria 2008
with coverage of Whistler

Available at bookstores everywhere.

CLOSED
due to accidental demolition

WEGEN BISSIGEN EICHHÖRNCHEN GESCHLOSSEN

CERRADO CABRAS

Κλειστό Μετεωρίτες

POOL CLOSED
ELECTRIC EELS
プールも 閉鎖中

Hotel closed for facelifting

FERMÉ POUR RAISON DE GRÈVE DES BONNES

FECHADO!
POR CAUSA DE ATAQUES DOS CROCODILOS

— I don't speak sign language.

A hotel can close for all kinds of reasons.
Our Guarantee ensures that if your hotel's undergoing construction,
we'll let you know in advance. In fact, we cover your entire travel
experience. See www.travelocity.com/guarantee for details.

travelocity
You'll never roam alone.

© 2007 Travelocity.com L.P. CST # 2056372-50.

There's a parking lot where my ocean view should be.

 À la place de la vue sur l'océan, me voilà avec une vue sur un parking.

 Anstatt Meerblick habe ich Sicht auf einen Parkplatz.

 Al posto della vista sull'oceano c'è un parcheggio.

 No tengo vista al mar porque hay un parque de estacionamiento.

 Há um parque de estacionamento onde deveria estar a minha vista do oceano.

 Ett parkeringsområde har byggts på den plats där min utsikt över oceanen borde vara.

 Er ligt een parkeerterrein waar mijn zee-uitzicht zou moeten zijn.

 هنالك موقف للسيارات مكان ما وجب ان يكون المنظر الخلاب المطل على المحيط .

 眼前に広がる紺碧の海・・・じゃない。窓の外は駐車場！

停车场的位置应该是我的海景所在。

I'm fluent in pig latin.

Hotel mishaps aren't bound by geography.
Neither is our Guarantee. It covers your entire travel experience, including the price. So if you don't get the ocean view you booked, we'll work with our travel partners to make it right, right away. See Travelocity.com/guarantee for details.

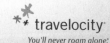
travelocity
You'll never roam alone.